SCHOOL OF ADVANCED STUDY UNIVERSITY OF LONDON
Institute of Germanic & Romance Studies

Technology's Pulse
Essays on Rhythm in German Modernism

igrs books

Established by the Institute of Germanic & Romance Studies, this series aims to bring to the public monographs and collections of essays in the field of modern foreign languages. Proposals for publication are selected by the Institute's editorial board, which is advised by a peer review committee of 36 senior academics in the field. To make titles as accessible as possible to an English-speaking and multi-lingual readership, volumes are written in English and quotations given in English translation.

For further details on the annual competition, visit:
http://igrs.sas.ac.uk/publications/IGRS_books_2011.php.

Editorial Board

Dr Maria-José Blanco (Hispanic)
Dr Martin Liebscher (Germanic)
Ms Maria-José Homem (Lusophone)
Dr Katia Pizzi (Italian)
Professor Naomi Segal (French)
Dr Ricarda Vidal (Visual Culture)
Dr Godela Weiss-Sussex (Germanic)

igrs books Volume 5

Volume Editor
Professor Naomi Segal

Technology's Pulse
Essays on Rhythm in German Modernism

by

Michael Cowan

SCHOOL OF ADVANCED STUDY UNIVERSITY OF LONDON
Institute of Germanic & Romance Studies
2011

Published by the

Institute of Germanic & Romance Studies
School of Advanced Study, University of London
Senate House, Malet Street, London WC1E 7HU
http://igrs.sas.ac.uk

© Michael Cowan, 2011

Professor Cowan has asserted his right under the Copyright, Designs and Patents Act 1988 to be identified as the author of this work.

All rights reserved. No part of this publication may be reproduced, stored in a retrieval system, or transmitted, in any form or by any means, electronic, mechanical, photocopying, recording or otherwise, without the prior permission of the author and the publisher.

Cover Image

Franziska Kantor, *Wiedergabe des rhythmischen Ablaufs einer Bewegung* (ca. 1921). Reproduced with permission of the Wien Museum, Vienna

First published 2011

ISBN 978 0 85457 230 4

Table of Contents

Acknowledgements	7
List of Illustrations	9
1. Introduction: Rhythm and the Mediation of Modern Experience	15
2. Poetry for Restless Times: Rhythm and Urban Experience in the Work of Gerrit Engelke (1890–1918)	49
3. Cinema as 'Heart Machine': Rhythm and the Ordering of Nature in Weimar Film	87
4. The Compulsory Power of Resonance: Rhythm, Attention and the Weimar Advertising Film	127
5. Surviving the Rhythms of America: Jazz and the Fantasy of Technological Mastery	167
6. Epilogue – Rhythm and Moving Image Media: Some Afterthoughts	209
Bibliography	229
Index	245

Table of Contents

For my parents

For Lu Daiyin.

Acknowledgements

While conceiving and writing this book, I have benefited from numerous forms of institutional, intellectual and collegial support. I would like first to thank the editors of IGRS books at the Institute of Germanic & Romance Studies for embracing this project three years ago and helping me see it through to publication. In particular, I am grateful to Naomi Segal for her feedback and her meticulous proofreading, and to Jane Lewin for her help in preparing the manuscript. I would also like to thank several colleagues who have offered helpful feedback, critique and motivation in various forms over the past few years including Nora Alter, Thomas Elsaesser, Oliver Gaycken, Tom Gunning, Laurent Guido, Barbara Hales, Anton Kaes, Viva Paci, Hélène Sicard-Cowan, Kai Sicks, Malcolm Turvey, Andrew Webber and William Wees. In addition, I send my sincere gratitude to several colleagues in Montreal who have helped provide the institutional and collegial support without which a project such as this would not be sustainable. This includes the faculty and staff in German studies – Karin Bauer, Lynda Bastien, Dimitris Karantanis, Annie Lisi, Paul Peters, Andrew Piper, Sylvia Rieger, Brigitte Weiss-Dittmann and Shawn Whelan – as well as several other colleagues from the Montreal universities. In particular, my gratitude goes out to Philippe Despoix, Yuriko Furuhata, André Habib, Volker Heins, Thomas Lamarre, Katie Russell, Will Straw, Alanna Thain, Till van Rahden and Haidee Wasson. Beyond Montreal, many other friends and colleagues in North America and Europe have helped – directly or indirectly – to shape my thinking about this project over the past few years, including Janelle Blankenship, Robert Brain, Gustav Deutsch, Paul Dobryden, Wolfgang Fichna, Paul Flaig, Jeanpaul Goergen, Robb MacFarland, Siegfried Mattl, Klaus Müller-Richter, Sabrina Rahman, Hanna Schimeck, Werner Schwarz, Georg Vasold and Raleigh Whitinger. This book also benefited directly from the help of archivists and librarians. I would like to thank in particular the staff of the Deutsche Kinemathek in Berlin for their generous help in accessing print, film and photo materials. I also thank the staff of the Filmarchiv/Bundesarchiv (Berlin) and the Wien Museum (Vienna), as well as Kendall Wallis from the McGill University Library, whose ability to track down sources has often bordered on the magical. I would be amiss not to thank the people who have invited me to share various parts of this project in research colloquia and conference panels in recent years: Katharina Aulls, Cornelius Borck, Marion Froger, Roman Horak, Christine Kanz, Ines Lindner, Lorna Martens, Clark Muenzer, Mihaela Petrescu, Bill Rasch, Rosemarie Schade, Frank Stanisch and Christopher Young. Finally, let me add that my ability to research and present various parts of this project over the past four years was facilitated by generous research grants from the Social Sciences and Humanities Research Council of Canada and the Canadian Foundation for Innovation, for which I remain humbly grateful. Shorter versions of chapters 2, 3 and 4 initially appeared in *The German Quarterly*, *Modernism/modernity* and *October* respectively. They are included here by kind permission of the editors.

Textual Note

Throughout this book, all translations into English, unless otherwise attributed, are my own and reference is given to the original text. Further references to a cited text will appear after quotations; passages without page reference are from the last-cited page and page-numbers without specified text are similarly from the one last named. Unless otherwise stated, all italics are the author's.

List of Illustrations

Chapter 1
1. Rhythmical gymnastics, pupil from the Institut Jaques-Dalcroze in Hellerau (1913), from *The Eurhythmics of Jaques-Dalcroze* (London : Constable & Company, 1913)
2. Rhythmical labour, illustration from Karl Bücher, *Arbeit und Rhythmus* (1924)
3. Sphygmograph, from Étienne Jules-Marey, *La méthode graphique* (Paris, 1878)
4. Isadora Duncan photographed by Arnold Genthe ca. 1915, courtesy of the Jerome Robbins Dance Division, The New York Public Library for the Performing Arts, Astor, Lenox and Tilden Foundations.
5. Rhythmical group gymnastics, from Rudolf Bode, *Rhythmus und Körpererziehung* (1923)

Chapter 2
1. Luigi Russolo, *Dinamismo di un'automobile* (1912/13), courtesy of Agence Photographique de la RMN
2. Franziska Kantor, *Wiedergabe des rhythmischen Ablaufs einer Bewegung* (ca. 1921), courtesy of Wien Museum
3. Umberto Boccioni, *Visioni simultanee* (1911/12)
4. Ferdinand Hodler, *Eurythmie* (1895), courtesy of the Kunstmuseum Bern
5. Loïe Fuller photographed by Frederick Glasier (1902)

Chapter 3
1. Snapshot of dancers, from Rudolf von Laban, *Gymnastik und Tanz* (1926)
2. Kinetische Versuche (1922), courtesy of Wien Museum
3. Advertisement for Walter Ruttmann, *Berlin. Die Sinfonie der Großstadt* (1927), courtesy of the Deutsche Kinemathek
4. Still from Wilhelm Prager and Nicholas Kaufmann, *Wege zu Kraft und Schönheit* (1925), courtesy of the Deutsche Kinemathek

5. Still from Fritz Lang, *Metropolis* (1927), courtesy of the Deutsche Kinemathek
6. Still from *Metropolis*, courtesy of the Deutsche Kinemathek
7. Still from *Metropolis*, courtesy of the Deutsche Kinemathek
8. Still from *Metropolis*, courtesy of the Deutsche Kinemathek

Chapter 4
1. Walter Ruttmann, *Der Aufstieg* (1926), still from Käthe Kurtzig, 'Die Arten des Werbefilms', *Industrielle Psychotechnik* (1926)
2. Sketch for an electric light advertisement, from Fritz Pauli, *Rhythmus und Resonanz als ökonomisches Prinzip in der Reklame* (1926)
3. Still from Julius Pinschewer and Guido Seeber, *Kipho* (1925), courtesy of the Deutsche Kinemathek
4. Stills from *Kipho* (1925), courtesy of the Deutsche Kinemathek
5. Guido Seeber, schema illustrating in-camera montage technique, from *Der Trickfilm in seinen grundsätzlichen Möglichkeiten* (1927)
6. Still from *Kipho* (1925), courtesy of the Deutsche Kinemathek
7. Still from *Kipho* (1925), courtesy of the Deutsche Kinemathek
8. Still from *Kipho* (1925), courtesy of the Deutsche Kinemathek
9. Still from *Kipho* (1925), courtesy of the Deutsche Kinemathek
10. Stills from *Kipho* (1925), courtesy of the Deutsche Kinemathek
11. Advertisement for *Das Cabinet des Doktor Caligari*, from *Der Kinematograph* (1919)
12. Advertisement for the Kipho exhibition, from *Kinematograph* (1925)
13. Still from *Kipho* (1925), courtesy of the Deutsche Kinemathek
14. Sketch for a traffic advertisement (for Elida cosmetics), from Fritz Pauli, *Rhythmus und Resonanz als ökonomisches Prinzip in der Reklame* (1926)
15. Poster for diving competition, from Fritz Pauli, *Rhythmus und Resonanz als ökonomisches Prinzip in der Reklame* (1926)

Chapter 5
1. *Jonny spielt auf*, cover page for piano score (1926)
2. Jazz on the assembly line, image from Fritz Giese, *Methoden der Wirtschaftspsychologie* (1927)
3. Paul Moran, *Moderne Tänze* (1926), cover page
4. Heinz Loew, untitled photo (1927/28), courtesy of the Bauhausarchiv (Berlin)
5. Shimmy Liddy, illustration from Franz Wolfgang Koebner, *Jazz und Shimmy* (1922)

6. Filmed dance steps, from Franz Wolfgang Koebner, *Das neue Tanz-Brevier* (1920)
7. Advertisement for *1000 Schritte Charleston* (1926), from *Der Film*
8. The Tiller Girls, illustration from Fritz Giese, *Girlkultur. Vergleiche zwischen amerikanischem und europäischem Rhythmus und Lebensgefühl* (1925)
9. Illustration from Fritz Giese, *Girlkultur. Vergleiche zwischen amerikanischem und europäischem Rhythmus und Lebensgefühl* (1925)
10. Advertisement for *Saxophone Susi* (1928), from *Lichtbild-Bühne*
11. Ernst Krenek, *Jonny spielt auf,* collage of elements from the opera (1927) © by kind permission of Universal Edition A.G., Wien
12. Promotional photograph for Fritz Lang, *Metropolis* (1927), courtesy of the Deutsche Kinemathek

1. Introduction: Rhythm and the Mediation of Modern Experience

Socialement et individuellement, l'homme est un animal rythmique.¹

[Socially and individually, man is a rhythmical animal.]

At one point in Thomas Grube and Enrique Sánchez Lansch's documentary film *Rhythm is it!* (2004), the conductor of the Berlin Philharmonic Orchestra, Sir Simon Rattle, explains his involvement with the project to have schoolchildren from Berlin's underprivileged neighbourhoods perform Stravinsky's *Le Sacre du printemps* as follows: 'I had somehow always wanted to do a project where you could bring young dancers and an orchestra together. Why not? Why does it always have to be professionals? [...] One of the things I think work on music can teach people is what joins them rather than what separates them'.² Rattle's words here provide a succinct summary of the film's argument; beyond documenting a pedagogical endeavour, the project behind *Rhythm is it!* was above all to offer a model of community in an era seemingly beset with individualism, competition and anomie. In classic documentary fashion, the film begins by setting up the problem and offers a solution in the latter

---

1   Marcel Mauss 1926

2   *Rhythm is it!* 3-Disc Collector's Edition, dir. by Thomas Grube and Enrique Sánchez Lansch (DVD, Boomtown Media, 2005), disc 1. Rattle's comments here were clearly important for the filmmakers, as they find an echo in another interview with Rattle included in the DVD version of the film, where he describes the project as follows: 'Let's find some big place [...] where everyone can come, all of these people who would not normally meet each other, some of whom would fight each other, whose parents wouldn't know each other, and who wouldn't necessarily speak the same language – let's bring them all together. If there's anything we have to do in this new century, it's this' (*Rhythm is it!*, disc 3).

parts.³ Set to the accompaniment of hip-hop music, the establishing sequence offers a vision of Berlin as a nightmarish ghetto: long shots of the cold and empty city, close-ups of chain-link fences and faces of children smoking cigarettes or engaged in acts of bullying converge to construct an atmosphere of isolation, aggression and affective distance. Subsequent scenes, documenting the schoolchildren's participation in the *Rite of Spring* project, will show them gradually emerging from their shells and exchanging their solitude for a newfound sense of community belonging – a process symbolized by the performance of *Rite of Spring* in Treptow Arena by some 250 children in the final shots of the film.

The inclusive model of this pedagogical project can be seen as a symbolic construct directly opposed to the elimination format recently imported into Germany in series such as *Big Brother* (first broadcast in Germany in 2000) and *The Weakest Link* (2001). As Zygmunt Bauman has argued, such reality TV shows can be understood precisely as 'pedagogical' projects, namely a training in neoliberal ethics, 'Verhaltenslehren' [guides for conduct] for a competitive and unstable world in which individuals are encouraged to enter only into tentative – and always revocable – alliances.⁴ Adopting a similar reality format, *Rhythm is it!* constructs a counter-pedagogy, one centred on the inculcation of a desire for community belonging. As the choreographers Royston Maldoom and Susannah Broughton explain repeatedly throughout the film, the purpose of the project is to teach children values not of individualism, competition and precarious attachments, but rather of responsibility, commitment and mutual support.

It would be an understatement to say that the project documented in *Rhythm is it!* spoke to concerns of the new millennium. Over the course of 2005, the film was honoured with no fewer than six prizes for documentary, including the German Critics Association Award, the Guild of German Art House Cinemas award, and Germany's most prestigious prize of all, the Deutscher Filmpreis for best documentary. Moreover, the project at the centre of the film has spawned several sequels: Maldoom's *Rite of Spring* project has been performed by schoolchildren in several cities including London and,

3 Bill Nichols has called this the 'problem solving' narrative. See Nichols, *Representing Reality. Issues and Concepts in Documentary* (Bloomington: Indiana University Press, 1991), 18.

4 See Zygmunt Bauman, *Society under Siege* (Cambridge: Polity Press, 2002), 61–66; the term 'Verhaltenslehren' comes from Helmut Lethen, *Verhaltenslehren der Kälte. Lebensversuche zwischen den Kriegen* [*Cool Conduct: The Culture of Distance in Weimar Germany*] (Frankfurt am Main: Surhkamp, 1994).

most recently, Carnegie Hall in New York in autumn 2007, followed by similar projects using different composers.[5] Given this goal of reaffirming community bonds, the filmmakers – and the organizers of the project on which it was based – could hardly have chosen a more symbolically charged ballet than Stravinsky's *Le Sacre du printemps*. Aside from its status as the catalyst of modernism's most infamous scandal, Stravinsky's ballet of ritual sacrifice embodied above all a fantasy of community for a 'New' Europe beset with a sense of anomie, an effort to re-imagine the authenticity of ritual and myth in an increasingly disenchanted and cynical cultural climate. These themes from Stravinsky's ballet find echoes in the film through a host of recurrent motifs: the acquisition of self-knowledge, the escape from modern distractions, the overcoming of cynicism and, above all, the rediscovery of the body.[6]

But more than all these modernist themes, what *Rhythm is it!* shares with Stravinsky – as the title suggests – is a concern with a particular notion and mythology of *rhythm*: rhythm as a medium of communal participation, a structuring principle of ritual time (as opposed to the linear time of industrial modernity) and an authentic force of vitality lying below the surface of a rationalized world. As Rattle describes it in a passage from which the filmmakers drew their title: 'There's a part of the brain, the pre-civilized human part of the brain [...] where rhythm is it. The first idea, I think probably the first communication, was through rhythm, before words. And I think when you get that as a child, somehow you're connecting with your origins' (*Rhythm is it!*, disc 1). Rattle's statement here recalls ideas generally attributed to another contemporary of Stravinsky from the modernist era, namely the conductor and Wagner disciple Hans von Bülow (1830–1894), who is generally held to have coined a statement that became one of the rallying cries of modernist music in the early twentieth century: 'Im Anfang war der Rhythmus' [In the beginning was rhythm].[7] Von Bülow's dictum, which circulated widely among turn-of-the-century musicologists, betokened an increasing emphasis

---

5   In his dance project *Overture 2012*, performed at the Royal Albert Hall in November 2008, Maldoom brought in 120 London-based young people to dance to Shostakovich's 10th symphony performed by the London Symphony Orchestra.

6   As the choreographer Susannah Broughton puts it at one point: 'The moment there is stillness, you can really listen to the body, you can really hear what's happening. Cause we're so unfamiliar with it. There's quite a fear connected to that' (*Rhythm is it!*, disc 1).

7   Theodor Pfeiffer, *Studien bei Hans von Bülow* [*Studies with Hans von Bülow*] (Berlin: F. Luckhardt 1896), 8.

on rhythm in modern music that would find its culmination in the early twentieth century in the work of composers such as Darius Milhaud, Paul Hindemith and of course Stravinsky himself. But the saying is perhaps less interesting in purely musicological terms than for the importance it gained in all sorts of unexpected cultural domains after 1900. To offer one example, the architect and founder of the Deutscher Werkbund, Hermann Muthesius, began a lecture on modern architecture at the Art Institute of Berlin in 1908 as follows:

> Im Anfang war der Rhythmus. Dieser Ausspruch des geistvollen musikalischen Denkers Hans v. Bülow bezieht sich nicht allein oder auch nur vorwiegend auf die Musik. Der Rhythmus ist jeder menschlichen Tätigkeit eigentümlich, er ist das erste Gesetz aller Äußerungen unseres Selbst. Und er ist noch deutlicher erkennbar im Jugendzustande des Individuums, und in den primitiven Kulturen, als in vorgerückteren Entwicklungsstadien.[8]

> [In the beginning was rhythm. This saying by the brilliant musical theorist Hans von Bülow refers not only and not even primarily to music. Rhythm characterizes every human activity; it is the first law of every expression of our being. And it is more clearly recognizable in youthful individuals, and in primitive cultures, than in more advanced developmental stages.]

Muthesius's words here would be repeated in countless variations by any number of artists, intellectuals and scientists around the turn of the century.[9] As they suggest, notions of rhythm stood at the centre of a broad anthropological effort, in modern culture, to understand the human ('the first law of every expression of our being'), an endeavour encompassing fields as diverse as philosophy, economics, sociology,

---

8   Hermann Muthesius, *Die Einheit der Architektur. Betrachtungen über Baukunst, Ingenieurbau und Kunstgewerbe* [*The Unity of Architecture. Observations on Building, Civil Engineering and the Applied Arts*] (Berlin: Curtius, 1908), 1.

9   To offer one other example here, the pedagogical theorist Gustav Klar, in the introduction to a treatise on the use of rhythm in education from 1922, explained: 'Hans von Bülow, einer der bedeutendsten Dirigenten der Neuzeit, hat gewiß recht, wenn er den Ausspruch tut: "Im Anfang war der Rhythmus". Er ist tatsächlich das dem Menschen von Natur innewohnende und in den verschiedenen Beziehungen zum Ausdruck kommende Urgefühl' [Hans von Bülow, one of the most significant modern conductors, is certainly correct when he states: 'In the beginning was rhythm'. Rhythm is indeed the most primitive sensation, which inhabits human beings by nature and finds expression in their various relations], Gustav Klar, *Der Rhythmus und seine Bedeutung für den Unterricht* [*Rhythm and its Significance for the Classroom*] (Langensalza: Verlag von Julius Beltz, 1919), 3.

history, biology, psychology, art history, anthropology and the 'science of work'.¹⁰ Indeed, as Christine Lubkoll has shown, 'rhythm' was one of European modernism's most fetishized keywords, one charged with a fantasy of overcoming modernity's malaise and returning to a more authentic state of being.¹¹ If, as Baumann has argued, the very sound of the term 'community' carries a warm affective valence in the English language today, one can make a similar argument for the term 'Rhythmus' in German and European culture around 1900, and this for a similar reason: the word evoked associations of communal participation, ritual renewal and a connection with nature and the body seemingly lost to modern technological civilization.¹²

Another major centre of modernity's preoccupation with rhythm, and one that formed something of a direct precursor to the pedagogical project documented in *Rhythm is it!*, was the Jaques-Dalcroze Institute in Hellerau. Founded by the Swiss composer, educator and dance theorist Emile Jaques-Dalcroze in 1910 (and partly designed by Muthesius), the Institute trained students in a rigorous system of 'rhythmical gymnastics' in which various complex rhythms were translated into standardized arm and leg movements (figure 1). Visitors to Hellerau, who often commented on the pupils' extraordinary bodily dexterity, were particularly impressed with their ability to perform multiple rhythms simultaneously; in the words of one observer, '[G]eradezu verblüffend für jeden Musiker sind die Taktierübungen, wo mit Kopfbewegungen ein 2/4 Takt, mit dem linken Arm ein 3/4 Takt, mit dem rechten Arm ein 4/4 Takt, den Beinen ein 5/4 Takt gleichzeitig angegeben wird' [Musicians are all truly amazed by scansion exercises in which the head beats a 2/4 time, the left arm 3/4, and the right arm 4/4, while the legs beat a 5/4

---

10   I borrow the term 'science of work', a direct translation of the French 'science du travail' and the German 'Arbeitswissenschaft', from Anson Rabinbach to designate a broad spectrum of research on labour efficiency and fatigue in the workplace in the late nineteenth and early twentieth centuries. See Anson Rabinbach, *The Human Motor. Energy, Fatigue and the Origins of Modernity* (Berkeley: University of California Press, 1992), 179–205. On the role of rhythm studies in work science, see pp. 172, 189–92.

11   Christine Lubkoll, 'Rhythmus. Zum Komplex von Lebensphilosophie und ästhetischer Moderne' [Rhythm. On the Connections Between Vitalist Philosophy and Modern Aesthetics], in Christine Lubkoll (ed.), *Das Imaginäre des Fin de siècle. Ein Symposion für Gerhard Neumann* [The Fin-de-Siècle Imaginary. A Symposium for Gerhard Neumann] (Freiburg: Rombach, 2002), 83–110.

12   See Zygmut Bauman, *Community. Seeking Safety in an Insecure World* (Cambridge: Polity, 2001), 1–7.

Fig 1. Rhythmical gymnastics, pupil from the Institut Jaques-Dalcroze in Hellerau (1913)

time].[13] As I have discussed elsewhere, one of the goals of Jaques-Dalcroze's exercises was to inculcate self-confidence in an insecure world by instilling in students a sense of control over the body and its movements,[14] and this project – along with many of Jaques-Dalcroze's trademark techniques such as warming students up by having them walk and stop on command – shows up verbatim in *Rhythm is it!* As Susannah Broughton describes it at one point, echoing the earlier body-culture theorists, one of the main goals of dance instruction is precisely to build self-confidence through bodily control: 'They have very little confidence. I mean it's quite scary, I find, to see such young people so out of control of their bodies' (*Rhythm is it!*, disc 1). But even more than individual confidence, the film takes up Jaques-Dalcroze's emphasis on group and community dance.

---

13 *Die Bildungs-Anstalt für Musik und Rhythmus E. Jaques-Dalcroze in Dresden-Hellerau. Ein Bericht mit 8 Abbildungen* [*The E. Jaques-Dalcroze Educational Institute for Music and Rhythm in Dresden-Hellerau. A Report with Eight Illustrations*] (Jena: Eugen Diederichs, 1910), 4.

14 See Michael Cowan, *Cult of the Will. Nervousness and German Modernity* (University Park, PA: Pennsylvania State University Press, 2008), 180–207.

In many ways, the much-celebrated Jaques-Dalcroze Institute – which trained such dancers as Mary Wigman and was visited by many of the most prominent intellectuals of Europe – served as a model for other efforts to harness rhythm in the service of cultural reform in the early twentieth century, particularly in the realm of education. In addition to numerous other dance schools in Germany such as Rudolf von Laban's 'Schulen der Bewegungskunst' [Schools of the Art of Movement] and the Elisabeth Duncan dance school in Berlin, the interest in rhythm as a pedagogical tool in the early twentieth century can be gleaned from the sheer number of print publications on the topic such as Gustav Klar's *Der Rhythmus und seine Bedeutung für den Unterricht* (1919) [*Rhythm and its Significance for the Classroom*], Rudolf Bode's *Der Rhythmus und seine Bedeutung für die Erziehung* (1920) [*Rhythm and its Significance for Education*], Bernhard Koch's *Der Rhythmus. Untersuchungen über sein Wesen und Wirken in Kunst und Natur und seine Bedeutung für die Schule* (1922) [*Rhythm, an Analysis of its Essence and Effects in Art and Nature and its Significance for Schools*] or Friedrich Struwe's *Erziehung durch Rhythmus in Musik und Leben* (1930) [*Education through Rhythm in Music and Life*]. But this interest in rhythm as an agent of cultural 'renewal' also extended well beyond the realm of education proper. Indeed, among those inspired by Jaques-Dalcroze's experiments were none other than Stravinsky's collaborators themselves; according to Modris Eckstein, Diaghilev and Nijinsky visited the Dalcroze Institute in 1912 to learn more about eurhythmical dance and persuaded one of the students, Marie Rambert, to join the Ballets Russes to assist in the group choreography for *Rite of Spring*.[15]

Such collaborations are indicative of a broader shared project. The very rhythmical structures at work in *Rite of Spring* resemble Jaques-Dalcroze's performances in several respects; in particular, the ballet recalls Jaques Dalcroze's rigorous training in polyrhythms with its use of constantly shifting time signatures. Thus the conductor Pierre Boulez describes his first encounter as a conductor with Stravinsky's work as follows:

> When I began to conduct, I began to face the problems [of *Le Sacre du printemps*], and the problems are mainly rhythmical problems. In a normal way, you beat 1-2-3, 1-2-3-4, but nothing exceptional. It does not change all the time. But in some parts of Stravinsky, especially the final dance, the *danse sacrale*, the metre changes constantly. You

---

15 See Modris Ekstein, *The Rites of Spring* (Boston: Houghton Mifflin, 1989), 37, 51–52.

have 2-3-5, 2-3-4, and so on. And so you have to adapt yourself to this constant change. [...] At first, I was very anxious.[16]

Similarly, in an interview for the DVD release of *Rhythm is it!*, Simon Rattle describes his own experience with Stravinsky's rhythms: 'Whenever you think you've got your rhythm, there's an extra beat. There's no point where you can get comfortable. But yet, you feel as though the whole planet is pulsating under you' (*Rhythm is it!*, disc 2). Contemporary observers clearly understood such pulsating polyrhythms as a return to primitive vitality. As one observer described it: 'Wenn Strawinsky in seinem polyrhythmischen "Sacre du printemps" [...] bahnbrechend vorangeht, so kehrt er eben zur Quelle aller Musik zurück' [If Stravinsky breaks new ground with his polyrhythmical *Sacre du printemps*, he also returns to the source of all music].[17]

If Stravinsky and other modern artists and intellectuals ascribed such great importance to the rediscovery of 'primitive' rhythms, this is because they hoped to find in art an answer to a problem that had been articulated elsewhere. For Jaques-Dalcroze and his associates, as for many invested in the rhythm debates around 1900, the most authoritative formulation of the problem could be found in a study largely forgotten today but widely influential in the early twentieth century: *Arbeit und Rhythmus* (1897) [*Work and Rhythm*] by the economist Karl Bücher. Studying a range of traditional work songs from anthropological publications and ethnographic exhibitions (so-called 'zoos humains' or 'Völkerschauen') at the Paris World's fair, Bücher claims to have discovered a lost world of rhythmical, collective labour, one attuned to the rhythms of the body and functioning to solidify community bonds rather than isolating workers – in the manner of modern factory work – in the performance of individual tasks (figure 2). For Bücher, rhythmical work not only pre-dated the division of labour characteristic of Taylorist production, but also knew nothing of the modern separation of life spheres into work and leisure. 'Arbeit, Musik und Dichtung,' Bücher claimed, '[müssen] auf der primitiven Stufe ihrer Entwicklung in *eins* verschmolzen gewesen sein. [...] Was sie verbindet, ist das gemeinsame Merkmal des Rhythmus' [In their primitive form, work, music and poetry must have been melded into *one*. [...] They were linked by the common

---

16 Pierre Boulez, interviewed in *Pierre Boulez Conducts Stravinsky. Le Sacre du printemps* (DVD, Image Entertainment, 1993).

17 Erwin Felber, 'Primitive und moderne Musik' [Primitive and Modern Music], *Der Auftakt* V (1925), 311.

Fig 2. Illustration of rhythmical labour from Karl Bücher, Arbeit und Rhythmus, *6th edn., 1924*

trait of rhythm].[18] Jaques-Dalcroze and his associates latched on to precisely this point; as the Institute's financial backer Wolf Dohrn wrote in an article for the Institute's yearbook *Der Rhythmus*: '[Bücher] führt den Nachweis, daß auf der primitiven Stufe der Menschheit alle Arbeit rhythmische Form hatte, daß es überhaupt nur eine Art menschlicher Betätigung gegeben habe, in welcher "Arbeit, Spiel und Kunst" eine Einheit gewesen sei' [Bücher demonstrates that, for primitive humanity, all work assumed rhythmical form, that there existed only one type of human activity, in which 'work, play and art' formed a unity].[19]

Bücher was hardly the first observer to associate rhythm and 'primitive' culture. Charles Darwin, for example, saw pleasure in rhythm as a universal characteristic of animal life activated in mating rituals, a fact which, he argued, explains why 'music, dancing, song, and poetry are such very ancient arts'.[20] Closer to Bücher, the art historian Ernst Grosse had argued, in his study *Die Anfänge der Kunst* (1894) [*The Origins of Art*], that rhythm formed the primitive basis of

18 Karl Bücher, *Arbeit und Rhythmus. Abhandlungen der philologisch-historischen Classe der königlichen sächsischen Gesellschaft der Wissenschaften* 39:5 (Leipzig: S. Hirzel, 1897), 78.

19 Wolf Dohrn, 'Aufgaben der Bildungsanstalt Jaques-Dalcroze' [Tasks of the Jaques-Dalcroze Educational Institute], *Die Schulfeste der Bildungsanstalt Jaques-Dalcroze* [*The School Festivals of the Jaques-Dalcroze Educational Institute*]. *Der Rhythmus* 2, Nr 1 (Jena: Diederichs, 1912), 7–8.

20 Charles Darwin, *The Descent of Man and Selection in Relation to Sex*, 2nd edn (London: John Murray, 1874), 572.

dance, poetry and music, arguing in particular that dance rhythm served as the first medium for forging a social bond: '[D]iese ganze Menge bewegt sich alsdann nach *einem* Gesetze, in *einem* Takt. [...] Während des Tanzes befinden sich die Theilnehmer im Zustande der vollkommenen Socialisierung; die tanzende Gruppe empfindet und handelt wie ein einheitlicher Organismus' [Thereupon the entire crowd moves according to *one* law, to *one* beat. [...] During the dance, the participants are in a condition of complete socialization; the dancing group feels and acts like a unified organism].[21] But while Bücher shared this association between rhythm and the 'primitive' arts of dance, music and lyric, it would be a mistake to see his study – or the Jaques-Dalcroze gymnastics influenced by it – only as an example of anti-modern nostalgia. For Bücher's understanding of rhythm was also steeped in the values of rationality and the rationalized body, subscribing wholeheartedly to the nineteenth-century view of the body – explored by Anson Rabinbach – as a 'human motor'.[22] Rhythm, for Bücher, was first and foremost a natural means of regulating bodily efficiency:

> Der Rhythmus entspringt dem organischen Wesen des Menschen. Alle natürliche Bethätigung des thierischen Körpers scheint er als das regulierende Element sparsamsten Kräfteverbrauchs zu beherrschen. Das trabende Pferd und das beladene Kamel bewegen sich ebenso rhythmisch wie der rudernde Schiffer und der hämmernde Schmied. (Bücher 101)

> [Rhythm arises from humanity's organic being. It regulates all the natural movements of the animal body to generate the most efficient use of energy. Trotting horses and loaded camels move rhythmically no less than oarsman in a ship or blacksmiths wielding the hammer.]

In particular, by rendering movements automatic, rhythm decreased the amount of conscious energy necessary to complete individual

---

21 Ernst Grosse, *Die Anfänge der Kunst* (Freiburg: Akademische Verlagsbuchhandlung von J. C. B. Mohr, 1894): 218–19. Wilhelm Wundt would later take up a similar line of argument in the third volume of his *Völkerpsychologie* (1908) dedicated to the evolution of art, where he argued that dance and song were united in primitive cultures, where affect 'ungehemmt sich ergießen kann' [can flow forth uninhibitedly], Wilhelm Wundt, *Völkerpsychologie. Eine Untersuchung der Entwicklungsgesetze [Folk Psychology. A Study of the Laws of Development]*, vol. 3, *Die Kunst*, 4th edn (Leipzig: Alfred Kröner Verlag, 1923), 470.
22 See Rabinbach, *The Human Motor*.

tasks and, as a result, rendered labour more pleasurable.[23] Precisely this effort to automate bodily movements would form a centrepiece of Jaques-Dalcroze's gymnastics programme, as he explained in another context:

> Eine hervorragende Rolle spielt der Rhythmus bei der täglichen Arbeit. Er ist es, der die einzelnen Bewegungen erleichtert, indem er sie automatisiert. Einerseits erregt er die Kräfte, andererseits schont er sie, steigert so die Leistungsfähigkeit und ermöglicht ein freudiges, von Widerwillen freies Arbeiten. Zur Stütze meiner Theorien lassen sich die Arbeitslieder anführen, die auf allen handwerklichen Berufszweigen vorkommen und dort eine wichtige Rolle spielen.[24]

> [Rhythm plays a prominent role in daily work. Rhythm is what facilitates individual movements by rendering them automatic. It both arouses energy and saves it, thus increasing productivity. It enables the worker to perform his tasks with joy and without reluctance. Evidence for this theory can be found in work songs, which play an important role in all manual trades.]

By claiming for rhythm the powers of automatization and increased productivity, Bücher clearly sought to appeal to readers subscribing to the values of work science no less than those of modern ethnography. Indeed, part of the appeal of Bücher's model of rhythmical labour resided not only in the claim to increased efficiency but also increased worker satisfaction – a topic taken up often in discussions of Bücher's arguments in turn-of-the-century work science.[25]

---

23   This link between rhythm and 'pleasure' is key to any understanding of the investment in rhythm in the late nineteenth and early twentieth centuries. As Michael Golston has shown, moreover, it was underpinned by a wide industry of physiological and psychological research. According to one American psychologist writing in 1902: 'The great pleasure which children find in rhythm is due to the efficacy of rhythm to set up vibrations in other organs of the body, and the consequent harmonious activity of the several bodily organs. The affective tone increases in proportion as the summation of excitation increases, till a state bordering on ecstasy may be reached', cited in Michael Golston, 'Im Anfang war der Rhythmus – rhythmic incubations in discourses of mind, body and race from 1850–1944', *Stanford Electronic Humanities Review*, supplement 5: *Cultural and Technological Incubations of Fascism* (1996). www.stanford.edu/group/SHR/5-supp/text/golston.html [accessed 20 July 2011].

24   Emile Jaques-Dalcroze, *Rhythmus, Musik und Erziehung* [*Rhythm, Music and Education*], trans. by Julius Schwabe (Basel: Verlag Beno Schwabe & Co., 1922), 62.

25   See, for example, Margaret Keiver Smith, *Rhythmus und Arbeit* [*Work and Rhythm*] (Leipzig: Wilhelm Engelmann, 1900), 152–53.

By thus projecting the values of productivity and energy efficiency back onto pre-modern cultures, Bücher's model of rhythm, along with the various research and movements that drew on it, presented a fundamental ambiguity. If rhythm figured as the object of a nostalgic reconstruction, the hallmark of holistic communities, it was *also* seen as the quintessential activity of the body understood as a 'human motor', the phenomenon by which the body's activity, regularized and automatized, most closely resembled that of machines. Writers and intellectuals often reflected on precisely this paradox. In his 1915 novel *Tropen* [*Tropics*], for example, the Austrian author Robert Müller mused:

> Mit dem Rhythmus verhält es sich seltsam. Es scheint, daß er das Wesen aller jener Kulturen darstellt, die der unsern entgegengesetzt sind, und die wir zu leugnen suchen: die im Süden und Osten. Aber der Rhythmus bringt dort am menschlichen Körper Leistungen hervor, denen wir nichts Gleichartiges entgegenzustellen haben und die in ihrer steifen und von uns aus unnachahmbaren Einseitigkeit nur mit unserer Spezialität Technik verglichen werden können.[26]

> [Rhythm is a strange thing. It appears to constitute the essential ingredient of all those cultures opposed to our own – cultures of the south and the east – and from which we like to distinguish ourselves. But within those cultures, rhythm spurs the body on to achievements that we cannot that we cannot hope to match, achievements whose rigid and inimitable uniformity can only be compared to our own speciality, technology.]

Rhythm thus appeared both as a criterion of difference, distinguishing the 'primitive' from the 'modern' or the 'organic' from the 'vital', *and* as a category of sameness, drawing a parallel between 'primitive' bodily labour and the labour of factory technology.

Grappling with this ambiguity, Bücher argued that the problem with factory work was not the emphasis on efficiency as such, but rather the imperative of *constant* energy expenditure to the detriment of the organic requirement of an alternation between work and rest, tension and relaxation. Bücher saw this new, inhuman temporality of machines embodied most centrally in the phenomenon of continuous rotation, which eliminated the pauses and rests – the downbeats and backstrokes – characteristic of rhythmical labour:

---

26 Robert Müller, *Tropen* (Munich, H. Schmidt, 1917), 37.

[E]s wird eine denkwürdige Tatsache in der Geschichte des Maschinenwesens bilden, dass viele der ältesten Arbeitsmaschinen rhythmischen Gang haben, indem sie [...] die Hand- und Armbewegungen des bisherigen Arbeitsverfahrens bloss nachahmen. [...] Mit der weiteren Entwicklung des Maschinenbaues strebt man darnach, den mit dem rhythmischen Gang des Mechanismus meist verbundenen todten Rückgang zu vermeiden und geht [...] von der wage- oder senkrechten zur gleichförmig rotierenden Bewegung über, die jenen Kraftverlust vermeidet. [...] Damit schwindet die alte Musik der Arbeit, welche die rhythmisch gehenden Maschinen noch deutlich erkennen liessen, aus den Werkstätten. (Bücher 114–15)

[It will remain a noteworthy fact for historians of industrial technology that the earliest machines displayed a rhythmical motion, in which they [...] imitated the hand and arm movements of traditional workers. But with the advancement of industrial machinery, one strove to eliminate the idle backstroke usually associated with rhythmical machine motion and [...] thus exchanged this horizontal or vertical movement for uniform rotation, which avoids that loss of energy. [...] This transition marks the disappearance from factory floors of the traditional music of labour, which could still be heard clearly in the machines that followed rhythmical movement.]

This transformation, Bücher argued, marked the moment at which the relation between people and machines was turned on its head, where people began to serve machines and not the other way around:

Der arbeitende Mensch ist nicht mehr Herr seiner Bewegungen, das Werkzeug sein Diener, sein verstärktes Körperglied, sondern das Werkzeug ist Herr über ihn geworden; es diktiert ihm das Mass seiner Bewegungen; das Tempo und die Dauer seiner Arbeit ist seinem Willen entzogen; er ist an den todten und doch so lebendigen Mechanismus gefesselt. (Bücher 115)

[The working man is no longer master of his own movements. His tools no longer act as his servants, as enhanced bodily limbs. Rather, the tools now lord it over him. They dictate to him the measure of his movements. The speed and duration of his labour no longer obeys his will. He has been chained to a mechanism that is dead and yet seems so alive.][27]

27 Here again, Jaques-Dalcroze agreed, and he saw his rhythmical pedagogy largely as an effort to restore man's centrality through bodily cultivation. As he explained in a later passage from the text already cited, rhythmical gymnastics were meant to compensate for the loss of rhythm (and of the human) in labour: 'Heutzutage hat die Maschine das Handwerk verdrängt, und der Mensch ist der Diener dieser Maschine geworden. Statt die Arbeit zu beherrschen, ist er

Of all the findings of Bücher's study, it was his diagnosis of technological modernization in terms of a subordination of human or organic temporality to the temporality of machines that had the strongest resonance with other contemporary thinkers. To take just one example, in his monumental *Philosophie des Geldes* (1900) [*Philosophy of Money*], Georg Simmel included a lengthy discussion of rhythm, clearly inspired by Bücher, in which he described urbanization as a transformation from organic to machinic rhythms.[28] Traditional societies, in Simmel's reading, are defined above all by their subordination to definite rhythms of 'Expansion und Kontraktion' [expansion and contraction] dictated by the alternation of day and night, the phases of the moon, the cycle of seasons and the needs of the body (554). In the modern urban habitat, on the other hand, such periodicity of tension and relaxation is replaced by a world in which factory technology, industrial transportation and – not least – the modern banking economy have made possible constant and uninterrupted activity.

> [W]enn die Kultur, wie man zu sagen pflegt, nicht nur den Raum, sondern auch die Zeit überwindet, so bedeutet dies, daß die Bestimmtheit zeitlicher Abteilungen nicht mehr das zwingende Schema für unser Tun und Genießen bildet [...]. Also: die generell dargebotenen Bedingungen sind vom Rhythmus befreit. (555)

> [If culture, as is customarily held, overcomes time as well as space, then this means that precise temporal intervals no longer form the compulsory framework for our activities and leisure [...]. Thus the general conditions of existence are freed from rhythm.]

Like other aspects of urban modernity in Simmel's thought, this liberation from natural rhythms grounded in the body or the seasons represented an ambivalent phenomenon: while it offered individuals hitherto unknown freedoms, it also entailed a loss of the security of community bonds. Like Bücher, moreover, Simmel saw the unpleasurable aspect of modern work as a result of the subordination of bodily rhythms to those of the industrial factory:

---

nunmehr ihr Sklave' (Jaques-Dalcroze, *Rhythmus, Musik und Erziehung*, 62–63) [Today, manual trades have been suppressed by machines, which have made people into their servants. Rather than controlling the work process, man is now the slave of the latter].

28 See Georg Simmel, *Philosophie des Geldes*, 4th edn (München: Duncker & Humboldt, 1922), 552–75.

Nun enthält zwar gerade der moderne Fabrikbetrieb wieder stark rhythmische Elemente; allein soweit sie den Arbeiter an die Strenge gleichmäßig wiederholter Bewegungen binden, haben sie eine ganz andere subjektive Bedeutung, als jene alte Arbeitsrhythmik. Denn diese folgte den inneren Forderungen physiologisch-psychologischer Energetik, die jetzige aber entweder unmittelbar der rücksichtslos objektiven Maschinenbewegung oder dem Zwange für den einzelnen Arbeiter, als Glied einer Gruppe von Arbeitern, deren jeder nur einen kleinen Teilprozeß verrichtet, mit den anderen Schritt zu halten. (559)

[Today, we can once again observe such pronounced rhythmical structures in, of all places, the modern factory. However, inasmuch as these structures bind the worker to the stringent requirement of performing repetitive identical movements, they have a completely different subjective meaning from the old work rhythms. For the latter followed the inner demands of physiological-psychological energies, while the new rhythms conform either to the indifferent and objective movement of the machines or to the compulsory requirement for the individual worker to keep up with the other workers in the group, each of whom performs only a small part of the work process.]

Transformed from an organic affirmation of the body (the 'inner demands of physiological-psychological energies') to a mode of compulsory machinic discipline, rhythm, for Simmel, constituted one variant of the basic 'conflict' of modern culture, in which the 'objective culture' of technology and institutions takes on a life of its own, threatening to overwhelm the very individuals who produced it (502–33). As the Weimar psychotechnician Fritz Giese would later describe it, in a study that points forward to Siegfried Kracauer's interpretation of the Tiller Girls and the aesthetic objectification of Fordist factory rhythms, the industrial milieu thus confronted its inhabitants with a profoundly inhuman rhythm, one that had emancipated itself from the grasp of its human creators:

> Ein Rhythmus, den jetzt diese neue künstliche Welt, wie losgelöst vom menschlichen Schöpfer, für sich lebt; den sie fordert. Die Großstadt hat uns, die Technik hat uns, die Wirtschaft hat uns: nicht wir sie! Das ist eine der interessantesten Entwicklungsformen und die Tragik des Schöpfers, dem die Kinder über den Kopf gewachsen.[29]

---

29 Fritz Giese, *Girlkultur. Vergleiche zwischen amerikanischem und europäischem Rhythmus und Lebensgefühl* [*Girl Culture. Comparative Studies of American and European Rhythm and Sensibility*] (Munich: Delphin-Verlag, 1925), 27.

[A rhythm that this new artificial world now develops and promotes on its own, as if detached from its human creator. The metropolis controls us; technology controls us; the economy controls us – not the other way round! This is one of the most interesting social developments and the tragedy of a creator whose children have outgrown him.]

As I hope this study will show, it was largely this 'conflict' – described elsewhere by Giese as a conflict between 'natural-biological' and 'artificial-technological' rhythms – that came to characterize the widespread preoccupation with rhythm in German culture after 1900, becoming particularly virulent during the Americanist decade of the 1920s.[30] In part, the proponents of that discourse saw in rhythm something of a rallying cry for an anti-technological stance. The key player in this story is surely the conservative philosopher Ludwig Klages, whose essay *Vom Wesen des Rhythmus* [*On the Essence of Rhythm*], written in 1922 for the Tagung für künstlerische Körperschulung [Conference for Artistic Bodily Education] in Berlin, became an influential manifesto of German Kulturkritik in the 1920s.[31] In it, Klages insisted on the strictest separation between the rhythms of life – which he identified with phenomena such as the heartbeat, breathing, tides and seasons – and machinic repetition, for which Klages reserved the term *Takt* (metre or cadence).[32]

Rhythm, of course, had long been associated with vital phenomena. In his study *First Principles* (1862), Herbert Spencer had argued that rhythm arises wherever forces come into conflict, but especially in vital phenomena: 'Perhaps nowhere are the illustrations of rhythm so numerous and so manifest as among the phenomena of life'.[33] Indeed, the emergence of the 'human motor' model of the body in the course of the nineteenth century went hand-in-hand with a broad process of medical mapping, in which the body's vital interior was reconceptualized as a force-field of overlapping rhythmical movements. Particularly influential, in this process, was the work of Étienne-Jules Marey, who – long before his better-known experiments in capturing phases of bodily movement on film via

---

30 See Giese 25.

31 The term *Kulturkritik* refers to a broad set of intellectual currents, in German thought of the late nineteenth and early twentieth centuries, that focused on the negative aspects of industrial capitalism such as alienation, reification, rationalization and levelling.

32 Ludwig Klages, *Vom Wesen des Rhythmus* (1923) [*On the Nature of Rhythm*] (Kampfen auf Sylt: Niels Kampmann Verlag, 1934).

33 Herbert Spencer, *First Principles*. 4th edn (New York: Appleton, 1883), 261.

chronophotography – had developed a whole series of apparatuses for the graphic inscription of recurrent internal movements such as the heartbeat (sphygmograph, cardiograph), breathing (pneumograph), and the curves of muscular and nervous energy (myograph) (figure 3).[34] By the early twentieth century, such work had given rise to a widespread association between two kinds of recurrence: the vital and the periodic. To take one oft-cited example, Wilhelm Fließ, in his biological treatise *Der Ablauf des Lebens* (1906) [*The Cycle of Life*, 1906], started out from menstrual cycles to identify rhythmical recurrence as the trademark of all living organisms.[35]

In many respects, one could see Klages's arguments as part of this broader constellation; like Fließ, he clearly identified the vital with rhythmical phenomena, and like Marey, he first approached the question of vital rhythm as a problem of graphic inscription – namely in his graphological writings, where he claimed to access the living rhythms of the body through the spatialized trace of subjects' handwriting.[36] However, unlike the proponents of the 'human motor' model, Klages insisted on the absolute dissociation of

---

34 On Marey and graphic inscription, see Rabinbach, *The Human Motor*, 90–97. For a fuller account of the medical mapping of the body in terms of internal rhythms, see Golston, 'Im Anfang war der Rhythmus'.

35 As Fließ explained: '[Die gegenwärtige Arbeit] soll uns lehren, daß der zeitliche Ablauf von Menstruation und Entbindung im letzten Grunde mit dem zeitlichen Ablauf der Lebensvorgänge überhaupt identisch ist. Daß durch alles Leben *ein* Puls geht und *ein* Rhythmus' [The present study should teach us that the temporal cycles of menstruation and childbirth are, in the last instance, identical to the temporal cycles of all vital phenomena. That all life is traversed by *one* pulse, *one* rhythm], W. Fließ, *Der Ablauf des Lebens. Grundlegungen zur exakten Biologie* [*The Cycle of Life. Fundaments of a Precise Biology*] (Leipzig: Franz Dueticke, 1906), 2. Fließ's study was widely received by proponents of the rhythm discourse. For example, in a 1922 study on rhythm in education, Bernhard Koch walked readers through several of the examples from Fließ's study to conclude: 'Es genügt [...], um zu erkennen, was Fließ beweisen will – daß nämlich "durch alles Leben *ein* Puls geht und *ein* Rhythmus"' [It suffices to understand what Fließ wishes to demonstrate – that namely all life is traversed by *one* pulse, *one* rhythm], Bernhard Koch, *Der Rhythmus. Untersuchungen über sein Wesen und Wirken in Kunst und Natur und seine Bedeutung für die Schule* [*Rhythm. Investigations into its Essence and Effects in Art and Nature and its Significance for School*] (Langenzala: Hermann Beyer & Söhne, 1922), 52.

36 Klages's first theorization of rhythm in opposition to metre can be found in his book *Ausdrucksbewegung und Gestaltungskraft*, first published in 1913 and reprinted – with a much longer discussion of rhythm – in 1923. See Klages, *Ausdrucksbewegung und Gestaltungskraft. Grundlegung der Wissenschaft vom Ausdruck* [*Expressive Movement and Formative Power. A Foundation of the Science of Expression*], 3rd edn (Leipzig: Johann Ambrusius Barth, 1923), 134–45.

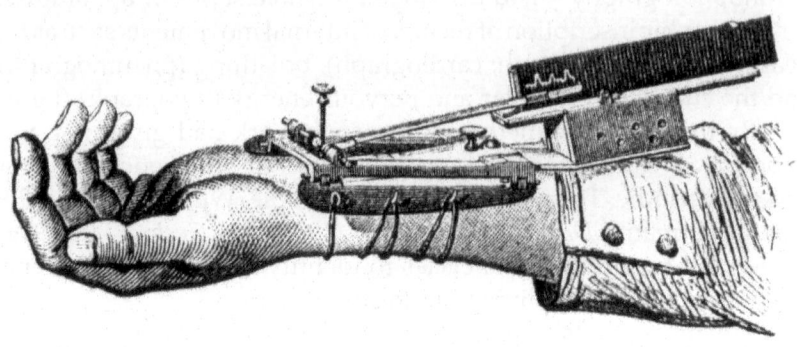

Fig 3. Étienne-Jules Marey, sphygmograph for the direct transcription of pulse curves

rhythm from anything resembling the movement of a machine: '[D]ie Maschinenbewegung *vernichte[t]* den Rhythmus' (Klages, *Vom Wesen des Rhythmus*, 15) [Machinic movement *destroys* rhythm]. In particular, Klages argued that rhythm manifested itself not in the repetition of identical elements, but rather in the *deviations* and irregularities that interrupt serial repetition:

> Niemals in grenzgenauen, wohl aber in ähnlichen Zwischenzeiten wechseln Helle und Dunkelheit, Ebbe und Flut, die Phasen des Mondes, die Jahreszeiten, die Bilder der Pflanzenwelt; und es wechseln in gleicher Weise Wachen und Schlafen, Frische und Müdigkeit, Hunger und Sättigung, Durst und Flüssigkeitswiderwille, ja beim ursprünglichen Menschen sogar das Paarungsverlangen mit geschlechtlicher Gleichgültigkeit. (33)

> [Light and darkness, high and low tide, the phases of the moon, the seasons and the cycles of plant life never succeed one another in identical intervals, but only in similar ones. And the same can be said for the alternation of waking and sleeping states, energy and fatigue, hunger and satiation, thirst and the aversion to fluids – and in primitive people even the alternation of mating seasons and periods of sexual indifference.]

But even more than the question of regularity and deviation, what separated rhythm from mechanized movement for Klages – here adapting Bergson's critique of segmented representations of time – was the criterion he termed *Stetigkeit* [continuity]. Arguing that the term 'rhythm' derives from the Greek verb for 'flow' ('ῥέω'), Klages insisted that we experience the rise and fall of genuine rhythm in the form of an undivided continuum, whereas mechanized repetition functions by cutting into nature and drawing boundaries, thus segmenting elements into discrete, isolated sections: 'Die Einteilungsleistung ist Teilungsleistung, und alles Teilen geschieht durch Grenzensetzung' (13) [The distribution of elements is an act of division, and all division functions by setting boundaries]. If the dividing activity (*teilen*) of *Takt* manifested itself most clearly in the punctual beats of clocks and metronomes, *Rhythmus* was most directly perceptible in the gradual ebb and flow of waves:

> Wie auf die Arsis die Thesis folgt, so folgt auf den Wellenberg das Tal; beide entsprechen den begrenzenden Schlägen, allein die Schläge sind nicht markiert. Vermittelt durch einen unauszählbaren Wechsel von Zwischenlagen gleitet die Aufbewegung in die Abbewegung hinüber und umgekehrt, derart daß weder am oberen noch am unteren Wendepunkt eine Kante entspringt. Im stattdessen erscheinenden Bogen wird uns anschaulich offenbar die unzergrenzte Stetigkeit einer Bewegung von nicht zu verkennender Gliederung, infolge des beständigen Wechsels nämlich einander entgegengesetzter Ausschläge von der Ruhelage. (17)[37]

> [Just as thesis follows arsis [in music and verse],[38] so the peaks of waves follow the valleys: both extremes correspond to the dividing beats of the metronome, but here, the beats are not marked. Mediated by an unquantifiable succession of intermediary phases, the upward movement glides into the downward movement and vice versa, so that no hard edges arise on either the upper or the lower transitions between waves. Rather, what we see is a curve, which clearly reveals the undivided continuity of an unmistakeably organized movement – organized on account of the continual alternation of opposing weights on either side of the balance.]

37   Among those influenced by Klages's theories, one can count Helmuth Plessner. In his treatise *Stufen des Organischen* [*The Stages of the Organic*], Plessner sees rhythm as key to vital phenomena and defines it as follows: 'Alles Lebendige zeigt Unstetigkeit im Stetigen, regelmäßige Unregelmäßigkeit. [...] Dynamisch tritt regelmäßige Unregelmäßigkeit [...] in den Phänomenen der Rhythmik auf. Ihre Verbreitung ist ungeheuer, so daß man sehr wohl verstehen kann, wie der Rhythmus geradezu zum Zentralmoment alles Lebendigen proklamiert werden konnte' [All living things show discontinuity in continuity or regular irregularity. [...] Regular irregularity appears dynamically [...] in the phenomenon of rhythm. This phenomenon is so widespread that we can easily understand how rhythm could be declared the central characteristic of all life], Helmuth Plessner, *Die Stufen des Organischen* (1928), *Gesammelte Schriften* 4, ed. Günter Dux, Odo Marquard und Elisabeth Ströker (Frankfurt am Main: Surkamp, 1981), 178.

38   In music and verse, 'arsis' and 'thesis' refer to accented and unaccented parts of a beat or a poetic foot.

Klages's celebration of the gliding movement of waves took up a longstanding interest in the seemingly non-quantifiable undulations of wave-movement in the arts and sciences of the late nineteenth century which had left a particularly strong imprint on the imaginary surrounding modern dance.[39] For Isadora Duncan, the undulating lines of wave motion formed the very model of natural movement. 'All the movements of the earth', Duncan had explained in a publication of 1909, 'follow the lines of wave motion' (figure 4).[40] Taking up the Bergsonian currents of turn-of-the-century art and thought, Duncan and other modern dancers sought to make the body into a conduit for such a structured, but nonetheless undivided, continuously flowing movement. Thus the above passage continues: 'If then one seeks a point of physical beginning for the movement of the human body, there is a clue in the undulating motion of the wave' (78). For Klages, there was no possible reconciliation between such wavelike motion and the serial movement of machines, between the process of organic 'renewal' characterizing life cycles and the serial 'repetition' of technology, or in Klages's more famous terminology between 'Seele' [soul] and 'Geist' [intellect]. At stake in this dichotomy was precisely the desire to draw a strict distinction between the experience of the body and that of the machine:

> Beobachten wir insbesondere das Leibes- und Seelenleben des Menschen, so stoßen wir vollends auf eine es Zug um Zug durchwaltende Rhythmik: man gedenke des Pulses, des Atems, der weiblichen Monatsregel, der Tages- und Jahresschwankung des Körpergewichtes [...], aber wir dürfen den Lebensvorgang niemals derart errechnen wollen, wie man es für die abgezogenen Vorgänge tut, die sprachgebräuchlich mechanische heißen. (Klages, *Vom Wesen des Rhythmus*, 34)[41]

39   Among other nineteenth-century researchers to take an interest in wave movement was Marey. See Georges Didi-Huberman, 'La danse de toutes choses', [The Dance of All Things] in Georges Didi-Huberman and Laurent Manoni, *Les mouvements de l'air. Étienne-Jules Marey, photographe des fluides* [*Movements of the Air. Étienne-Jules Marey, Photographer of Fluids*] (Paris: Gallimard, 2004), 177–317 (249–67, 281–317). On the predilection for liquid flows in modern art, see especially Christoph Asendorf, *Ströme und Strahlen. Das langsame Verschwinden der Materie um 1900* [*Streams and Rays. The Gradual Disappearance of Matter c. 1900*], Werkbund-Archiv 18 (Gießen: Anabas, 1989).

40   Isadora Duncan, *The Art of the Dance* (New York: Theater Arts Inc., 1970), 78.

41   All Klages's criteria for distinguishing rhythm and metre can be found in his graphological writings as well. In them, Klages sought to separate 'vital' handwriting from anything resembling automatic or reproducible inscriptions. 'Ausdruck des Lebens', he argued, 'ist der Rhythmus, Ausdruck des Geistes die

Fig 4. Isadora Duncan photographed by Arnold Genthe c. 1915, courtesy of the Jerome Robbins Dance Division, The New York Public Library for the Performing Arts, Astor, Lenox and Tilden Foundations

Verdrängung des Rhythmus durch die regelnde Kraft des Gesetzes. Je mehr im "Inneren" der Geist das Leben überwältigt hat, umsomehr tritt an der *Erscheinung* des Lebens der Rhythmus hinter der Regel zurück. Wie aber niemals die bloße Nachahmung eines schon vorhandenen Gebildes den Namen einer Schöpfung verdient, ebensowenig den der Ursprünglichkeit eine Körperbewegung, soweit sie nichts als Befolgung einer vorgeschriebenen Regel bietet' (Klages, *Ausdrucksbewegung und Gestaltungskraft*, 139) [Rhythm is the expression of life,

[If we observe the bodily and spiritual life of human beings in particular, we discover that they are regulated through and through by rhythm: one need only think of the pulse, the breath, the monthly menstrual cycle of women, the daily and yearly fluctuations of body weight [...], but we must never try to calculate life processes in the way that we would for those abstract processes that we habitually refer to as mechanical.]

Unlike Bücher, Klages has no use for notions of the body as a human motor regulated by principles of efficiency, rationality or calculability. On the contrary, if 'rhythm' was the phenomenological manifestation of the vital, this was true precisely to the extent that it resisted rational control. Criticizing in particular the understanding of rhythm developed by experimental psychologists such as Wilhelm Wundt, Ernst Meumann and Theodor Lipps, who saw rhythm as a manifestation of the mind's fundamental capacity to order its perceptions (10–12), Klages insisted that the genuine experience of rhythm entailed a wholesale relinquishing of rational control and the adoption of a mystical attitude he labelled 'Ergriffenheit' [a state of being seized or transported].[42]

while the suppression of rhythm through the regulating power of law is the expression of the spirit. The more the spirit has overpowered life in its 'inner' aspects, the more the *appearance* of life is characterized by a receding of rhythm in favour of regularity. But just as the mere imitation of an already present structure never deserves to be called a creation, no more does a bodily movement merit being called originary inasmuch as it offers nothing more than the execution of a predetermined rule]. In the many handwriting samples he examines, Klages thus claimed to perceive the visible imprint of an 'eternal struggle' between creativity and imposed patterns, spontaneous life and rigid law, rhythm and metre. The more the handwriting deviated from acquired, mechanical techniques, the more vitality Klages claimed to find in it. In his description of Nietzsche's handwriting we read: 'Trotz größter Leserlichkeit hat [Nietzsches Schrift] vollendete Eigenart [...] und einen perlenden Rhythmus, der die Schärfen zahlreicher Winkel spielend einverleibt' (141) [Despite its high degree of legibility, Nietzsche's handwriting possesses a perfect originality and a sprightly rhythm that playfully absorbs the hard edges of numerous angles].

42 'Als Zuschauer erleben kann ich den Rhythmus nur, sofern ich über das bloße Zuschauertum hinaus von ihm *ergriffen* werde, und als Bildner leisten kann ich den Rhythmus nicht kraft meiner Willkür, die freilich Maße und Takte zu erzeugen gestattet, sondern wiederum nur aus Ergriffenheit. Die Eigentätigkeit auch des Bildners wird genau in soweit Rhythmus bilden, als sie bei entmächtigter Willkür vom rhythmischen Pulse *getragen* ist' (Klages, Vom Wesen des Rhythmus, 57) [As spectator, I can only experience rhythm to the extent that I transcend the position of mere spectator and allow myself to be *seized* by it. As creator, I cannot achieve rhythm by the power of my will, even if the will allows me to produce measure and metre. Rather, once again, I can only achieve

Klages's effort to draw a phenomenological line in the sand between vital and mechanical movement was not without its contradictions; these are visible throughout the text as he struggles with the possible imbrications between the two modes. At one point, for example, he asks why the very regularized rattling of a train car rolling over evenly spaced tracks – a symbol of industrial modernity if ever there was one – is able to put passengers into a trance-like state no less than the irregular lapping of waves. In order to explain the problem, Klages speculates that what lulls the passengers to sleep are not the percussive noises themselves, marking as they do dividing intervals, but rather the uninterrupted forward movement of the train that these noises indicate. But despite this explanation, a philosophical doubt remains: if modernity's fixation on mechanical metre has largely extinguished our access to rhythm, it nonetheless sometimes allows rhythm to appear: 'Der periodische Wechsel, dessen es bedarf, damit die Stetigkeit der Bewegung zum Rhythmus werde [...] *kann* offenbar auch durch Einführung eines Taktes entstehen, vorausgesetzt, der Stetigkeitswert des Bewegtseins behalte die Vormacht vor dem Teilungswert der zergrenzenden Schalle' (29) [The periodic alternation necessary in order that continuous movement may assume the form of rhythm, [...] clearly *can* arise through the introduction of metre, provided that the continuity of movement retains precedence over the divisions of ordering sounds]. The hesitancy palpable in this passage will become much more pronounced by the end of Klages's study, where he begins to suspect that, for modern individuals no longer immersed in vital and cosmic rhythms, it is *only* through the ordering presence of mechanical or intellectual metre that rhythm can manifest itself at all. Thus the very phenomenon so detrimental to rhythm might be, paradoxically, the precondition for the latter's continued phenomenological presence:

> Wenn darnach der Rhythmus, ungeachtet er fraglos *verdrängt* wird durch überstarke *Betonung* des Metrums, offenbar auch sich *verflüchtigen* kann durch *Aufhebung* des Metrums, so liegt zunächst einmal die Erwägung nahe, ob nicht im geistbehafteten Eigenwesen dem Geiste im Verhältnis zum Leben günstigenfalls die Rolle des *Gegenspielers* zuteil werden könne, mit dessen *Überwindung* allererst dieses seine rhythmischen Möglichkeiten entfalte. (51–52)

> [Accordingly, we see that rhythm, although clearly *suppressed* by an *overemphasis* on metre, can also *disappear* through the *abolition* of

rhythm from a state of seizure. The creator's action can create rhythm only to the extent that its will is disempowered and it is *carried* by the rhythmical pulse].

metre. It thus stands to reason that, for the intellectualized individual, the intellect can, in fortunate cases, assume the role of an *adversary* to life, and that it is through overcoming this adversary that life first unfolds its rhythmical possibilities.]

Foreshadowing his later study *Der Geist als Widersacher der Seele* (1929) [*The Intellect as Adversary of the Soul*], Klages's model of the interplay between intellect and life offers a textbook case of 'supplementary' logic: the very presence of intellectual, metric and machinic modernity (everything Klages understood under the term *Geist*) which is responsible for the death of rhythm appears at once as the only thing allowing rhythm to survive.[43]

Klages's essay was picked up by numerous theorists of body culture – particularly in its more 'volkisch' variants – during the 1920s, though for the most part they ignored such philosophical intricacies to insist on the utter incompatibility of living rhythm and machinic repetition. Writing in 1923, the gymnastics teacher and future proponent of Nazi body culture Rudolf Bode – who had devised a school of eurhythmical gymnastics designed to restore the alternation between tension and relaxation – attacked the theories of Bücher and Jaques-Dalcroze in particular, arguing that both had confused the instrumental and mechanical world of *Takt* for the experience of authentic rhythm (figure 5).[44] As a mark of primitive cultures still swimming in the 'Strom des Lebens' (25) [stream of life] and 'eingebettet in einem größeren Zusammenhang' (29) [embedded in a greater rhythmical whole], rhythmical expression, Bode insisted, was inevitably destroyed by any attempt to subject it to the regularity of technological order: '[J]ede "Technik", sei es die Technik eines Instruments, sei es die Technik der Körperbeherrschung, ist dem Rhythmus antagonistisch, weil jede "Technik" auf "Gliederung" und

---

43   On this point, see Lubkoll, 'Rhythmus', 84; for the logic of the supplement, see of course Jacques Derrida, *De la grammatologie* [*On Grammatology*] (Paris: Minuit, 1967), 203–35.

44   See Rudolf Bode, *Rhythmus und Körpererziehung* [*Rhythm and Bodily Education*], 2nd edn (Jena: Eugen Dietrichs, 1925), 21. On Bode's career under Nazism, see Karl Toepfer, *Empire of Ecstasy. Nudity and Movement in German Body Culture, 1910–1935* (Berkeley: University of California Press, 1997), 127–29. In his espousal of a specifically 'Germanic' rhythm, Bode was a key player in what Inge Baxmann has labelled the 'nationalization of rhythm' in Germany beginning in the 1920s and continuing in the conception of racial rhythms under the National Socialists. See Inge Baxmann, *Mythos: Gemeinschaft. Körper- und Tanzkulturen in der Moderne* [*The Myth of Community: Cultures of the Body and Dance in Modernity*] (Munich: Fink, 2000), 232–52. On the connection of rhythm and race, see also Golston, '"Im anfang war der rhythmus"'.

Fig 5. Rhythmical group gymnastics from Rudolf Bode, Rhythmus und Körpererziehung *(1923)*

"Kombination" beruht!' (35) [*Every* form of technology, be it that of an instrument or that of bodily discipline, is antagonistic to rhythm. For all technology relies on 'division' and 'combination'!].[45] Whereas Heidegger would see the essence of technology in the spatializing category of the 'Gestell' [enframement], Klages and his disciples, in the wake of new Taylorist and Fordist production processes, located it above all in the act of segmenting a temporal flow.

Focusing on such vitalist models of rhythm, much of the recent work on rhythm in the German context has interpreted the intense preoccupation with the topic in the art and science of the Wilhelmine and Weimar periods largely as a proto-fascist phenomenon and a

---

45 Similarly, in a text of 1926, another Klages disciple, Max Merz, would present rhythmical gymnastics as an effort precisely to oppose the separating function of machines: 'Es kann kein Zufall sein, daß gerade in unserem Maschinenzeitalter die Körperkultur mit solcher Bestimmtheit ins Zentrum des menschlichen Bewußtseins rückt. In ihr haben wir die Antithese, die elementare Einführung in die Welt des Organischen' [It cannot be an accident that body culture has moved so decisively into the forefront of human consciousness precisely in our industrial era. It is the antithesis of industry, the elemental introduction into the world of the organic] Max Merz, *Körperbildung und Rhythmus* [*Body Building and Rhythm*] (Vienna: Duncan, 1926), 7

prelude to the racial politics of the Third Reich.[46] But while notions of rhythm as a marker of national or racial difference certainly figured into the debates, this is surely not the entire story.[47] On the one hand, the interest in rhythm was hardly unique to Germany; not only among international dancers such as Duncan, but also in domains as diverse as psychology,[48] anthropology,[49] anthroposophy,[50] art criticism[51], media and film,[52] rhythm formed the object of a

46 See Michael Golston, *Rhythm and Race in Modernist Poetry and Science* (NY: Columbia University Press, 2008); Michael Mackenzie, 'From Athens to Berlin: The 1936 Olympics and Leni Riefenstahl's Olympia', *Critical Inquiry* 29:2 (2003), 302–36. Laure Guilbert, *Danser avec le IIIe Reich. Les danseurs modernes sous le nazisme* [*Dancing with the Third Reich. Modern Dancers under Nazism*] (Paris: Éditions Complexe, 2000).

47 Cf. Siegfried Behn, *Der deutsche Rhythmus und sein eigenes Gesetz. Eine experimentelle Untersuchung* [*German Rhythm and its Specific Law. An Experimental Investigation*] (Strassburg: Verlag von Karl J. Trübner, 1912).

48 See for example the influential essay by Thaddeus Bolton, 'Rhythm', *The American Journal of Psychology* 6:2 (1894), 145–238. In Germany, the research on rhythm in experimental psychology was extensive, particularly in Leipzig where Bücher was active. See for example Ernst Meumann, *Psychologie und Ästhetik des Rhythmus* [*Psychology and Aesthetics of Rhythm*] (Leipzig: Wilhelm Engelmann, 1894); Kurt Koffka, *Experimenal-Untersuchungen zur Lehre vom Rhythmus* [*Experimental Investigations into the Theory of Rhythm*] (Leipzig: Barth, 1908); Wilhelm Wundt, *Grundzüge der physiologischen Psychologie* [*An Outline of Physiological Psychology*], 6th edn (Leipzig: Kröner, 1911), 141.

49 The key figure here is surely Marcel Mauss, who described the human being as an 'animal rythmé' [rhythmical animal] in his lectures at the University of Paris. See Mauss, *Manuel d'ethnographie* [*Manual of Ethnography*] (Paris: Payot, 1947), 85.

50 See for example Archibald Keightley, *The Rhythm of Life: Character Building as an Aid to Health* (London: Henry J. Glasisher, 1907).

51 See for example C. G. Holmes, 'Stray Thoughts on Rhythm in Painting', *Rhythm* 1: 3 (1911), 1–3. Holmes article appeared in *Rhythm* (1911–13), a journal founded by the British writer Middelton Murray to cover the latest movements in literature and art. In Germany and Austria, rhythm was also a central topic of debate in the burgeoning field of art history. See for example Hermann Russack, *Der Begriff des Rhythmus bei den deutschen Kunsthistorikern des XIX. Jahrhunderts* [*The Concept of Rhythm among German Art Historians of the 19th Century*] (Weida in Thüringen: Thomas & Hubert, 1910). For an excellent discussion of rhythm in art history around 1900 (focusing on debates between Alois Riegl in Vienna and August Schmarsow in Leipzig), see see Georg Vasold, 'Optique ou haptique: le rythme dans les études sur l'art au début du 20e siècle', *Intermédialités* 16 (automne 2010), 35-55.

52 For an excellent treatment of the question of rhythm in French film theory, see Laurent Guido, *L'Âge du rythme. Cinéma, musicalité et culture du corps dans les théories françaises des années 1910–1930* [*The Age of Rhythm. Cinema, Musicality and Body Culture in French Theory from the 1910s to the 1930s*] (Lausanne: Payot, 2007).

thoroughly transnational modernist discourse. On the other hand, this discussion – both within and outside Germany – stretched across the political and ideological spectrum. If questions of rhythm attracted conservative thinkers such as Klages, they also attracted liberal intellectuals such as Simmel and socialist theorists such as Georg Lukács, who drew on Bücher's derivation of aesthetic rhythms from work to argue for an understanding of rhythm in lyric poetry – particularly in its opposition to metre – as a 'Wiederspiegelung' [reflection] of the human being's productive labour and ordering powers over nature.[53]

Most importantly, perhaps, many writers saw in rhythm not simply an organic force opposed to the machine, but rather the very hallmark of machinic productivity. And they could cite Bücher's theories of rhythm, pleasure and efficiency as their authority. In a treatise on the use of rhythm for education from 1922, to take just one example, the physician Bernhard Koch explicitly defended Bücher and Dalcroze against Bode's critiques, arguing that rhythm, although a natural phenomenon, constituted above all a mode of calculable alternation serving to regulate energy expenditure:

> Wir können deshalb der Meinung Bodes nicht beitreten, der das Gesetzmäßige als den Tod des Rhythmus bezeichnet. Vielmehr muß hinter jeder Bewegung, die doch an Zeit und Raum gebunden ist, ein Gesetz, ein Wille stehen, der nötigt, sie mit Selbstbeobachtung auszuführen, der die Kräfte nach Zweck und Ziel genau abwägt. [...] Desgleichen können wir uns der Ansicht Büchers und Dalcrozes anschließen, daß der Rhythmus, als den Kräfteverbrauch regulierend, als ökonomisches Prinzip zu betrachten ist. (Koch 32)[54]

---

53   See Georg Lukács. *Ästhetik 1 [Aesthetics 1], Werke* 11 (Neuwied: Luchterhand, 1972), 266, 279, 281. While thus subscribing to a productivist notion of rhythm, Lukács also concurred with Bücher's insistence that rhythm ended where the human worker became a servant of the machine: 'Sobald die Arbeit [...], mit der Herrschaft der Maschine, nicht mehr konkret vom Menschen aus bestimmt ist, hört der Rhythmus auf, in diesem Sinne zu existieren und zu wirken, obwohl – rein objektiv angesehen, begrifflich betrachtet – die Maschine ebenfalls einen Rhythmus der Bewegungen haben kann' (283) [As soon as, with the rule of machines, labour ceases to be determined concretely by human beings, rhythm ceases to exist and function in this sense, although – considered from a purely objective or conceptual standpoint – machines can also display a rhythm in their movements].

54   Koch also took issue with Klages's derivation of the term 'Rhythmus' from 'ῥέω' ('flow'), arguing instead that the word derived from the Greek 'ῥύω' ('pull'). As such, rhythm would designate a volitional, instrumental activity: 'In der Bedeutung von "ziehen" ist der Rhythmus nicht nur ein passives Geschehenlassen, wie z. B. der Tropfenfall, sondern ein aktives Tun, eine Energie,

[For this reason, we cannot agree with Bode's argument that conformity to rules and laws means the death of rhythm. Rather, since all movements are bound to time and space, each one must be driven by a law and a will, which requires us to execute it self-consciously, carefully applying our energies according to our aims and purposes. [...] Likewise, we can agree with Bücher and Dalcroze that rhythm, as a means of regulating energy expenditure, can be seen as an economic principle.]

Indeed, the very vehemence with which Klages and his disciples insisted on limiting the usage of the term 'rhythm' to designate irrational phenomena should be understood as a reaction to the term's de facto ambiguous – or, if one prefers, 'polysemic' – status, its ability to designate phenomena understood as both organic and mechanical, both the 'natural-biological' *and* the 'artificial-technological'. As a key term in modernity's perception of modernization, 'rhythm' was thus up for grabs, and it would be a mistake on the part of contemporary cultural historians to reduce what served as the object of conflicting interpretations of modernization and its meanings to a univocal narrative of anti-technological thought.[55]

If the 'rhythm' discourse in Germany encompassed several voices and positions, however, those voices were nonetheless responding to a shared set of concerns about the transformations in bodily experience and forms of community in the wake of Germany's rapid industrialization around 1900. One of the central stakes in modernity's rhythm debates was thus precisely an effort to come to terms with the increasingly palpable changes in the interfaces between the body and technology, the organic and the machinic, resulting from such processes as urban expansion and migration, new forms of rapid transit, the increasing reach of industrial production and, not least, the influence of Taylorist and Fordist work principles. And while some observers of these new interfaces might have sought an imaginary restoration of natural purity through phenomenological

ein Druck und Gegendruck. In dieser Auffassung haben wir alle wesentlichen Merkmale des Rhythmus vor uns, nämlich Kräfteverbrauch, Kräftesammlung, Heben und Senken, Wirkung und Gegenwirkung, Stoß und Zug, Spannung und Lösung' (31–32) [Understood in the sense of 'pulling', rhythm is not simply a passive motion like that of falling drops but rather an active intervention, an energy, a pressure and counter-pressure. Conceiving of rhythm in this way, we perceive all of its essential characteristics, namely the expenditure of energy, the collection of energy, lifting and lowering, effect and counter-effect, push and pull, tension and relaxation].

55   In his study on rhythm in French film theory, Laurent Guido makes a similar point: see Guido, *L'Âge du rythme*, 7.

meditations or bodily performance, many tended to see the problem as one of *adaptation:* adaptation to new forms of perception, temporal experience, movement and energy expenditure – in short, new rhythms – characteristic of work and leisure in urban and industrial milieus. The latter stance became increasingly prevalent under the influence of 'Americanist' forms of work and leisure during the Weimar Republic (1919–33), the period to which all but one of the following chapters refer. However, if I have reviewed several pre-Weimar discourses on rhythm here, this is because I do not believe that the discourses and representations concerning rhythm in the 1920s appeared on the scene out of nowhere in 1918. On the contrary, those discourses took up and sharpened debates already begun in earlier decades in works such as Bücher's *Arbeit und Rhythmus* (which had its sixth edition in 1924).

In setting out to examine some of the key stations of this rhythm discussion in the 1910s and 1920s, this study joins a great deal of research on rhythm in recent scholarship, particularly from Germany and France.[56] If my contribution differs from some of these other

---

56   In Germany, the Research Group 'Kulturen des Performativen' [Cultures of the Performative], based in the Institut für Theaterwissenschaft [Institute for Drama Studies] at the Freie Universität in Berlin, has carried out particularly productive research into rhythm and the arts. The 2004 conference *Rhythmus im Prozeß* [*Rhythm in Process*], which included contributions covering periods from the medieval to the postmodern and disciplines from linguistics to biology to art history, gave rise to an extensive volume of various rhythm theories. See Christa Brüstle, *et al.* (eds.), *Aus dem Takt. Rhythmus in Kunst, Kultur und Natur* [*Out of Time. Rhythm in Art, Culture and Nature*] (Bielefeld: Transcript, 2005); and for a similar multidisciplinary collection of rhythm studies, see Barbara Naumann (ed.), *Rhythmus. Spuren eines Wechselspiels in Künsten und Wissenschaften* [*Rhythm. Traces of an Interplay in the Arts and Sciences*] (Königshausen und Neumann, 2005). In France, the most prolific writers on rhythm have been Pierre Sauvanet and the group of researchers involved in the seminar 'L'Homme et ses rythmes' [The Human and Its Rhythms] directed by Christian Doumet et Aliocha Wald-Lasowski (2006–08). Sauvanet, in particular, has published a series of monographs and essay collections dedicated to the philosophy and aesthetics of rhythm. See in particular Pierre Sauvanet, *Le Rythme grec d'Héraclite à Aristote* [*Greek Rhythm from Heraclitus to Aristotle*] (Paris: Presses Universitaires de France, 1999); Pierre Sauvanet, *Le rythme et la raison* [*Rhythm and Reason*], vols. 1–2 (Paris: Kimé, 2000). See also Pierre Sauvanet and Jean-Jacques Wunenburger (eds.), *Rythmes et philosophie* [*Rhythms and Philosophy*] (Paris: Kimé, 1996). For an overview of rhythm in modernist film theory, see Guido, *L'Âge du rythme*. In North America, several recent works have focused on the intersections between rhythm in modern physiology and modernist aesthetics. See especially Robert Brain, 'The Pulse of Modernism: and Aesthetic Avant-Gardes circa 1900', *Studies in the History and Philosophy of Science* 39 (2008), 393–417; Michael Golston, *Rhythm and Race in Modernist Poetry and Science*.

projects, this is, perhaps, first of all in the light of what it does *not* do. Unlike some recent scholarly studies of rhythm, I do not make any claims about what rhythm *is* objectively or engage in philosophical debates with modern thinkers such as Bergson or Nietzsche. Nor does this study set out to provide an empirical history of modern scientific (physiological, psychological or otherwise) research on rhythm, or of any particular rhythmical practices. In particular, readers expecting a history of modern dance or dance schools will be disappointed. Although both science and dance figure in my analyses as key domains for conceptualizing and visualizing different models of rhythm, this book is by no means a catalogue of such practices. Rather, it attempts, through a select number of close analyses, to examine how people imagined, talked about and represented rhythm at a certain pivotal moment in an effort to come to terms with industrial modernity.

More specifically, I am concerned with the ramifications of this preoccupation with rhythm for the understanding of temporal media and art-forms in the German modernism of the 1910s and 1920s. One of my arguments is that the new focus on rhythm served not only to work through questions of community but also to conceptualize new media – particularly the dynamic medium of cinematography – or to rethink 'old' forms such as lyric poetry and music in the light of urban and industrial transformations in the early twentieth century. To put the argument on the table: the preoccupation with rhythm generated a view of artistic media not only as vehicles of information or representation, but also as *mediators* in a very precise sense – forums for mediating between organic and machinic movement, between the vital and the rational experiences of time, between the body and technology, and ultimately between tradition and modernity. In recent decades, media historians such as Friedrich Kittler and Jonathan Crary have highlighted the extent to which the experience of media became an increasingly embodied affair in the nineteenth century, when media were largely reconceived in terms of their material effects on the bodies of receivers.[57] Building on these insights, the present study examines a particular variant of such 'embodied' understandings of media and their effects on receivers, one in which artistic media were charged with the performative function of assimilating perception and the body to the new world of technological rhythms.

---

57 See Friedrich Kittler, *Discourse Networks 1800/1900,* trans. by Michael Metteer (Stanford University Press, 1992) [*Aufschreibesysteme 1800/1900* (Munich: Fink, 1985)]; Jonathan Crary, *Techniques of the Observer. On Vision and Modernity in the Nineteenth Century* (Cambridge: MIT Press, 1992).

With no pretence to thematic exhaustiveness, the chapters making up this book are intended as a series of case studies, some of them interpreting well-known works anew and some of them uncovering less familiar aspects of modernist art and culture in the 1910s and 1920s. Chapter 2 focuses on a representative effort to refashion a traditional form – that of lyric poetry – in terms of this new understanding of artistic media. The work of the expressionist poet Gerrit Engelke (1890–1918) offers a good example of efforts to mediate between 'primitive' and 'modern' rhythms. Like many other expressionist writers, Engelke was fascinated by the phenomenon of rhythm, which he saw as the source of a primitive vitality utilizable for both artistic and cultural renewal. Unlike other poets of his generation (such as Georg Heym), however, he saw poetry as a means not to critique or mythologize the urban environment, but rather to come to terms with it. 'Unsere rastlose Werkzeit,' he wrote in his notes, 'ist so eisenstark [...] daß sich die Tagesmenschen vor ihrem unerkannten Hammerrhythmus, vor ihrer tausendtürmigen Größe ängstigen. Sie sollen sie lieben lernen! Darum reden die Dichter zu ihnen' [Our restless era of factories is so powerful [...] that most people are afraid of its unfamiliar hammer rhythm, of its towering enormity. But they should learn to love it! And this is why poets speak to them].[58] This technological 'hammer rhythm' celebrated by Engelke had all the characteristics of industrial rhythm as described by Bücher: speed, inexhaustibility and absolute efficiency. Examining Engelke's poetry, diaries and notes, I show how he sought to use lyric – in poems such as 'Der Mittler' (1913) [The Intermediary] – as an interface between vital and technological rhythms, and specifically to locate a universal vital rhythm behind the surface appearance of industrial life and thus to reinvest technology with a spiritual and vital dimension.

Building on my arguments from Chapter 2, the third chapter turns to the 1920s to examine the impact of debates on rhythm for the understanding of its newest temporal medium: cinematography. Film, I argue here, was also understood as an interface between primal and technological rhythms. Whereas more recent film theorists such as Gilles Deleuze have read modernist film as an effort to undo mechanized movement in order to access a primary Bergsonian flux underneath, I present a more contextual and historicized account of

---

58   Gerrit Engelke, *Rhythmus des neuen Europa. Das Gesamtwerk* [*Rhythm of the New Europe. Complete Works*] (Hannover: Postskriptum, 1979), 225.

Weimar's 'movement images'.[59] While some works (such as Arnold Fanck's *Der heilige Berg* (1926) [*The Holy Mountain*], in which Leni Riefenstahl performed Klagesian dances before a raging sea) did seek to use the cinema as a means of accessing vital rhythm through technology, many others (e.g., Hans Richter's rhythm films *Rhythmus 21* and *Rhythmus 23* from the early 1920s or Walter Ruttmann's *Berlin: die Sinfonie der Großstadt* (1927) [*Berlin: The Symphony of a Great City*] imagined film as an eminently technological art form, serving to submit primal rhythm to the precise order of technology. Chronophotography and film, after all, had been considered a quintessential instrument of mechanized time since at least Bergson's critique of the 'cinematographic illusion' in *L'Évolution créatrice* (1907) [*Creative Evolution*], and the staccato movements of the projector exemplify the form of *Takt* described by Klages.[60] This chapter culminates in a rereading of Fritz Lang's *Metropolis* as a film about the rhythmical possibilities of the filmic medium itself. Central to my interpretation is a reconsideration of the film's main allegory of the beating heart as mediator between the head and the hands. This 'mediating' function, I argue, should be understood not sentimentally but rather in a precise technological sense – one embodied by the formidable 'heart machine' at the centre of the industrial apparatus in *Metropolis*. Mediating between technology and nature by submitting the power of primal rhythm to the order of a technological will, the pumping heart machine offers a metaphor both for industry and for film understood as an industrial art form.

Having explored the impact of rhythm debates on writing and film in Chapters 2 and 3, I then go on to consider in Chapter 4 their interaction in theories of advertising and advertising film from the 1920s. In direct analogy to the theories of Bücher and his followers, advertising theorists such as Fritz Pauli argued that the rhythmical presentation of letters, syllables, words and images in advertising functioned to increase the 'productivity' of the consumers' mental apparatus (their attention) and thus incite viewers to consume the product on display. Pauli devised all sorts of means for the rhythmization of advertising, including rhythmical layouts for posters, animated electric advertisements, series of commercial

---

59 The term 'movement images' comes from Gilles Deleuze, who uses it to distinguish the pre-WWII cinema of movement from the post-war cinema of time. See Gilles Deleuze, *Cinéma I. L'image-mouvement* [*Cinema 1: The Movement Image*] (Paris: Minuit, 1983).

60 See Henri Bergson, *L'Évolution créatrice*, 10th edn (Paris: PUF, 2003 [1907]), 305–15.

billboards to be placed at precise intervals along public transport lines and – not least – the use of film to animate images and letters. With Pauli's theories as a backdrop, this chapter focuses on the work of the pioneer of advertising film in Germany, Julius Pinschewer. Specifically, I offer an extended reading of the famous avant-garde film *Kipho* (1925), which Pinschewer made together with cinematographer Guido Seeber as an advertisement for a major exhibition of the film industry in Berlin in 1925. The *Kipho* film – which Standish Lawder later described as a compendium of 'the most advanced artistic vocabulary of its day' – also represents a case-study in the application of theories of rhythm to advertising.[61] On the one hand, the film restages Bücher's narrative of modernity visually by demonstrating the integration of working bodies into a vast cinematic apparatus, consisting of cranks, reels, platters and gears spinning in accelerated and continuous rotation. Indeed, writing itself is absorbed into this rhythmical movement, as we gather from the rhythmical presentation of titles and the iconic image of a 'Drehbuch' [script; *literally* turning book] now shown turning on the spot rather than advancing according to a narrative trajectory. On the other hand, the film also attempts to absorb spectators into this same rhythmical apparatus with its final injunction: 'Du musst zur Kipho!' [You must go to the Kipho exhibition!]. The filmmakers explicitly adapted this phrase from the expressionist thriller *Das Cabinet des Dr. Caligari,* where the words 'Du musst Caligari werden!' [You must become Caligari!] functioned to objectify the protagonist's exposure to the occult power of an ancient book. In Pinschewer's and Seeber's citation however, the Caligari phrase now functions to advertise the hypnotic power of rhythm described by theorists such as Pauli. In this rationalization of hypnosis, *Kipho* thus exemplifies the impact of rhythm theories on modernity's understanding of cinematography as a medium that absorbed both writing and spectators into its rhythmical pulse.

Efforts to forge a rhythmical cinema or rhythmical advertisements were, of course, imbued with musical analogies, and in chapter 5 I turn my attention to music itself – in particular to the phenomenon of jazz in Germany, which was widely understood as a means of 'educating' the body for modern times. Drawing on the writings of work scientists such as Fritz Giese, this chapter shows how jazz confounded the dichotomies in the rhythm discourse of the 1920s, representing at once a manifestation of 'primitive' and precise

---

61 Standish Lawder, *The Cubist Cinema* (NY: New York University Press, 1975), 180–81.

'technological' rhythms. As such, jazz constituted yet another model of mediating between the traditional and the modern, and one that specifically responded to European desires and anxieties in the age characterized by the increasing influx of 'Americanist' forms of work and leisure. Although many practitioners of eurhythmics and vitalist dance categorically rejected jazz, intellectuals such as Max Brod or Fritz Giese saw jazz as providing answers to specific questions of German modernity in the 1920s. For these thinkers, I argue, the figure of the African-American dancer or jazz drummer, who displayed a remarkable ability to manipulate rhythm through syncopation, embodied a fantasy of survival among and adaptation to the inhuman rhythms of Americanist rationality. In a foreshadowing of the 'White Negro' phenomenon described by Norman Mailer in the 1950s, Weimar thinkers thus projected their own fears of existential or cultural annihilation onto jazz performers, seeing them as figures who had turned the tables on the dominant culture of white America.

Despite the persistence of obvious racial stereotypes in jazz reception, this engagement with rhythm marks a different kind of negotiation of race from those which the monological narratives of proto-fascism can account for. No doubt, reactionary modernists in the Third Reich had every reason to take an interest in rhythm, which held out the promise of lending to technological modernity an aura of primitive ritual, inducing an ecstatic sense of participation in the performance of the nation and, not least, controlling mass movements. But the story of modernity and rhythm extends beyond fascism in both a synchronic and a diachronic sense; efforts to understand, harness or manipulate rhythm were inherent to modernity's confrontation with technology as such. Moreover, as I explore in my epoligue to this book, this preoccupation with rhythm extends – albeit with varying degrees of intensity – from the era of industrialization to our own post-industrial society. If 'rhythm is it' for modern society, this is above all because rhythm held out and still holds out the promise of assimilating new technologies, adjusting to new modes of discipline and calibrating the body to new forms of mediated experience.

2. Poetry for Restless Times: Rhythm and Urban Experience in the Work of Gerrit Engelke

> Wir brauchen die neue Landschaft der Stadt,
> Den Tanz der Turbinen,
> Den öligen Atem der Maschine.[1]
>
> [We need the new landscape of the city,
> the dance of the turbines,
> the oily breath of the machine.]

Modern Poetry and the 'Rediscovery' of Primal Rhythm

While modernity's 'rediscovery' of vital rhythm occurred across many different domains and media, one that resonated widely around 1900 was that of lyric poetry. Not least on account of its diachronic presentational mode and metred structure, poetry, like music and dance, appeared as an obvious medium in which to work through or counter the new temporal experiences associated with technology, labour and the urban environment. As Christine Lubkoll has argued, the modernist 'revolutions' in lyric form – from Mallarmé's 'vers libre' [free verse] in France to Arno Holz's 'Mittelachsenlyrik' [middle axis poetry] in Germany – shared with vitalist dance, philosophy and music a desire to loosen the constraints of metre, now understood negatively as a mode of mechanical repetition, in order to access the natural rhythm or flux thought to lie below the ordered sphere of rationality (Lubkoll 99–110).[2] As Karl Freiherr von Levetzow described

---

1   Claire Goll, 'Zwanzigstes Jahrhundert' [Twentieth Century] (1922)

2   Not the least of Lubkoll's merits in her wide-ranging article is to offer a more historically precise reading of this project than Julia Kristeva, whose generalized account of modernist literature as a struggle between the ordered sphere of the symbolic and the rhythmical pulsations of 'semiotic chora' reifies a conceptual opposition that arose in very specific historical circumstances. On this point,

it in an article of 1899, rhythm represented a force of nature directly opposed to the quantifiable beats of metre: '[Ü]berall ist Rhythmus, in der ganzen Natur, im geistigen und körperlichen Menschen. [...] Nicht die Silben werden gezählt oder gemessen, sondern der Wert des Begriffs ist maßgebend, die Vertheilung und Harmonisierung der geistigen Accente' (cited in Lubkoll 102–3) [Rhythm is everywhere, in all nature and in the mental and bodily being of the human. [...] It is not a matter of counting or measuring out syllables; rather the essential thing is the value of the concept, the distribution and harmonizing of spiritual accents]. Largely prefiguring the theories of Klages and Bode (although not the latter's ideology), these poets hoped to access such primal rhythms by interrupting the mechanics of metre.

In Germany, this project found its most prominent spokesman in Arno Holz. Holz saw his later 'middle axis poetry' – in which lines of various lengths and feet are centred around a middle axis on the page rather than justified at the left – as a means of undoing conventional metre in order to liberate the 'natural rhythms' of words, syllables and objects. Such a non-mechanical rhythm, he argued, constituted the one universal element in poetry and the utopian object of a future verse-form freed from all historical constraints of metrical, rhyming or accent schemas: 'Als formal Letztes in jeder Lyrik, das überhaupt uneliminierbar ist, bleibt für alle Ewigkeit der Rhythmus' [Rhythm remains for all eternity the most basic formal element in every lyric form and can never be eliminated].[3]

Like Klages's phenomenology, however, this *fin-de-siècle* poetic project ran up against a central paradox. For if the effort to access primal rhythm required the destruction of mechanical metre, it was at the same time dependent upon that metre. Indeed, conceived by definition as a force that interrupts mechanical succession, primal rhythm could only appear through and by means of such a mechanized medium. Thus metre acted not only as that which blocks rhythm, but also as the very medium enabling access to rhythm – a 'Gegenspieler' [adversary to life], in Klages's description cited in the chapter 1, the overcoming of which first allows rhythm to arise (Klages, *Vom Wesen des Rhythmus*, 52).

But while these poets may have shared in the vitalist conceptual opposition that later informed thinkers like Klages, it would be a mistake to reduce the discourse on rhythm in modernist poetry to

---

see Lubkoll 85–86; Julia Kristeva, *La Révolution du langage poétique* [*Revolution in Poetic Language*] (Paris: Seuil, 1986).

3   Arno Holz, *Das Werk* (Berlin: J. H. W. Dietz, 1924), X: 141.

a reactionary 'flight out of time'. Rather, modernist explorations in rhythm should be seen as part of a broad effort to come to terms with the transformed temporal experience of industrial modernity in the temporal medium of poetry – and more specifically to *mediate* between two poles of modern and traditional (mechanical and vital) rhythms. While such mediations often took the form of an effort to transform metre in order to access vital rhythms through lyric, one can observe an increasing tendency – particularly in works of Weimar poetry such as Johannes Becher's *Maschinenrhythmen* (1926) [*Machine Rhythms*] – to reconceive of poetry as a medium for adapting to modernity's technological pulse.[4]

Before turning to Weimar culture proper in the following chapters, I would like to use the present chapter to explore the work of a poet on the cusp of this transformation: the expressionist poet Gerrit Engelke. With the exception of a few poems such as 'Auf der Straßenbahn' (1913) [In the Tram], Engelke – whose life and career were cut short at the age of 28 just days before the armistice of the First World War (WWI) – has received little attention in scholarship on German modernism. Where he has been discussed, his writing has generally been relegated to the category of 'Arbeiterdichtung' [proletarian poetry],[5] a designation usually based on a biographical reading of Engelke's working-class background in Hannover.[6] In what

---

4 On Becher's work, see Peter Demetz, 'The Futurist Johannes R. Becher', *Modernism/modernity* 1:3 (1994), 179–94.

5 Examples of this reading of Engelke can be found in Hans Hermann Schulz, *Das Volkstumserlebnis des Arbeiters in der Dichtung von Gerrit Engelke, Heinrich Lersch und Karl Bröger. Ein Beitrag zur Morphologie des Problems* [*Workers Encountering National Culture in the Poetry of Gerrit Engelke, Heinrich Lersch and Karl Bröger. A Contribution to the Morphology of the Phenomenon*], Arbeiten aus dem Germanistischen Seminar der Universität Berlin 5 (Würzburg: Triltsch, 1940); Christoph Rückler, *Ideologie der Arbeiterdichtung 1914–1933. Eine wissenssoziologische Untersuchung* [*Ideology of Proletarian Poetry 1914–1933. A Sociological Investigation*] (Metzler, Stuttgart, 1970); Alfred Klein, *Im Auftrag ihrer Klasse. Weg und Leistung der deutschen Arbeiterschriftsteller 1918–1933* [*In the Service of One's Class. Paths and Accomplishments of German Proletarian Authors 1918–1933*] (Berlin und Weimar: Aufbau, 1972). Essays going beyond this paradigm can be found in a more recent volume based on a symposium hosted by the Gerrit-Engelke-Gedächtnisstiftung in Hannover for the poet's 100th anniversary. See Kurt Morawietz, et. al. (eds.), *Zwischen Wolken und Großstadtrausch. Warum Engelke lesen? Dokumentation zum 100. Geburtstag des hannoverschen Dichters Gerrit Engelke* [*Between the Clouds and Factory Smoke. Why Read Engelke? Documentation of the 100th Birthday of the Hannover Poet Gerrit Engelke*] (Hannover: Postskriptum-Verlag, 1992).

6 For more on Engelke's life, see Kurt Morawietz, *'Mich aber schone, Tod': Gerrit Engelke 1890–1918* [*'But spare me, Death': Gerrit Engelke 1890–1918*] (Hannover: Postskriptum, 1979).

follows, however, I would like to argue that Engelke's poetic œuvre – and particularly his posthumously published collection *Rhythmus des neuen Europa* (1921) [*Rhythm of the New Europe*] – deserves another look. More than any other poet of the expressionist generation, Engelke made rhythm *the* theme of his poetry, and his project reveals a great deal not only about modernity's understanding of rhythm in general but also about modernism's investment in rhythm as a component of poetic aesthetics.

Like Holz and the theoreticians of dance, Engelke saw rhythm not simply as a component of poetic aesthetics, but as a primordial natural force. A good starting-point for examining Engelke's understanding of rhythm can be found in a 1913 poem entitled 'Rhythmus':

Rhythmus

Vom Stoff, daraus das Große wie Geringe
Den offenbaren festen Wuchs beginnt,
Vom Stoff, daraus von Anfang alle Dinge,
Vom Grund, daraus Begriff und Dasein sind:

Vom Rhythmus, der sich selber heißt: das Leben,
Der unsichtbar den schweren Stoff durchfließt,
Ihn wälzt, ihn schmilzt in ungeheurem Streben,
Ihn fort und fort in andre Formen gießt:

Von Stoff und Kraft in Schöpfungswerk-Durchdringung,
Im tiefsten Sein erzeugt, im Schoß versenkt,
Genährt vom Stoff, durchpulst von Rhythmusschwingung,
Vom Rhythmus-Strom geboren, hochgedrängt –

Kam ich: ein Auferstehn mit heller Schwinge
In Neu-Gestalt, aus dunklem Labyrinth
Zur Oberflächen-Welt, in neue Ringe
Als Lebens-Teil, als Anfangsmensch: als Kind! (Engelke 186)

[**Rhythm**

From the element from which all things great and small
Begin their apparently solid growth,
From the element that has given rise to everything since the beginning
From the ground of which concept and being grow:

From rhythm, the form life gives to itself,
Which flows, invisible, through all weighty matter,
Rolling it, melting it, in a great burst of energy,
Continually pouring it into changing forms:

From the matter and energy penetrating the work of creation,
Conceived in the deepest folds of being and embedded in nature's womb,
Nourished by this element, pulsed through and through by the undulations of rhythm,
Born of the rhythm-stream and propelled to the heights –

I came: resurrected with a light wing
In New-Form, from a dark labyrinth
To the surface-world, in new rings
As vital force, as primal man, as child!]

In accordance with what Jacques Rancière has called the modern 'utopie [...] de la matière dissoute en energie' [utopia of matter dissolved into energy] or what Christoph Asendorf has described as modernity's tendency to dissolve solids into so many 'Ströme und Strahlen' [streams and rays], Engelke depicts rhythm here as an eminently Dionysian force, an invisible pulse that animates ('durchpulst') all matter, dissolving and reconstituting visible forms.[7] As the hidden origin ('Anfang', 'Grund') of all things, rhythm appears as the essence of life itself ('Rhythmus, der sich selber heißt: das Leben') and above all as a force of vital renewal: submerged in the flowing stream of primal rhythm, the poet returns as a primitive human being ('Anfangsmensch') and as a child. Like many of Engelke's poems, 'Rhythmus' also attempts to awaken in the reader a feel for the very phenomenon the poet describes; in particular, the poem's many abstractions (e.g. 'das Große') and neologisms ('Schöpfungswerk-Durchdringung', 'Neu-Gestalt', 'Lebens-Teil') suggest a vision of language as malleable material, a mass ('Stoff') continually shaped and reshaped by the vital energy of the poem's rhythm.

Along with Holz and many expressionist poets, Engelke sought to revitalize modern poetry by accessing such organic rhythms. He experimented with middle axis poetry like that of Holz, and he also sought to differentiate the aesthetics of rhythm from any slavish adherence to metre. As he wrote in a journal entry in 1914:

> Sonett, Stanzen usw. mit Worten aufzufüllen, dazu bedarf es keines besonderen Abwägungsgefühls beim Dichter, während die 'lockeren' Formen ein stark entwickeltes Großrhythmus- und Feinrhythmusgefühl bedingen. Das ganze Gedicht und jedes einzelne

---

7 See Jacques Rancière, *La fable cinématographique* [*Film Fables*] (Paris: Seuil, 2001), 10; Asendorf, *Ströme und Strahlen*.

Wort hat das Blutgefühl des neuen Dichters genau abzuwägen, ehe das Ganze als ausmodulierter Klang dasteht. Also keine willkürliche Formlosigkeit, sondern Mußform. Dieses starke Rhythmusgefühl des neuen Dichters konnte erst unsere starke Zeit erregen. (223)

[Filling up sonnets, stanzas and the like with words does not require poets to possess any particular feeling for balance, whereas 'looser' forms demand a highly developed sense of micro- and macro-rhythms. The new poet must rely on his blood-feeling to balance out the entire poem and every word precisely before the poem can exist as a well-modulated tonal ensemble. Thus [what is needed is] not haphazard formlessness, but rather a compulsory form. The new poet's strong sense of rhythm could only be spurred on by our strong times.]

Rhythm, Engelke argues here, is something much more chthonic and vital – anchored in the blood ('Blutgefühl') – than the mechanical succession of metre. And yet, as this passage also suggests, Engelke did not strive to undo form altogether. On the contrary, while he did write much of his poetry in 'looser forms' – in particular employing a frequent alternation of metre – most of Engelke's poems employ very deliberate rhyme schemes and many, including 'Rhythmus' with its consistent iambic pentametre, are striking precisely in their metrical regularity. This regularity, as I will further elucidate below, serves in Engelke above all to convey the sense of a consistent and unitary vital force behind the manifold sensations of modern life.

Writing in 'Restless' Times

It is precisely this question of modern life – what Engelke describes as 'our strong times' in the passage above – that motivated Engelke's extended engagement with rhythm. When he called for a 'strong' sense of rhythm for 'strong times', he was attempting to imagine a form of poetry attuned to an industrial era that has unleashed unimaginable energies. In many ways, *Rhythmus des neuen Europa* picks up where Bücher and Simmel's analyses left off. In Engelke's poetry, icons of industrialization, from the train to the factory, are almost all described in terms of their rhythmical movement – and of their indifference to the organic conditions of the human body. In a poem of 1912 entitled 'Stadt' [City], for example, Engelke depicts the city as a great system of coordinated moving parts, which pays no heed to the fate of individuals dying of exhaustion:

Fünfhunderttausend Menschen rollt das große Leben
Durch alle Rinnen fort und fort in ungeheuerem Streben.
Und karrt der Tod auch Hundert täglich fort,
Es braust der Lärm wie sonst an jedem Ort
Schleppt er vom Hammer-Block den Schmied,
Schleppt er vom Kurven-Gleis den Wagenleiter:
Noch stärker brüllt das Straßenlied:
Der Wagen fährt – der Hammer dröhnt weiter. (47)

[Five hundred thousand people are carried along by the great life,
On and on through all channels with unfathomable force.
And should Death whisk away one hundred each day,
The thundering noise continues all around as before.
Should Death drag the smith from his hammer-block,
Or the train conductor from the sinuous tracks:
The street's song only roars more loudly:
The train car rolls on, and the hammer keeps pounding.]

Like the traffic rolling indifferently over the bridge at the end of Kafka's 'Das Urteil' (1916) [The Judgment], the noisy hammers and railway carriages of Engelke's city have no use for individual tragedies. Similarly, in another poem from the same year entitled 'Die Fabrik' [The Factory], Engelke describes the factory as a rhythmically pumping energy-machine identifiable from its roaring industrial noise:

Zuckend schwillt, schrill und brutal
Aus den Toren Maschinen-Musik (51)

[Trembling machine-music swells
From the gates, violent and shrill]

Most centrally, the factory's music is characterized by an utter disregard for the organic rhythms of the body or the diurnal rhythms of nature; the factory functions day and night, whether or not its human occupants can keep up:

Tag und Nacht: Lärm und Dampf,
Immer Arbeit, immer Kampf:
Unerbittlich schröpft das Moloch-Haus
Stahl und Mensch um Menschen aus.

[Day and night, noise and steam
Continuous work, never-ending struggle:
Unrelentingly, the Moloch house
Bleeds out steel and streams of people.]

Engelke's syntax here reduces people and steel to the same level: not that of modernism's heroic steel body, but rather that of passive material for the new rhythms of industrial production.

With its 'Moloch'-like consumption of its human workers and its utter disregard for human time, Engelke's factory looks ahead to the thoroughly Taylorized city of Fritz Lang's *Metropolis* with its rationalized ten-hour clock;[8] like Lang's film, Engelke's poetry clearly attempted to work through the rationalization and acceleration of time brought about by urbanization and industrialization. In poems such as 'Der rasende Psalm' (1912) [The Racing Psalm], 'Die Stadt lebt' (1914) [The City is Alive], 'Die große Uhr' (1914) [The Great Clock] and 'Sonne' (1918) [Sun], Engelke depicts a world in the grips of acceleration due to flows of traffic, bodies, communications technologies and an array of productive forces – a world that has forgotten the diurnal and seasonal alternations that characterized the rhythm of country. The speaker of 'Die Stadt lebt' for example, in a rejection of the traditional Herbstgedicht [autumn poem] genre (and in lines looking forward to the poetry of New Objectivity such as Bertolt Brecht's 'Über das Frühjahr' (1928) [On Spring] 1928), proclaims:

> Ob Ebene und Wald in welkes Sterben fallen,
> Ob draußen tost Vergänglichkeit,
> Im Stadtberg brüllen Straßen, Hämmer hallen:
> die Lärmstadt dampft in Unrast ohne Zeit. (53)

> [Even if the plains and forests whither and die,
> Even if the world outside radiates transience,
> In the city, the streets roar, the hammers resound:
> The noisy city steams in unrest without time.]

If Engelke describes the activity of the city's hammers as being 'without time' this is because they know nothing of the traditional rhythms – in this case the seasons – that structure temporal experience in rural settings and pastoral poetry. In contrast to time calibrated to the alternation of work and rest, tension and relaxation, Engelke's urban time is characterized by an imperative of constant and sustained energy flow, a state captured in Engelke's epithet 'unrest' (Unrast). In this sense, Engelke's understanding of industrial technology bears a distinct affinity to that of Bücher; like Bücher's continually rotating machine or Simmel's city liberated from rhythmical periodicity, the urban apparatus in Engelke has surpressed the rhythmical alternation

---

8 On *Metropolis*, see Chapter 3 below.

between tension and relaxation, expenditure and pause, work and rest.

Again and again, one finds this restlessness expressed in Engelke's poetry through long series of jarring impressions strung together – in a configuration reminiscent of futurist writing – with no verbs or adjectives.[9] In his best-known poem 'Auf der Straßenbahn' (1913) [In the Tram], for example, fragmented impressions fly past the poet caught in the grip of modern acceleration:

> Scharf vorüber an Laternen, Frauenmoden,
> Bild an Bild, Ladenschild, Pferdetritt, Menschenschritt. (48)

> [Flying past lights, women's fashions
> image upon image, store sign, trotting horse, human step.]

Similarly, the following lines from 'Stadt' present the city as a great maelstrom of simultaneous impressions and events:

> In Kaufhaus, Werkstatt, Saal und Bahnhofshalle,
> In Schule, Park, am Promenadenwalle,
> Im Fahrstuhlschacht, im Bau am Kran,
> Treppauf und ab, durch Straßen über Plätze,
> Auf Wagen, Rad und Straßenbahn:
> Da schäumt des Menschenstrudels wirre Hetze. (47)

> [In department stores, workrooms and railway stations,
> In schools, parks and city walls,
> In lift shafts, in crane-lined construction sites,
> Up and down steps, through streets and over squares,
> By train, bicycle or tram,
> The tumultuous throng of the human maelstrom churns forth.]

Indeed, Engelke raises this 'tumultous throng' (wirre Hetze) to a poetic principle. According to 'Der rasende Psalm', the task of modern poetry is precisely to capture all these impressions in their very heterogeneity:

---

9 On the futurist call for the elimination of adjectives, see Filippo Tommaso Marinetti, 'Manifesto tecnico della letteratura futurista' (1912) [Technical Manifesto of Futurist Literature], in Luciano De Maria (ed.), *Teoria e invenzione futurista* [*Futurist Theory and Invention*] (Milan: Arnoldo Mondadori, 1968), 41–42); 'Distruzione della sintassi. Immaginazione senza fili. Parole in libertà' [Destruction of Syntax. Wireless Imagination. World in Freedom], in *Teoria e invenzione futurista*, 64–66.

Alle Telegraphendrähte,
Alles Krankenhaus-Gestöhn,
Aller Hammer Schlag-Gedröhn,
Alle krummen Straßenstränge,
Allen Wirtshaus-Lärm,
Militärkapellen-Klänge,
Alles Mensch-Gedärm
Will ich auf die Pauke spannen,
Daraus Groß-Gesänge bannen. (44)

[All the telegraph wires,
All the moaning of hospitals,
All the din of pounding hammers,
All the crooked lines of streets,
All the noise of bars,
The sounds of military bands,
And the guts of man –
I want to stretch them all across my drum
And from it beat out great songs.]

Cultivating such heterogeneous series, Engelke's poetry recalls contemporary descriptions of neurasthenia and its relation to the increasing fragmentation and acceleration of urban perception. Simmel himself had famously described the experience of urban life as a 'Steigerung des Nervenlebens' [intensification of nervous life] due to changes in perceptual conditions that look forward to Engelke's poetry: 'die rasche Zusammendrängung wechselnder Bilder, der schroffe Abstand innerhalb dessen, was man mit einem Blick umfaßt, die Unerwartetheit sich aufdrängender Impressionen' [the rapid and dense throng of alternating images, the sharp discontinuities between phenomena visible in a single glance, and the unexpectedness of onrushing impressions].[10] Simmel's description was also undergirded by a veritable industry of medical research into changing modes of urban perception. The psychiatrist and cultural critic Willy Hellpach, for example, in one of the most revealing *fin-de-siècle* treatises on neurasthenia, spoke of city-dwellers' growing 'Wechseltrieb' [drive toward alternation], which was leading to an alarming spread of psychic instability.[11] Similarly, the Berlin neurologist Johannes Marcinowski described the jarring impressions of city traffic, noise

---

10 Georg Simmel, 'Die Großstädte und das Geistesleben', in *Aufsätze und Abhandlungen 1901–1908*, vol. 1 (Frankfurt am Main: Suhrkamp, 1995), 16–17.

11 Willy Hellpach, *Nervosität und Kultur* [*Nervousness and Culture*] (Berlin: Johannes Räde, 1902), 72.

and spectacles as a 'fortgesetzte Reihe "psychischer Traumata"' [continuous series of 'psychic traumas'].[12]

Occasionally, Engelke's poems do appear to search for some respite from the throng of urban rhythms. In the poem 'Die große Uhr', for example, the poet finds respite from the modern tempo in the midnight hours, when time appears to slow down:

> Einen Augenblick hält jede Stunde
> Mich mit Lärm und Licht umschlossen
> Eingetaucht im Wirbel-Straßengrunde,
> Wirft mich dann gelangweilt und verdrossen
>
> Neuem Stundenbrausen in die Mitte:
> Wieder branden, klirren sechzig Eilminuten
> Durch mein Blut, – überstürzen meine Schritte:
> Neue Stunde! – Weiter tosen Straßenfluten.
>
> Nur die Mitternacht ist tröstend gütig,
> Langsam summen ihre Stunden, sternenflütig,
> Blau dahin; und ich weiß dann nicht im Traum,
> Daß ich nur Atom der Stunden bin im Weltraum. (138)
>
> [Every hour envelops me
> For a moment in light and noise,
> Submerged in the maelstrom of the street,
> Only then to throw me, bored and tired,
>
> Into the midst of a new din of hours:
> Once again, sixty rapid-transit minutes crash and clatter
> Through my blood – overtake my steps:
> A new hour! – Again the street floods roar.
>
> Only midnight provides the comfort of respite;
> Its hours hum by slowly, flooded with stars,
> Blue; then, in my dream, I do not know
> That I am only an atom of the hours in the cosmos.]

In the first two stanzas of this poem, Engelke's poet describes himself in terms that specifically evoke Simmel's most famous urban type (itself a variant of the growing *Wechseltrieb* diagnosed by Hellpach

---

12   Johannes Marcinowski, *Im Kampf um gesunde Nerven. Ein Wegweiser zum Verständnis und zur Heilung nervöser Zustände für Ärzte und Laien* [*In the Struggle for Healthy Nerves. A Guidebook for Understanding and Healing Nervous Conditions for Doctors and Laypeople*], 4th edn (Berlin: Otto Salle, 1911), 64.

and the neurologists): the 'blasé' (blasiert) personality.[13] Frazzled by the velocity and intensity of urban sensations, the poet can only muster up a feeble reaction before boredom sets in and he is thrown headlong into a new sensation. Indeed, this sense of lurching from one sensation to the next is borne out formally in the enjambment that erases the boundary between the first two stanzas. Both the speaker and readers find themselves 'thrown', in mid-sentence, from the 'Wirbel' of the first stanza into the renewed din of acceleration ('neuem Stundenbrausen') of the second. The second stanza then describes this accelerated lurching from one experience to another in terms of the poet's being permeated by modern tempo. Replacing the beat of the heart, the hasty seconds ('Eilsekunden') race through his bloodstream like high-speed trains ('Eilzüge') and overtake his own steps. In contrast to this racing tempo, the third stanza – now demarcated from the first two by a full stop – seems to offer some sense of rest; midnight is described as 'comforting' ('tröstend') and 'benign' ('gütig'); its hours hum by slowly; and above all, midnight seems to connect the poet back to the diurnal rhythms of stars. But if anything, this connection with nature is represented here as illusory, as part of a dream that allows him to forget ('ich weiß dann nicht im Traum') his knowledge of his own insignificance within the great race of universal time. Told from the perspective of a waking poet – and therefore a poet who *does* know that he is merely an atom in the hours of the universe – this poem operates according to the logic of 'sentimental' longing:[14] longing for a state of naiveté from the knowledge of modern time, a state only imaginable in a midnight dream – or Klagesian phenomenology.

In thematizing the 'maelstrom' of urban experience, Engelke's poems occasionally strike an ambivalent tone. In addition to 'Die große Uhr', one could cite in this context poems such as 'Seele' (1913) [Soul] and 'Ich will heraus aus dieser Stadt' (1914) [I Want Out of This City], with their echoes of the lyric from the *Lebensreform* movement such as Richard Dehmel's 'Predigt ans Großstadtvolk' (1906) [Sermon to City Dwellers]. But these moments are few and far between in Engelke. Much more central, in *Rhythmus des neuen Europa,* is an effort

13   Simmel saw the blasé personality as a 'Folge jener rasch wechselnden und in ihren Gegensätzen eng zusammengedrängten Nervenreize' (Simmel, 'Die Großstädte und das Geistesleben', 121) [result of that rapidly alternating throng of disparate nervous sensations].

14   See of course Friedrich Schiller, 'Über naive und sentimentalische Dichtung' (1795) [On Naive and Sentimental Poetry], *Werke und Briefe in zwölf Bänden* 8: *Theoretische Schriften [Theoretical Writings]*, ed. Rolf-Peter Janz (Frankfurt am Main: Bibliothek deutscher Klassiker, 1992), 707–810.

– pointing forward to 1920s texts such as Joseph Roth's *Bekenntnis zum Gleisdreieck* (1924) [*Ode to the Triangular Railway Junction*] or the urban poetry of Claire and Yvan Goll – to affirm the city and its new rhythms.[15] A case in point can be found in 'Auf der Straßenbahn', in which the poet describes his submission to the rhythms of technology in rapturous terms:

> Schütternd walzt und wiegt der Wagenboden,
> Meine Sinne walzen, wiegen mit!:
> Voller Strom! Voller Strom!
>
> Der ganze Wagen, mit den Menschen drinnen
> Saust und summt und singt mit meinen Sinnen.
> Das Wagensingen sausebraust, es schwillt! (48)
>
> [Quaking, the car rolls and sways,
> And my senses roll and sway with it!:
> Full of electricity! Full of electricity!
>
> The whole tram, with the people inside,
> swishes, hums and sings with my senses.
> The car-song roars, speeds and swells up!]

In a configuration once again reminiscent of Italian Futurism, with its fantasy of melding the human body with the car and the aeroplane, Engelke here depicts a ride in the tram as an ecstatic experience of being suffused with technological rhythms.[16] As in 'Die Große Uhr', the senses here become the conduit whereby the rhythms of industrial modernity – the clattering of motors, the crackling of electric wires, the trotting of horses and the march of pedestrians – permeate the body and fill it with industrial energies ('Meine Sinne walzen, wiegen mit'). Like the 'Straßenlied' of the poem 'Stadt' or the 'Maschinen-Musik' of 'Die Fabrik', the energetic sensations condensed in the tram ride are described in musical terms through verbs such as 'singen' and 'summen' (a few lines later, the poet will refer to the tram's music as a 'Stromgesang' [electric chant]) (48). Indeed, it is perhaps no coincidence if Engelke repeatedly employs the term 'walzen' [to roll or to dance] in 'Auf der Straßenbahn' – a word that, alongside

---

15   See Joseph Roth, *Bekenntnis zum Gleisdreieck* (1924), www.berlin-gleisdreieck.de/Seiten/projekte/projekte_Frameset.htm [consulted 15 August 2011]; Claire Goll, *Lyrische Films* [*Lyrical Films*] (Basel and Leipzig: Rhein Verlag, 1922).

16   See Filippo Tommaso Marinetti, 'L'uomo moltiplicato e il Regno della macchina' [The Multiplication of Man and the Reign of the Machine], in *Teoria et invenzione futurista*, 255–59.

'Wirbel' [maelstrom], recurs in several of his poems – to describe the common activity of the tram and his own senses. Recalling its etymological derivative *Walzer* (a waltz), 'walzen' here suggests the experience of being swept up by the rhythmical dance of technology. 'Auf der Straßenbahn' is an ode to machinic rhythms, the waltz of the great city.

Engelke's image of the body swept up into the dance of technology reads like an allegory of the rhythm problem as described by theorists such as Bücher, Simmel and Giese, and one could point to numerous poems in *Rhythmus des neuen Europa* that echo these images of the body being suffused with the rhythms of modernity.[17] In 'Ich weiß: ich bin ein Leben' (1912) [I Know: I am a Life], for example, the poet speaks ecstatically of being filled with the city's tremendous energies:

> In der Ferne, Automobile knattern
> Hart vorbei: es stampft und walzt in meinem Sinn:
> [...]
> Von nun ab geh ich durch die Häuserstraßen-Enge,
> Die übervoll von Schritten, Hufen, Straßenbahn-Gebimmel,
> Von nun ab geh ich durch die Promenaden-Menschenmenge,
> Durch das frauen-, früchtebunte Wochenmarkt-Gewimmel,
> [...]
> Wie mit elektrisiertem Leibe hin! (64)

> [In the distance, automobiles rattle by
> loudly: my senses are filled with pounding and rolling
> [...]
> From now on, I walk through the narrow house-lined streets,
> Which overflow with human steps, hooves, the bells of trams;
> From now on, I walk through the human crowds in the promenades,
> Through the marketplace with its colourful throng of women and fruits,
> [...]
> As with an electrified body!]

For readers familiar with Baudelaire, Engelke's image of the city-dweller's 'electrified body' will surely recall the famous depiction of the *flâneur's* urban milieu as an 'immense réservoir d'électricité'

---

17 In Giese's words, 'Industrie, Technik, Handel, Verkehr und Großstadt entwickeln ihr Eigenleben. Sie werden Giganten, sie spannen den Einzelnen und die Menge in ihre Kräfte ein' (Giese, *Girlkultur*, 26) [Industry, technology, trade, traffic and the city develop their own life. They become giants, which yoke the individual and the group to their energies].

[giant reservoir of electricity].[18] Like Baudelaire, moreover, Engelke was clearly attempting to create new forms of lyric appropriate to an increasingly electrified world. But if Engelke's electric body recalls the porous body of the *flâneur*, his focus on urban traffic situates his poetry more squarely in Benjamin's post-*flâneur* world of motorized shocks.[19] Above all, however, Engelke's vitalist investment of this technological world bears close affinities to Italian Futurism. Like the futurists, Engelke celebrated the new modes of industrial transportation – trains, cars and aeroplanes – as icons of modernity's restless tempo. In his poem 'Weltgeist' [World Spirit] (1914), for example, Engelke sings an ode to an all-encompassing rhythmical energy (an 'unruhevoller Rhythmus' [restless rhythm]), visible in the shipping industry ('Wo Docks und Hellinge Schiffsbauten umkrampfen' [where docks and launchways squeeze the ships under construction]) and in air travel:

Da steigt, da fliegt, da siegt über Erdenschwere der Unruh-Geist:
Der neue Schönheit, neue Tatenwege weist:
Der Weltgeist! (101)

[Climbing, flying and triumphing over gravity, the spirit of unrest
Displays a new beauty and new paths of action:
The world spirit!]

---

18 'Ainsi l'amoureux de la vie universelle entre dans la foule comme dans un immense réservoir d'électricité' [Thus the lover of universal life enters into the crowd as if into a giant reservoir of electricity]. Charles Baudelaire, *Curiosités esthétiques, L'Art romantique et autres Œuvres critiques* (Paris: Garnier, 1962), 463–64.

19 On the demise of the Baudelairean *flâneur*, see Walter Benjamin, 'Über einige Motive bei Baudelaire' [On Some Motifs in Baudelaire] (1939), *Illuminationen* (Frankfurt am Main: Suhrkamp, 1977), 204–05. Like Simmel and Giese, Benjamin saw the traffic-laden city as an environment characterized by new technological rhythms, which found their paradigmatic incarnation in the conveyer-belt. Hence Benjamin's interest in film as a training ground for the shock-like rhythms of urban life: 'So unterwarf die Technik das menschliche Sensorium einem Training komplexer Art. Es kam der Tag, da einem neuen und dringlichen Reizbedürfnis der Film entsprach. Im Film kommt die chockförmige Wahrnehmung als formales Prinzip zur Geltung. Was am Fließband den Rhythmus der Produktion bestimmt, liegt beim Film dem der Rezeption zugrunde' (208) [Technology thus submitted the human sensorium to a complex form of training. The day came when film corresponded to a new and urgent need for stimulation. In film, the experience of shock came into its own as a formal principle. That which determines the rhythm of production on the conveyor belt forms the basis of reception in film].

In referring to the restless rhythm of industry as a 'neue Schönheit [new beauty], Engelke specifically recalls the futurists' insistence on the new 'bellezza della velocità' [beauty of speed].[20] Like the futurists, with their elimination of weighty adjectives and punctuation, Engelke sought to forge a dynamic aesthetics adapted to a world in perpetual movement, one whose heavy rhythms and endless linguistic variations entail a rejection of any notion of stasis or rest. 'Jede Ruhe', he explained in his notes, 'ist Stillstand: der geringe Wert der "stillen Dichter" und der "Stillen im Lande" für fortschreitendes Leben und Kunst!' (219) [Every form of rest means stasis: 'still poets', like 'the quiet ones in the country', are of little use for advancing life and art].[21]

Poetry, Painting and the Aesthetics of Rhythm

If this rejection of stasis informs Engelke's understanding of poetic aesthetics, it also informs a media-theoretical reflection on the function of lyric poetry. In his notes, Engelke argued that, because of its dynamic, temporal character, poetry could better represent the

20 Filippo Tommaso Marinetti, 'Fondazione e manifesto del futurismo' (1909) [Foundation and Manifesto of Futurism], in *Teoria et invenzione futurista*, 10.

21 If Engelke rejects the model of aesthetic production as other-worldly meditation contained in the metaphor of pietistic devotion ('die Stillen im Lande' [the quiet ones in the country]), his critique of rest here echoes an energetic imperative visible in numerous other domains in the early twentieth century. A good example can be seen in contemporary self-help manuals for overcoming neurasthenia. The author of one 1912 manual entitled *Wie werde ich energisch?* [*How Do I Increase My Energy?*] spoke for many when he argued against the nineteenth-century rest cure: 'Absolute Ruhe gibt es ja nur im Tode; so lange wir leben, sind wir thätig, und es kommt nur darauf an, wie' [Absolute rest exists, after all, only in death; as long as we are alive, we are active, and it is only a question of how], Wilhelm Gebhardt, *Wie werde ich energisch*, 9th edn (Leipzig: Verlag von F. W. Gloeckner & Co, 1912), 75. Similarly, in his popular treatise *Gymnastik des Willens* [*Gymnastics of the Will*], the neurologist Reinholt Gerling insisted that life and rest were incompatible: 'Bewegung ist Leben, Ruhe ist Tod. Das Leben ist wie ein rieselnder Bach, der über Stock und Stein fließt; wird es ein stillstehendes Wasser, so versumpft es. Darum sollen wir die Ruhe als ein notwendiges Übel betrachten, lediglich dazu bestimmt, uns neue Gedanken und Kräfte zur Arbeit zuzuführen' [Movement is life, while rest is death. Life is like a rippling stream that flows over sticks and stones; if the water stands still, it turns into a dirty marsh. For this reason, we should consider rest a necessary evil, intended only to provide us with new thoughts and new energy], Reinholt Gerling. *Die Gymnastik des Willens*, 5th edn (Oranienburg bei Berlin: Verlag von Wilhelm Möller, 1920), 61. On this point, see also Cowan, *Cult of the Will*, 69–78; Rabinbach, *The Human Motor*.

'maelstrom' of modern life than visual art, which can only capture one moment and one event:

> Wirbelndes Leben, Bewegtheit kann nur (und nur in einigen Fällen) der Dichter (der vor dem bildenden Künstler über umfassendere, beweglichere Ausdrucksmittel verfügt) – oder der lautmalende Orchesterkomponist darstellen. [...] Der bildende Künstler (im stärksten Maße natürlich der Plastiker) kann jeweils immer nur eine Erscheinung (ausnahmsweise wohl einige, wenn sie ganz in Ruhe verharren) aus dem Leben greifen und sie dann zum vollkommenen Kunstwerk [...] ausgestalten; nie aber Dutzende rastlos bewegter Erscheinungen. (220)

> [Only poets (and only then in rare cases) – or tonal orchestra composers – can represent life's churning and movement. (For they have at their disposal more agile, mobile and copious means than visual artists). [...] The visual artist (above all the sculptor) can only ever latch onto one phenomenon (in exceptional cases a few phenomena if they remain absolutely still) and shape it into a perfect artwork [...], but never dozens of ceaselessly moving phenomena.]

Engelke's reflections here are of interest not only for biographical reasons – he himself had trained as a painter before turning to poetry – but also because of the insight they offer into the early twentieth century's understanding of artistic media and what they should do. To be modern, Engelke argues, media must be above all *dynamic*; only a medium capable of constant transformation can keep pace with modernity's restless movements and alternations, the 'dozens of ceaselessly moving phenomena' all around.

Of course, one can criticize Engelke's dichotomy between poetry and the visual arts. Largely inherited from the 18th-century aesthetics of G. E. Lessing's *Laokoon* (1766) in its insistence on associating visual representation with stationary poses and reserving temporal succession for poetry,[22] this characterization of visual art takes no account of developments in modernist painting and sculpture – not least by the futurists themselves, whose novel forms in painting, as is well known, revolved precisely around an effort to transcribe dynamic rhythms in static visual media. Nor was Futurism alone in this respect: in the wake of new recording media such as snapshot and chronophotography, modernist movements

---

22 'Die Zeitfolge', Lessing famously claimed, 'ist das Gebiet des Dichters, sowie der Raum das Gebiet des Malers' [Duration is the domain of the poet, while space is the domain of the painter], G. E. Lessing, *Laokoon, Gesammelte Werke 5*, ed. Paul Rilla (Berlin: Aufbau, 1955), 130.

Fig 1. Luigi Russolo, Dinamismo di un'automobile *(1912/13), courtesy of Agence Photographique de la RMN*

of all sorts – from the vitalist art of the *Lebensreform* movements to Viennese Kinetismus to Dada (e.g. Marcel Duchamps) – sought to translate temporal experience into spatial media.[23] Not surprisingly, this dynamic aesthetics was often employed to depict the same icons of modernity that interested Engelke, such as the train and the motor car (figure 1).[24] That this endeavour was bound up with modernity's

23 As Sabine Autsch has argued, the energetic aesthetics of the *Lebensreform* movement in Germany, inspired as it was by snapshot photography, revolved around the effort to capture bodies in motion. See Sabine Autsch, 'Von Lichtbildern und Lichtfreunden. Zur Beziehung von Fotografie und Lebensreform um 1900' [From Projection Lights to Light Worship. On the Relation between Photography and Life Reform Movements ca. 1900], in Kai Buchholz, *et. al.*, *Die Lebensreform. Entwürfe zur Neugestaltung von Leben und Kunst um 1900* [*Life Reform: Models for Redesigning Life and Art around 1900*], vol. 1 (Darmstadt: Häusser, 2001), 303–6. On Viennese Kineticism, see Monika Platzer and Ursula Storch (eds.), *Kinetismus. Wien entdeckt die Avantgarde* [*Kinetismus. Vienna Discovers the Avant-Garde*] (Ostfildern: Hatje Cantz Verlag, 2006).

24 For images of a train in movement, see for example Luigi Russolo's *Dinamismo di un treno* (1912) [*Dynamism of a Train*] and Erika Giovanna Klein's *Lokomotive* (1926). The latter painting is reprinted in *Kinetismus. Wien entdeckt die Avantgarde*, 78.

fixation on rhythm can be seen in the many references to rhythm in works by futurist artists and movements inspired by Futurism. Giacomo Balla's painting *Ritmo + rumore + velocità d'automobile* (1913) [Rhythm, Noise and Speed of an Automobile], for example, offers one of the many examples of futurist efforts to reduce matter to pulsing energies. Even the medium of sculpture was dynamized, as it were, to facilitate the focus on rhythm; the sculpture *Wiedergabe des rhythmischen Ablaufs einer Bewegung* (1921) [*Representation of the Rhythmical Progression of a Movement*] by the Austrian artist Franziska

Fig 2. Franziska Kantor, Wiedergabe des rhythmischen Ablaufs einer Bewegung *(ca. 1921), courtesy of Wien Museum*

Fig 3. Umberto Boccioni, Visioni simultanee *(1911/12)*

Kantor, for example, would be unthinkable without the model of chronophotography (figure 2). Nor did Futurism or the avant-garde movements influenced by it (Dada, Cubism, Kinetismus) lack efforts to represent the 'maelstrom' of urban impressions. A case in point can be seen in Umberto Boccioni's painting *Visioni simultanee* (1911) [*Simultaneous Visions*], which could well be understood as the visual counterpart for a poem such as 'Stadt' (figure 3).

Clearly, then, Engelke had many affinities with the futurists and their avant-garde successors, and his project for a poetry of modern rhythms can hardly be understood outside this context. It would seem, moreover, that Engelke was well aware of these connections, as he makes repeated references to Futurism and Cubism in his notebooks. Despite their proximity, however, Engelke sought to distinguish his own urban aesthetic from that of the artistic avant-garde. The problem with such movements, as he understood them, had to do specifically with the question of mimesis:

> Warum solch ein Geschrei um die Futuristen und Kubisten? –Sie geben doch nur unvollkommene Kunst, glänzende Einseitigkeit. Sie geben chaotischen Inhalt ohne zusammenzwingende Form. Gewiß ist der umschließende Bogen der Form in allen Künsten weiter gespannt vor der wachsenden Fülle der Zeitereignisse; hier aber ist er überhaupt nicht da – und er *muß* immer da sein. (220)

[Why all this buzz around the futurists and the cubists? –They really only create imperfect art, flashy but one-dimensional. They render chaotic content without containing it through form. Certainly, the increasing abundance of events today has stretched the surrounding arc of form further in all the arts; but in these artists' work, that arc is absent altogether – and it *must* always be present.]

Futurism, Engelke argued, captured the maelstrom of modern existence, but it did so – like Impressionism before it – only in terms of surface appearance, failing to bind the chaos of modern life into any aesthetic form.

On one level, Engelke's rejection of mere mimesis for a deeper penetration of reality points forward to the analyses of realist theorists such as Siegfried Kracauer and Georg Lukács.[25] Coming in 1914, however, his arguments show a more immediate affinity with the aesthetic debates of German Expressionism. The notion of the artist as an agent who gives form to reality rather than passively imitating chaotic impressions stood at the very heart of Expressionism's self-understanding.[26] Echoing this expressionist credo, Engelke argues in his notes that artistic creation is 'nicht Wiedergabe (Photographie) sondern Umschaffung – ja, Schöpfung eines ganz Neuen' (215) [not reproduction (photography) but alteration – indeed the creation of something completely new]. Behind this aesthetic affinity with Expressionism, there is, I think, a more consequential question at stake here. As I have argued elsewhere, Expressionism's preoccupation with overcoming mimesis through the creative act had everything to do with reimagining agency in an age characterized by what Georg

---

25 See for example Kracauer's critiques of Walter Ruttmann's surface aesthetics in S. Kracauer, *From Caligari to Hitler. A Psychological History of the German Film* (Princeton: Princeton University Press, 1947), 187–88; Georg Lukács, 'Es geht um den Realismus' [The Subject is Realism] in *Werke 4: Probleme des Realismus* [*Works 4: Problems of Realism*] (Berlin: Luchterhand, 1971), 313–44.

26 As Thomas Mann would later describe it: 'Expressionismus [...] ist jene Kunstrichtung, welche, im heftigen Gegensatz zu der Passivität, der demütig aufnehmenden und wiedergebenden Art des Impressionismus, die Nachbildung der Wirklichkeit aufs tiefste verachtet, jede Verpflichtung an die Wirklichkeit entschlossen kündigt und an ihre Stelle den souverän, explosiven, rücksichtslos schöpferischen Erlaß des Geistes setzt' [Expressionism [...] is the artistic direction which, in opposition to the passivity of Impressionism with its humbly receptive and reproductive manner, profoundly detests the imitation of reality, decisively renounces all duty to reality, and posits in its place the sovereign, explosive, disrespectfully creative order of the spirit]. Cited in Thomas Anz and Michael Stark (eds.), *Expressionismus: Manifeste und Dokumente zur deutschen Literatur* [*Expressionism: Manifestoes and Documents of German Literature*] *1910–1920* (Stuttgart: Metzler, 1982), 90.

Simmel called the 'conflict' of culture—i.e. the apparent emancipation of 'objective culture' (technology, bureaucracy, institutions, etc.) from the control of individual subjects. In early expressionist theory, the creative poet was understood as someone who could master the new world of shocks and hyperstimulation rather than being mastered by it.[27] Thus the Austrian critic Hermann Bahr, in his 1916 treatise *Expressionismus*, interpreted the 'activist' turn of early Expressionism as a push to liberate humanity from its enslavement to technology: 'Darum geht es: daß der Mensch sich wiederfinden will. [Unsere Zeit] macht ihn zum bloßen Instrument, er ist ein Werkzeug seines eigenen Werkes geworden, er hat keinen Sinn mehr, seit er nur noch der Maschine dient' [This is the issue: The human being wishes to find itself once more. [Our epoch] has made people into mere instruments; they have become the tools of their own creations; their existence has no more meaning now that they only serve the machine].[28] Like Simmel and like Bücher, Bahr saw the problem of nervousness – embodied by the Nervenkunst [nervous art] of Impressionism – as the symptom of a greater discrepancy between subjective and objective culture, one in which human beings had become the tools of their own productions.

Like other expressionist poets, Engelke associated the slovenly imitation of reality with what he described as 'eine neurasthenische Überhitztheit' (221) [a state of neurasthenic hyperstimulation]. Like other expressionist poets, moreover, he associated this emphasis on external details with mechanistic materialism and called for a counter-turn inward toward the spirit: 'Wir konstruieren ganz erstaunliche Wunder der Technik', Engelke wrote in a passage reminiscent of Bahr:

> kilometerlange Brücken, wolkenhohe Häuser, Luftschiffe und andere rasendschnelle Beförderungsmittel – und denken nicht, daß wir nicht glücklicher dadurch werden, daß wir schneller leben – und daß wir uns immer mehr vom Materiellen, von Stahl und Dampf und Elektrizität, daß wir immer mehr von den neuen Mitteln zu neuen Bedürfnissen, die wir unnötiger- und zweckloserweise uns schaffen, – *knechten lassen!* Wann werden die Kräfte, die jetzt nur für den äußeren Menschen angewandt werden, auf den inneren Menschen gerichtet? (221–22)

---

27 See Cowan, *Cult of the Will*, 3–6. On Simmel's notion of the conflict of culture, see Simmel, *Philosophie des Geldes*, 502–33.

28 Hermann Bahr, *Expressionismus* (Munich: Delphin-Verlag, 1916), 122.

Fig 4. Ferdinand Hodler, Eurythmie *(1895). Courtesy of Kunstmuseum Bern*

[We construct astounding wonders of technology, mile-long bridges, skyscrapers, aeroplanes and other means of rapid transit, but we never stop to think that living faster will not make us happier – and that all this material, this steel, steam and electricity, these new means of creating new needs, which we have amassed unnecessarily and aimlessly, *is enslaving us* more and more. When will we turn all the powers today applied to our external lives towards inner life?]

Faced with humanity's increasing enslavement ('knechten') to material forces, Engelke, like Bahr and other expressionists, calls for the revitalization of 'inner' life or, in terms of Simmel's conflict, a revalorization of subjective culture to counter the hypertrophic expansion of technology and urban institutions.

For Engelke, such a turn inward was tantamount to an effort to reconnect with the vital flows of rhythm, the underlying principle animating all matter. The task of modern art, as he understood it, was first and foremost to access the primal rhythms behind the chaotic surface-culture of urban modernity. Thus to the surface aesthetics of Futurism, Engelke opposes, in his notebooks, the ritual-rhythmical compositions of the Swiss Symbolist painter Ferdinand Hodler: 'Aus unserer Malerei wird vor dem Gericht der Zeit nur Hodler bestehen. (Der Mann hat Rhythmus im Leibe!)' (214) [Among our contemporary painters, only Hodler will stand the test of time. (This man has rhythm in his body!)]. Engelke's praise for Hodler is significant: an acquaintance of Jaques-Dalcroze from Geneva, Hodler sought to adapt the aesthetics and ethics of eurhythmics into the realm of visual art.[29] Like Jaques-Dalcroze, Hodler associated rhythm in particular with collective ritual, as one can see in some of his most famous paintings such as *Eurythmie* (1895) [*Eurhythmics*] or *Tag* (1900) [*Day*], where the harmonious composition of figures – recalling specifically Jaques-Dalcroze's group choreography – seems to connote a sense of communal togetherness lost to modern capitalist society (figure 4).[30] Holding up Hodler's symbolist painting against the futurist cultivation of urban speed, Engelke clearly found affinities between Hodler's more harmonious compositions and his own search for primal rhythm behind the maelstrom of appearances, a rhythm that would contain the latter within the arc of a unifying form.

But although some of Engelke's surviving sketches treat similar themes of mythology or ritual,[31] his project ultimately differed from that of the 37–years-older Hodler in at least two respects. First, as already stated, Engelke saw rhythm as above all the domain of lyric poetry rather than painting (although the very fact that he praised Hodler's works would suggest that what really bothered Engelke was the dissonant aesthetics of avant-garde painting and collage painting, not painting as such); second, unlike Hodler's symbolist paintings, Engelke's poetry sought to cultivate primal rhythm less for its own sake than as a means of coming to terms specifically with *urban* experience. More precisely, Engelke sought – here by contrast with the futurists – to invest urban and technological modernity with a new spiritual significance. Again and again, he insists on using rhythm not to escape technological modernity, but rather to 'respiritualize' it. 'Keine Zeit', he wrote in 1914,

> kann sich vom Materiellen frei machen. Darum wollen wir nicht: Überwindung des Materialismus, sondern Durchgeistigung desselben.

---

29 On Hodler's relation to Jaques-Dalcroze, see Verena Senti-Schmidlin, *Rhythmus und Tanz in der Malerei. Zur Bewegungsästhetik im Werk von Ferdinand Hodler und Ludwig Hoffmann* [*Rhythm and Dance in Painting: On the Aesthetics of Movement in the Work of Ferdinand Hodler and Ludwig Hoffmann*] (Hildesheim: Georg Olms Verlag, 2007), 37–117.

30 On the affinities of *Eurythmie* and *Der Tag* with Jaques-Dalcroze, in particular, see Senti-Schmidlin 61–82. 'Was Hodler zeichnerisch zu realisieren suchte, erarbeitete Jaques-Dalcroze in choreographischen Bildern' (81) [What Hodler attempted to create on the canvas, Jaques-Dalcroze worked out through choreography].

31 See for example Engelke's sketch *Schicksal* (1914) [*Fate*], reprinted in Morawietz, 131.

Solches ist uns bitter not. Ein Freund sagt mir: 'Du wiederholst dich in deinen Gedichten.' (Im Anschauen der Welt, kann er nur meinen.) Ich: 'Schließlich gibt es ja auch nur *ein* Thema. Alle Millliarden von bunten und wirbelnden Erscheinungen des Daseins sind nur Variationen des *einen* Themas vom Leben, vom Lebensrhythmus!' (219–20)

[No era can free itself from material concerns. For this reason, we do not seek to overcome materialism, but rather to permeate it with spirit. We desperately need this. A friend tells me: 'You repeat yourself in your poems.' (He can only be referring to my world-view.) My answer: 'After all, there really is only *one* subject. All the millions of life's colourful and chaotic phenomena are only variations of the *one* subject of life, of life's rhythm!']

Such a 'Durchgeistigung' [spiritual permeation] of material reality, which would overcome the tragedy of modern culture, depended upon recognizing the creative energy underlying and animating objective things.[32] Engelke thus insists on the presence of a 'divine' rhythm behind the maelstrom of appearances:

Der Rhythmus, der Rhythmus!
Alles Geschehen in der Welt – Variationen eines göttlichen Themas
(220)

[Rhythm, rhythm!
All occurences in the world – variations on a divine theme.]

It is this relation between between the apparent chaos of material phenomena and a vital force underlying and animating the whole that Engelke's declamatory style, with its endless chains of words unfolding and transforming around a basic metre, attempts to convey.

---

32   In aesthetics terms, such a 'spiritualization' of art entailed a turn from surface impressions – the material of the medium – towards the soul: 'Dichtung der Jungen, die sich in verstandesscharfer Zuspitzung der Ausdrücke gar nicht genug tun kann. [...] Malerei, die sich in Ölfarbe und deren mehr oder weniger raffinierter Verwendung erschöpft. Musik, die zu den tausend Nerven, mitunter gar nur zu den Trommelfellen spricht – statt zur Seele. Unser kluger Materialismus ist jetzt schon fast restlos "vollkommen". Möge uns zertechnisierte Menschen bald wieder *ein* panisches Grundgefühl beseelend durchdringen' (222–23) [The writing of young poets, who cannot get enough of exaggeratedly witty expressions. [...] Painting that exhausts itself in oil colours and their more or less sophisticated application. Music that speaks to a thousand nerves, and sometimes only to the ear-drums, instead of speaking to the soul. Today, our clever materialism is nearly 'perfect'. Would that a *single* all-encompassing feeling might soon suffuse our overly technologized age with soul].

The effort to interpret the disparate activities of the city as variations on primal rhythm can be seen clearly in Engelke's poem 'Gott braust' (1914) [God Roars], which describes the city as one great dance of providential rhythm:

> Weißt du, was die Mittags-Straße schüttert, lebt,
> Wenn chaotisch tausend Lebenstakte schlagen
> Aus den Menschen, Häusern, Pferden, Wagen?
>   Gottesrhythmus!
> [...]
>
> Und du selbst, du Mensch in diesem Herzschlag-Leben,
> Von Tränen überspült, vom Straßenbraus gepackt,
> Bist der höchste Rhythmus, vollster Blutstrom-Takt:
>   Denn in Dir ist Gott! (54)
>
> [Do you know what living force shakes the midday street,
> When a thousand beats of life resound chaotically
> From people, houses, horses and trams?
>   God's rhythm!
> [...]
>
> And you yourself, you human being in this heartbeat-life,
> Awash in tears, seized by the noise of the street,
> You are the highest rhythm, the most perfect bloodstream-cadence:
>   For God is within you!]

Here, recognition of the divine rhythm ('Gottesrhythmus') animating all things not only promises to reveal the continuity behind the chaotic maelstrom of nervous impressions, but also to overcome the chasm between subjective and objective culture; recognizing themselves as 'the highest rhythm', Engelke's readers are meant to understand themselves as part of the creative agency underlying all visible phenomena. Reinvesting objective culture – and specifically urban impressions – with the spiritual force of rhythm, Engelke's poetry sought precisely to 'resubjectify' that culture, undoing its status as an autonomous entity standing overagainst the human.

The City-Body and the Poet as Mediator

As the closing stanza of 'Gott braust' suggests, a master metaphor for this resubjectification of urban rhythms in Engelke's poetry is that of the heartbeat ('Herzschlag') and blood flow ('Blutstrom-Takt'). In poems such as 'Blut-Strom' (1912) [Blood-Stream], 'Von innen nach außen' (1913) [From the Inside Out], 'Der ewige Herzklang' (1915) [The Eternal Sound of the Heart] and 'Weltfrühling' (1917) [World Spring], Engelke repeatedly characterizes rhythm as the activity of a great pumping and life-giving heart. 'Blut-Strom' offers a paradigmatic case. Again foreshadowing the city in Lang's *Metropolis*, which is powered at its centre by the famous 'heart machine' of pumps and spinning turbines, Engelke's poem represents the city as a giant organic body driven by a tirelessly pulsating 'heart-turbine'. I quote Engelke's poem here in full:

Blut-Strom
    Pochend, pochend, fort und fort
    Treibt die Lebensgas-Maschine.
    Pochend, pochend, fort und fort
    Treibt im Kreis die Herz-Turbine
Durch das Lungen-Schwammgekräuse,
Durch des Hirnes Labyrinth-Gehäuse,
Durch die Leber-, Nieren-Schleuse,
Durch der Nährungs-Adern Vielkanäle:
    Blutes roten Fluß. –
Weiter fließt der Fluß:
Schmilzt mit Lava-Glut die Aderschäle
Wellend, schwellend, fort und fort:
    Springt als Ton: als Schrei, als Wort
In die Straßen-Dissonanz-Choräle,
Geht als Meter-Schritt auf Pflastersteinen,
(Tausendteiliger Druck von allen Beinen)
Wächst als Arbeits-Griff, als Händerücken
In das armgetürmte Steinhausblock-Gewirr,
Saust als Peitschenhieb auf Lastpferd-Rücken,
Schwillt als sichtbarwachsend Werk aus Werk-Geschirr.
    Pochend, pochend, fort und fort
    Treibt im Kreis die Kraft-Maschine
    Pochend, pochend, fort und fort
    Treibt im Kreis die Herz-Turbine:
Blut durch Leib- und Stadt-Atom. –
    Fließt und fließt der warme Strom:
Fließt als Licht aus Bogenlampen:
Zischt als ‚Fertig-Pfiff' von Hochbahn-Rampen:
Schwerer Qualm aus Bahnsteigshallen:
Kaufgeschwirr aus Warenhallen:
Stundenschall vom Kirchenturm:
Fließt als Wort vom Telefunken-Turm:
Wellend, schwellend, fort und fort. –

Siebzehn blutdurchdrängte Straßen-Stunden
Voller Lärm und Arbeits-Drang,
Siebzehn rotdurchströmte Körper-Stunden,
Siebzehn Kreislauf-Stunden lang:
   Pocht und treibt die Herz-Turbine. –

   Dann stellt die Alles-Hand
   Die Saug- und Speimaschine,
   Den Hebelschaft
   Auf zehntel Kraft.
   Es ruht das Kraftgewelle eine Nacht.
Doch früh beim Sechs-Uhr-Morgen-Pfiff
Verstellt die Hand mit großem Griff:
Das Herz- und Stadt-Getrieb auf volle Macht. (97–98)

[Bloodstream
   Pulsing, pulsing, on and on
   The life-gas machine turns
   Pulsing, pulsing, on and on
   The heart-turbine turns in a circle.
Through the lung's spongy alleys,
Through the brain's labyrinthine chamber,
Through the liver and kidney sluices
Through the many canals of veins
   The red river of blood. –
The river flows on:
It melts the walls of the arteries with lava-fire,
Swelling, undulating, on and on:
   It leaps as sound: as cry, as word
Into the street's dissonant chorals
Walks, as giant steps, on the paving stones
(a thousand-fold pressure from all the legs),
Grows, as the gesture of workers, the movement of hands,
Within the tangle of poor stone-block buildings.
Resounds as the crack of whips on the backs of packhorses,
Swells up as a work taking form.
   Pulsing, pulsing, on and on,
   The energy-machine turns in a circle.
   Pulsing, pulsing, on and on,
   The heart-turbine turns in a circle.
Blood through the atoms of the body and city
   The warm stream flows and flows:
Flows as light from arc-lamps:
Hisses from the whistles of elevated trains:
Heavy steam from railway stations:
The buzzing of sales in department stores:
The sounding of hours from church bell towers:

Flows as words from the telegraph-towers
Undulating, swelling, on and on. –

Seventeen blood-soaked street hours
Full of noise and the bustling of work,
Seventeen red-soaked body hours,
For seventeen hours of circular flow,
    The heart-turbine pulses and turns.

    Then the all-powerful hand
    Turns the sucking and spitting machine,
    The lever,
    To low power.
    The energy waves rest for a night.
But early, at the six-o'clock whistle,
With a great gesture, the hand turns
The heart- and city-gears to full power.]

Body and city here undergo a complete amalgamation, both driven by an invisible heart-machine whose activity – reminiscent of Bücher's factory technology – is characterized by continuous circular movement (the rotation of the turbines, the circular pathways of the blood-energy). The poem renders these frenetic machinic rhythms above all through the use of a relentless trochaic metre ('pochend pochend, fort und fort...') – a pattern that significantly gives way to calmer iambic feet after the caesura that separates day from night and high power from low ('Dann stellt die Alles-Hand...'). That the poem's images meld the organic and the machinic around this frenetic rhythm could be understood in two distinct senses. On the one hand, the poem could be understood as a commentary on the mechanization of the body; after all, Engelke's bodies are utterly subordinated to the rhythms of industry (controlled by the invisible 'Alles-Hand' that operates the levers of the heart machine at precisely timed intervals). On the other hand, however, the metaphor of the heart and blood seems to imbue technology itself with the force of organic rhythm. Absent from this poem is any notion of a cold, rational modernity of the type propagated by *Neue Sachlichkeit* [New Objectivity]. On the contrary, Engelke's city is ecstatic, pumping away and spewing out vital flows ('Blutes roten Fluß', 'Lava-Glut', 'der warme Strom', etc.). Indeed, in this poem, images of vitality distinctly precede the images of technology to function as a kind of grounding metaphor for the latter; the 'Blut-Strom' of the title first flows through a decidedly organic body (the lungs, brain, liver, kidneys, veins, etc.), before taking a figurative leap – as the verb 'springen' in the 13th line suggests – into the chaotic phenomena of urban life: the shouts and marching of crowds, the hands of workers, the glow of electric lights, the whistling of elevated trains, the bustle of department stores, and so on. What Engelke hopes his readers will detect underneath all the multifarious and teeming energies perceptible in the urban environment is the universal living pulse that makes and unmakes forms and holds all things together. The continuous activity – the 'fort und fort' – of the great heart in 'Blut-Strom' thus recalls the activity of rhythm in the poem 'Rhythmus' cited in the opening of this chapter ('Der unsichtbar den schweren Stoff durchfließt, [...] Ihn fort und fort in andre Formen gießt' (186)).

Engelke thus saw rhythm as synonymous with the activity of the blood, and he hoped that his rhythmical poetry would help to transcend the 'maelstrom' of nervous impressions to the vital blood flow underneath. 'Stil', he wrote in his notebooks, 'ist gesteigertes Nervengefühl. Rhythmus ist Blutgefühl' (213) [Style is increased nervous feeling. Rhythm is blood feeling]. Such a 'blood feeling' represented not only the criteria of poetry for 'strong times', but also its intended effect on readers. Again and again, Engelke's poetry attempts to convey to readers an ecstatic sense of participation in the stream of rhythmical energy flowing behind appearances: 'Und Du', we read in Engelke's poem 'Der ewige Herzklang',

> du Mutter-Erde-Sohn,
> Hörst du deinen Herzens-Ton?
> Hörst aus Milliarden Dingen
> *Einen* Herzklang um dich schwingen?
> Horch! in Allen Herzen braust die Welt!
> Immerzu! (79)

> [You, you son of Mother Earth,
> Do you hear the sound of your heart?
> Hear in the billion things
> *One* heart beat oscillating?
> Listen! The world resounds in all hearts!
> Incessantly!]

In this effort to convey a sense of participation in the rhythms of the world, Engelke's poetry bears close affinities to the projects of modern dance which, as we saw in the previous chapter, sought to use the dancing body as a conduit with which to channel the Dionysian energies flowing through nature. As Inge Baxmann has argued, though many of these movements ostensibly called for a flight from rational modernity, their cultivation of Dionysian intoxication and 'dissolution' in fact constituted an attempt to come to terms with a modern world set into perpetual motion by the flows of technological energies.[33] Similarly, for Engelke, recognizing the rhythmical ground behind appearances hardly amounted to a 'flight out of time'; rather, that recognition was meant to help readers learn to live within the time of the modern.

This question of learning to live in modern time stands at the centre of Engelke's poem 'Der Mittler' (1913) [The Intermediary], which depicts self-reflexively the task of the poet as he understood it. There, in lines approaching free verse, Engelke describes a poet inextricably caught up in the 'maelstrom' of the urban milieu:

> Dich, Dichter und Denker,
> Umstürzt das tosende Meer der Lärm-Welt:
> Kreischende Wellen, zischende Gischt hasten wie Springflut,
> Dich umbrüllend, dir zu.
> Wellen um Wellen schleudert die Welt um dich auf:
> Fabriken, von fauchenden Eisenbahnen durchtummelt,
> Laufende Menschen, schreiende Menschen,
> Ineinander geschobene Pferde und Wagen,
> Straßenbahnen,
> Aufgesprengte Domtürme, Sing-Prozessionen,
> Boot-Gewimmel,
> Dampfer mit Heul-Sirene,
> Und Qualm, Lärm, Qualm, Hammerlärm –
> Alles
> Stürzt zusammen
> Und fällt hämmernd rasselnd blitzend schreiend
> Über dich her! (45)

---

33 'Um die Spezifik der Erfahrungen der Moderne auszumachen, kehrte man folglich zu jenen Praktiken zurück, die seit Beginn der Menschheitsgeschichte durch Wahrnehmungen außerhalb einer linearen und geometrischen Raum- und Zeitwahrnehmung charakterisiert sind, nämlich Traum, Tanz, oder Rausch. Die Spurensuche unterhalb der Kultur diente der Verarbeitung der Herausforderungen der Moderne, an deren erster Stelle die technologische Herausforderung stand. Einen Beitrag dazu lieferten auch jene Überlegungen, die auf den ersten Blick als Flucht vor ihr erscheinen' (Baxmann, *Mythos: Gemeinschaft*, 131) [In order to understand the specificity of the experience of modernity, theorists thus looked back to those practices which, since the beginning of human history, have involved perceptions beyond the confines of linear and geometric space and time: namely dreams, dance and intoxication. The search for traces below culture served to work through the challenges of modernity, the most significant of which was the challenge of technology. This was the goal of those reflections that seem at first to amount to a flight from modernity].

> [You, Poet and Thinker,
> Are tossed about in the raging sea of this noisy world:
> Pounding waves, hissing foam race toward you,
> Roaring about you like a flood.
> Waves upon waves hurl the world up all around you:
> Factories, rocked by churning trains,
> People running, people yelling,
> Horses and cars shoved into one another,
> Trams,
> Cathedral towers ripped open, musical parades,
> The noise of boats,
> Steamers with howling sirens,
> And steam, noise, steam, hammer noise –
> Everything
> Collapses together
> And hammering, rattling, flashing, screaming,
> Tumbles around you!]

With its rapid alternation of shock-like auditory and visual perceptions ambushing the traditional 'Dichter und Denker', Engelke's dynamic description of the city seems to visualize the neurasthenic conflict of culture as understood by Simmel. Within this context, Engelke takes up a classic image of stoicism and spiritual hygiene: that of the tumultuous 'raging sea' (tosendes Meer), which the stoic individual – most famously in Lucretius's *De rerum naturae* – was supposed to learn to observe from the safe vantage-point of a stable shore.[34] And yet, by contrast to Lucretius, Engelke no longer sees any possibility of defining a point of stasis *outside* the raging sea. As he put it in his notebooks, there is simply no vantage point for artists and intellectuals beyond the 'maelstrom' of modern energies: 'Leben und Denken: Chaos. Es gibt keine absolute Einheit in Welt und All. Überall Gegenlinien, Gegenbewegungen, immer neue und wiederneue: Leben! Die großen Denker sind [...] nur Menschen: Daseinspunkte im Chaos umhergewirbelt, wie alle anderen' (218–19) [Life and thought: chaos. There is no absolute unity in the world or the universe. Everywhere conflicting lines and counter-movements in ever new variations: life! The great thinkers are [...] merely human beings: points of existence whirled about, like all other points, in

---

34   See Lucretius, *On the Nature of Things* (ca. 50 B.C.E.), trans. by W. H. D. Rouse. Loeb Classical Library (Cambridge MA: Harvard University Press, 1975), 95: 'Pleasant it is, when on the great sea the winds trouble the waters, to gaze from shore upon another's great tribulation: not because any man's troubles are a delectable joy, but because to perceive what ills you are free from yourself is pleasant.'

chaos]. But if one could not escape the 'chaos' of modern experience, one could learn to move within the rhythms of modern time. Thus as 'Der Mittler' continues, the 'du' of the poem learns to ride the stormy waves like a surfer:

> Da faßt dich eine rasende Springwoge
> Und schleudert dich hoch!
> Höher –
> Ein letzter Gischtspritzer leckt dir den Fuß
> Und – da schwebst du in Sphären-Klarheit
> Erlöst über der Dampf-Welt,
> Über der Kampf-Welt da unten, tief unten –
> Sink wieder hinab,
> In die Welt,
> Dichter und Denker!
> Öffne den Menschen
> Die Sinne mit deinem Wort,
> Laß sie erkennen, die Menschen,
> Den Welt-Trieb-Geist,
> Den Gottgeist. (45)

> [Then a surging wave seizes you
> And hurls you high up!
> Higher –
> A final splash of foam licks your foot
> And – then you hover, released, in heavenly clarity
> Above the world of steam,
> Above the world of struggle below, deep below –
> Sink down once again
> In the world,
> Poet and thinker.
> Open people's senses
> With your word.
> Let them recognize, these people,
> The world-driving-spirit
> The divine spirit.]

In Engelke, it is no longer a question of locating a resting-point outside modernity's tumultuous throng. But he does believe that one can learn to ride *within* the rhythms of modern energy flows, as it were, like a surfer riding a wave, and thus to attain a kind of participatory insight into the force – the 'world-driving-spirit' ('Welt-Trieb-Geist') – underlying the whole.

If the raging sea of 'Der Mittler' bears affinities with Lucretius, Engelke's allegory of surfing the waves of rhythm once again recalls the project of modern dance. Indeed, as we saw in the first chapter, no

Fig 5. Loïe Fuller photographed by Frederick Glasier (1902)

other motif was more central to efforts to reimagine the rhythmical body in dance than that of the wave. For Isadora Duncan, the very goal of dance was to absorb the movement of waves, which she saw as the universal structure of vital and cosmic rhythms: 'The movement [of dance] should follow the rhythm of the waves' (Duncan 99). Like many of her contemporaries, moreover, Duncan associated such wave-like movement not only with nature, but also with modern forms of energy such the x-ray, electricity, light and sound waves. 'All energy', she wrote, 'expresses itself through this wave movement. For does not sound travel in waves, and light also?' (69).[35] Held to be the secret, dynamic structure of both nature and energy currents, such oscillating waves found another visual representation in the undulating flows of Loïe Fuller's serpentine dances (figure 5).[36] It was perhaps such dances that Paul Valéry had in mind when he argued that the quintessential model for the modern dancer could be found in the figures of jellyfish, whose 'corps de crystal élastique' [bodies of elastic crystal], by espousing the ebbs and flows of their liquid

35   Elsewhere, she wrote: 'The [dancer's] flesh becomes light and transparent, as shown through the X-ray' (51).

36   On Fuller, see especially Tom Gunning, 'Loïe Fuller and the Art of Motion. Body, Light, Electricity and the Origins of Cinema', in Richard Allen and Malcolm Turvey (eds.), *Camera Obscura. Camera Lucida. Essays in Honor of Annette Michelson* (Amsterdam: Amsterdam University Press, 2003), 75–90.

environment, represented (in Valéry's words) 'l'idéal de la mobilité' [the ideal of mobility].[37] Engelke's poem, in depicting the modern poet as someone who learns to ride the waves of modern rhythms ('Wellen um Wellen', 'eine riesige Springwoge'), espouses a model of poetic aesthetics that feeds on the same imaginary as modern dance. Like the dancer, the poet must become porous to the energies of the modern world. Thus to Valéry's image of the translucent jellyfish, Engelke could oppose his image of the poet as a sponge with 1,000 pores: 'Des heutigen Dichters Nervennetz (es ist ein Schwamm mit tausend Poren) hat sich verzehnfacht vor der ungeheueren Fülle der Zeit; er ist in allen Dingen hingegeben – doch reißt er wieder Stück um Stück aus dem Leben und ballt es zur Gestalt auf' (225–26) [The nervous system of today's poet (it is a sponge with 1,000 pores) has been multiplied by a factor of ten due to the incredible plenitude of our times; he is given over to all things – but he also tears piece after piece from life and packs it all together into a form]. Like the modern dancer, the poet was supposed to absorb the streams and flows of an energetic world. At the same time, lest he be overwhelmed and submerged in this new sea of energy, he was also supposed to recognize the universal rhythm underlying those flows.

For Engelke, then, the task of the modern poet involves a delicate balancing-act: that of opening oneself up to the nervous life of

---

37 Paul Valéry, 'Degas, danse, dessin' [Degas, Dance and Drawing], in Œuvres, vol. 2 (Paris: Gallimard, 1960), 1173. Interestingly, given my discussions in subsequent chapters, Valéry tells of first seeing the jellyfish on a film screen. 'La plus libre, la plus souple, la plus voluptueuse des danses possibles m'apparut sur un écran où l'on montrait de grandes méduses. [...] des êtres d'une substance incomparable, translucide et sensible, chairs de verre follement irritables, [...] aussi fluides que le fluide massif qui les presse, les épouse, les soutient de toutes parts, leur fait place à la moindre inflexion et les remplace dans leur forme. Là, dans la plénitude incompressible de l'eau qui semble ne leur opposer aucune résistance, ces créatures disposent de l'idéal de la mobilité, y détendent, ramassent leur rayonnante symétrie. [...] Point de solides, non plus, dans leur corps de cristal élastique, point d'os, point d'articulations, de liaisons invariables, de segments que l'on puisse compter.' [The freeest, most supple and most voluptuous of possible dances appeared to me on a cinema screen wher a film was showing giant jellyfish. [...] These were creatures of an incomparable substance, transluscent and sensitive, with their unbelievably excitable flesh of glass, [...] as fluid as the massive fluid that presses them, weds their form, supports them on all sides, gives way to their slightest inflection only to place them back into their former shape. Here, in the irreducible plenitude of water that seems to pose no resistance to their movement, these creatures enjoy the ideal of mobility, extending and retracting their radiant symmetry. [...] There are no solids and no bones in their bodies of elastic crystal, no articulations or fixed linkages, no segments one could count].

the modern world without being overwhelmed by the enormity of technological and industrial culture. To the question 'wozu Dichter?' Engelke thus proposed a very different answer from that of Heidegger.[38] Far from any lament about the flown gods, the rhythmical poet detects a pantheistic force at work everywhere *within* the industrial world. Rather than turning backwards, he uses poetry to help readers learn to live in the contemporary world with its frightening 'hammer rhythms'. 'Unsere rastlose Werkzeit ist so eisenstark', Engelke wrote, 'so gesund an allen unendlich verzweigten Gliedern, daß sich die Tagesmenschen vor ihrem unerkannten Hammerrhythmus, vor ihrer tausendtürmigen Größe ängstigen. Sie sollen sie lieben lernen! Darum reden die Dichter zu ihnen, zu allen!' (225) [Our restless work era is so powerful, so robust in all of its endlessly branching limbs, that most people are afraid of its unfamiliar hammer rhythm, of its towering enormity. But they should learn to love it! And this is why the poet speaks to them and to everyone!]. With the poet as 'mediator', the poetic medium, for Engelke, would serve to mediate between traditional and modern rhythms, adapting readers to the new temporality of the city.

It was precisely this 'hammer rhythm' that Engelke sought to integrate into his own lyric: the poems of *Rhythmus des neuen Europa* fashion the poet in turns as a drummer ('Der rasende Psalm') and a hammerer ('Ich klopfe mit dem Schallwort-Hammer' (1912) [I pound the hammer of sonic words]). As a training ground for the hammer rhythms of the modern world, Engelke's poetry thus sought to provide an answer, in the aesthetic realm, to the problem diagnosed by Bücher and Simmel. Rather than fleeing the rhythms of modernity, it conveyed an ecstatic experience of swimming within modern rhythm, one that would help readers overcome the gulf between subjective and objective culture through participation in the universal creative force behind appearances. In his late poem 'Heimkehr' (1917) [Homecoming], written from the front, Engelke opposes the poetry of nostalgia with a story about going 'home' to the big city. Taking leave of the countryside and village, the 'du' of the poem makes its home among the vital rhythms of the city:

---

38 See Martin Heidegger, 'Wozu Dichter?' [What are poets for?], *Holzwege* [*Paths in the Forest*] (Frankfurt am Main: Vittorio Klostermann, 2003), 269–320.

Heimkehr
Nun hat die Stadt dich angerührt,
Du hast der pauselosen Pulse Hieb gespürt,
Und alle Wucht, die dort bezwungen noch gewittert,
Macht, daß dein Blut in neuem Rhythmus zittert!
Es klopft an deines Leibes Wandung
Die monotone Brandung:
Dampf
Der von Flüssen zehrt,
Dampf
Der die Kraft vermehrt,
Kraft
Die um Achsen saust,
Kraft
Die den Rhythmus braust,
Von befahrenen Doppelschienen hallt,
Und mit muskelwilder Taktgewalt
Glut in deine Glut verschweißt,
Dich ins übervolle Leben reißt. –
Du kamst aus Einsamkeit –
Hier ist Gemeinsamkeit!
Hier rast die Stundenzeit
Durch aller Menschen Werk-Verbundenheit.
Tritt ein!
(145)

[Homecoming
Now the city has taken hold of you,
You can feel the stroke of its uninterrupted pulse.
And all the force that still thunders in submission,
Makes your blood tremble in a new rhythm!
There's a knocking on the walls of your body
The waves' monotone surge:
Steam
That feeds from rivers,
Steam
That increases power,
Power
That turns on axes,
Power
That roars with rhythm,
That resounds from well-worn tracks of trains,
And with the pounding violence of savage muscles
Welds hot embers to your fire,
Thrusts you into the throng of brimming life. –
You came from solitude –
Here is community!
The hours here race
Through the work joining all men together.
Step inside!]

Like 'Auf der Straßenbahn', this poem paints an ecstatic picture of a body ('Leib') traversed by the rhythmical energies of the city ('Dampf", 'Kraft'), its blood welded ('verschweißt') with the flowing vital energy of industrial production. With its uninterrupted circular motion, the turbine-like city bears the hallmark of industrial rhythms as defined by Bücher. But Engelke's poem also speaks about poetry itself. For the line 'Power that turns on axes' also points to the very activity of this 'middle axis poem': turning on its axis, Engelke's poem imitates the 'stroke of the uninterrupted pulse' ('der pausenlose Pulse Hieb') of the vital turbines he found so fascinating. Summoning the reader into this energetic frenzy in the manner of a circus barker ('Tritt ein!'), Engelke's poetry argues that the ecstatic participation in modernity's rhythm would help to overcome the sense of isolation and anomie characteristic of urban life through an experience of communal melding ('Gemeinsamkeit') with all people and things. Forged through rhythmical poetry, that sense of community would be established not in opposition to modernity but rather in and through modern technology itself.

3. Cinema as 'Heart Machine': Rhythm and the Ordering of Nature in Weimar Film

> So sieht das Herz der Erde aus, die tausendmal schneller um ihre Achse kreist, als es Tag-und-Nacht-Wechsel uns lehren will, deren unaufhörliche, unsterbliche Rotation Wahnsinn scheint und Ergebnis mathematischer Voraussicht ist.[1]
>
> [Thus appears the heart of the world which rotates on its axis a thousand times faster than the alternation of day and night would have us believe, whose perpetual, immortal rotation seems like insanity and is the result of mathematical foresight.]

Rhythm and the Embodied Spectator

If the discourse on rhythm provided a catalyst for rethinking the functions and forms of lyric poetry in industrial modernity, it also played a pivotal role in efforts to conceptualize the possibilities of modernity's newest time-based medium: cinematography. As we saw in the last chapter, there was in fact no shortage of artists attempting to capture rhythmical perception in traditionally static visual media. To the examples from painting and sculpture discussed in chapter 2, one might add the indexical medium at the basis of film: photography. Snapshot photography played an essential role in disseminating the iconography of modern dance and eurhythmics from Duncan to Jaques-Dalcroze and Bode and beyond. Indeed, as media theorists have pointed out, the medium was central to defining a new representational regime for a world (and bodies) in movement, a world no longer concerned with Lessing's privileged or 'pregnant' moments, but rather with what Gilles Deleuze has termed the 'instant quelconque' [any-instant-whatever], a moment determined not by its proximity to any transcendental or pre-given form but rather by the

---

1   Joseph Roth, *Bekenntnis zum Gleisdreieck* [*Affirmation of the Triangular Railway Junction*] (1924)

Fig 1. Snapshot of dancers from Rudolf von Laban, Gymnastik und Tanz *(1926)*

arbitrary cut into the flow of time.² If photography began by imitating painting in its predilection for the pose, the development of faster emulsions in the late nineteenth century made it possible to capture arbitrary phases of movement formerly not considered the domain of visual representation, a process most clearly visible in the fascination with chronophotography around the turn of the century (e.g. Eadweard Muybridge's shots of the galloping horse with all four hooves in the air).³ Given these imbrications between photography and the representation of movement, it should hardly be surprising that proponents of body-culture, attempting to construct a new energetic model of the body, would latch on to snapshot photography and chronophotography. This accounts, as I have argued elsewhere, for the particular obsession with snapshots and chronophotographic representations of the jumping body caught in mid-leap in the publications of body-culture groups in the early twentieth century

---

2   See Gilles Deleuze, *Cinéma I. L'image-mouvement* [*Cinema 1: The Movement Image*] (Paris: Minuit, 1983), 13–16. See also Mary Ann Doane, *The Emergence of Cinematic Time. Modernity, Contingency and the Archive* (Cambridge MA: Harvard University Press, 2002), 179–83.

3   See Rabinbach 84–119; Asendorf 16–18.

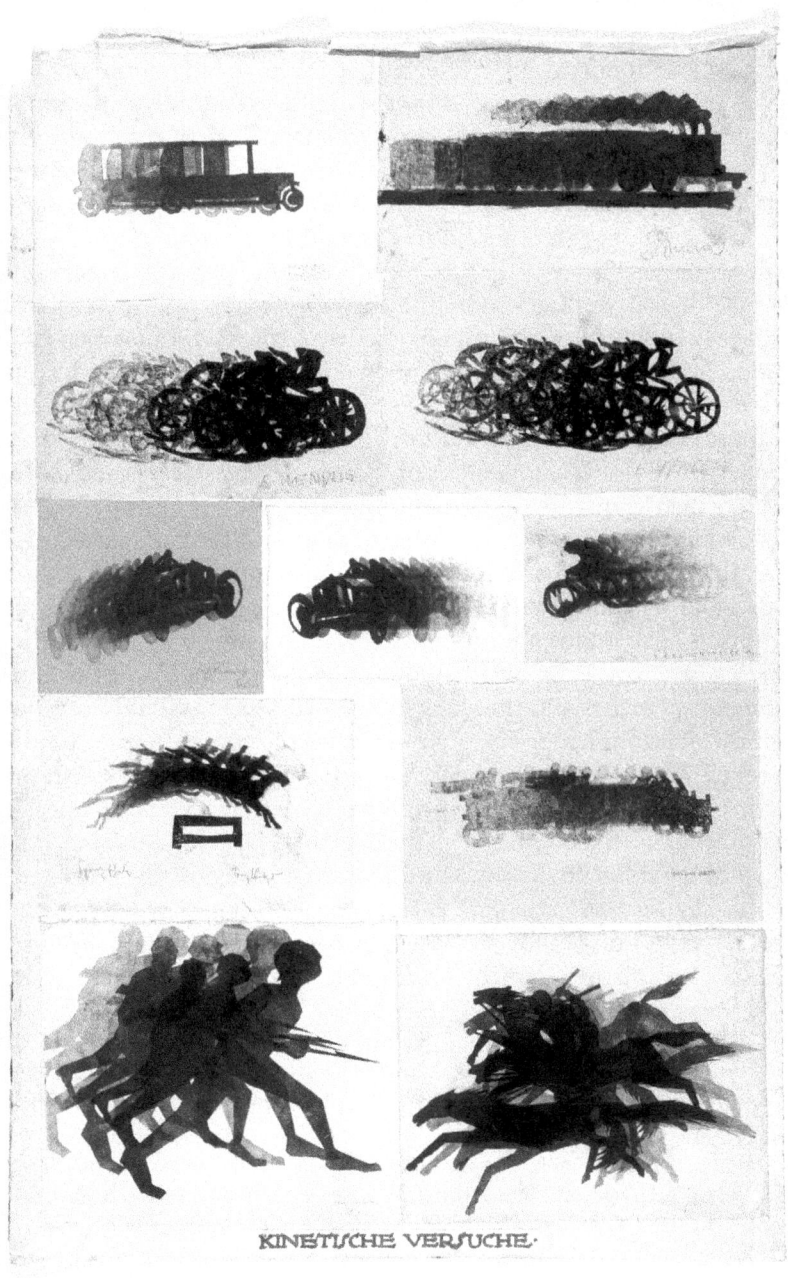

Fig 2. Kinetische Versuche *(1922), sketches by various artists from the Wiener Kinetismus circle, courtesy of Wien Museum*

(figure 1).⁴ Such images would still find use in the 1920s, for example in the many displays of athletic jumps at the Gesolei exhibition of athletics and hygiene in Düsseldorf in 1926, which simulated the phases of chronophotographic representations in three-dimensional models.⁵ As others have shown, moreover, such photographic iconography also had a reverse effect on the domains of painting and sculpture around 1900, where one can see the emergence of new forms for representing bodies caught in movement.⁶ As is well known, the visual art of Italian Futurism and Viennese Kinetismus was also directly influenced by the chronophotographic experiments of Marey, Muybridge and others (figure 2). Indeed, Luigi Russolo's famous image of a speeding car reproduced in the last chapter was itself clearly inspired by a famous snapshot: Ernst Mach's celebrated photograph of a speeding bullet published in 1884, which made visible the wave-like movement of the air around the projectile.⁷ But Russolo also transformed Mach's photograph by multiplying the waves of air to suggest the rhythmical phases of the car's movement, a painting strategy clearly indebted to chronophotography.

If visual art gained a new impetus from the ability of photography to capture a world in motion, however, it was above all the medium of *motion pictures*, as Laurent Guido has shown in the French context, that inspired artists and theorists to reflect on the possibility of a new rhythmical art for a new age obsessed with the presence of oscillating energies. This should be hardly surprising given film's inherently metric projection format in which a fixed number of frames succeed one another at fixed intervals. Writing in 1931, the Austrian critic René Fülöp-Miller thus wondered aloud, in his book on Hollywood cinema *Die Phantasiemaschine* [*The Fantasy Machine*], whether film's seemingly hypnotic effect was not based, in the last instance, precisely on this mechanical succession. Citing the Viennese writer

4 See M. Cowan, 'Imagining the Nation through the Energetic Body: The Royal Jump', in *Leibhaftige Moderne. Körper in Kunst und Massenmedien 1918–1933* [*Modernity in the Flesh. The Body in Art and Mass Media 1918–1933*] (Bielefeld: transcript-Verlag, 2005), 55–74.

5 For images, see Angela Stercken, 'Die Gesolei als Schaubild des Körpers. Sektionen, Überblick', in Hans Körner and Angela Stercken (eds.), *Kunst, Sport und Körper / GeSoLei 1926–2002* (Düsseldorf: Hatje Cantz Verlag, 2002), 117.

6 Klaus Wolbert, 'Das Erscheinen des reformerischen Körpertypus in der Malerei und Bildhauerei um 1900' [The Appearance of the Reform Body in Painting and Sculpture around 1900] in *Die Lebensreform*, vol. 1, 215–22.

7 On this point, see Andreas Braun, *Tempo, Tempo! Eine Kunst- und Kulturgeschichte der Geschwindigkeit im 19. Jahrhundert* [*Tempo, Tempo! A History of Speed in the Art and Culture of the Nineteenth Century*] (Frankfurt am Main: Anabas, 2001), 104–05.

Joseph Gregor, Fülöp-Miller explains: 'durch das physiologische Phänomen der Bildzerteilung (soundso viele Bilder in der Sekunde, die zusammen das lebende Bild ergeben) wird eine Art Suggestion ausgeübt, die man bei jeder Kinovorführung beobachten kann. Wie schwer ist es, den Blick von der "Leinwand" wegzulenken!' (Fülöp-Miller 135) [The physiological phenomenon of frame division (so-and-so many images per second which together generate the moving image) exercises a type of suggestion observable in any cinema presentation. How difficult it is to avert one's eyes from the 'screen'!]. For Fülöp-Miller, film's rapid-fire cadence represented the true realization of the futurist call for a new aesthetics of velocity. As he puts it (summarizing futurist doctrine):

> Da 'wir alle in einer anderen Geschwindigkeit rotieren als bisher', sei das Kino die Basis für jede neue, kommende Kunst, wie die Bewegung ja überhaupt den Urstoff unseres gesamten technischen Zeitalters bilde. Die 'neue Schönheit der Schnelligkeit', die schon von den Futuristen verkündet worden sei, finde in dem Rhythmus des Films ihren vollkommensten Ausdruck. (134)

> [Since people say that nowadays 'we all rotate at a very different speed from before', the movies are surely the basis of a new, emergent art form in much the same way that movement itself is said to form the primal matter of our entire technological era. The 'new beauty of speed', already announced by the futurists, would then find its most complete expression in the rhythm of film.]

But such a rhythm, he continued, might represent at the same time one of the most primitive aesthetic forces, the very force that gave rise to aesthetics in the first place: 'Der Urrythmus bei der Umarmung der Geschlechter habe von jeher alle Kunst hervorgebracht, und dieser Urrhythmus feiere nun im Film seine unserem Zeitalter entsprechende Auferstehung' (135) [The primal rhythm of the embrace of the sexes has brought forth all art from the beginning of time, and this primal rhythm celebrates its contemporary resurrection in film]. Thus film could be seen at once as the quintessential embodiment of technological precision and as a revival of the most primitive vitality.

Fülöp-Miller was hardly alone in his understanding of film as a medium able to exert a suggestive influence by tapping into primal rhythm; by the time he published *Die Phantasiemaschine*, the notion of film as an art of rhythm already had a long history among avant-garde filmmakers and theorists. Although, as Guido has shown,[8]

---

8 See Guido 148–51.

attempts to harness film's rhythmical capacities stretch back to the 1910s, when symbolist and futurist artists carried out experiments with synaesthetic colour organs and visual pianos (whose keys activated various coloured lamps), the desire to refashion cinema from a narrative to a rhythmical art-form became especially prevalent with the emergence of accelerated montage in the early 1920s. Specifically, as Standish Lawder argued already in 1975 in *The Cubist Cinema*, projects for a 'rhythmical' cinema emerged most forcefully in the wake of Abel Gance's 1922 film *La Roue [Wheels of Fate]*, in which Gance and Blaise Cendrars (Gance's editor at the time) introduced the accelerated montage sequences that would come to characterize French filmmaking throughout the decade.[9] Developing what would come to be known as 'external' rhythm (rhythm imposed by cutting as opposed to 'internal' rhythmical movement within the frame), Gance's montage sequences of Sisyphus's speeding train would form a model for the efforts of avant-garde filmmakers such as Germaine Dulac, Jean Epstein, Fernand Léger and Marcel L'Herbier, who saw these sequences as a demonstration of the cinema's unique ability to capture modern experience.[10] Léger and Dudley Murphy, in particular, seem to have drawn upon the montage of the train in *La Roue* for their own experiments in rhythmical filmmaking in *Ballet mécanique [Mechanical Ballet]* (1924), in which the rhythmical movements of human bodies and industrial objects are juxtaposed in an effort to underscore 'the reaction of man to his mechanical environment' (Lawder 90).[11]

Like other key concepts from the early cinema debates such as that of a 'universal language' or an art of 'hieroglyph', the notion of cinema as an art of 'rhythm' was suffused with the kind of progressive aspirations that broadly characterized what Gilles Deleuze has called the cinema of 'l'image-mouvement'[movement image] in the

---

9 On the influence of *La Roue*, see Lawder 79–99; see also Guido 69–70, 118.

10 It is perhaps no accident that Gance's film – the first to use montage specifically for capturing modern perception – also returns again and again to the leitmotif of circular motion, from the wheels of the speeding train to the dancing children at the end of the film.

11 For a frame-by-frame analysis of the film, see Lawder, 117–69. In a more recent reading of *Ballet mécanique* relevant to my arguments in this chapter and Chapter 5, James Donald argues that the film's formal structure integrated the rhythm of jazz as it was understood in the 1920s: i.e. a rhythm that was 'at *the same time the rhythm of the machine and the rhythm of "Negro music"'*. See James Donald, 'Jazz Modernism and Film Art: Dudley Murphy and *Ballet mécanique*', *Modernism/modernity* 16:1 (2009), 41.

interwar years.[12] Certainly, the appeal exerted by the fantasy of a rhythmical cinema on avant-garde artists stemmed in large part from a problem of legitimacy: the cinema's ability to visualize movement differentiated it not only from literature but also from painting and static photography and so seemed to offer a key to claiming a unique aesthetic domain. This was largely the motivation behind the famous matinee screening 'Der absolute Film' [Absolute Film] organized by the Novembergruppe and the Kulturabteilung [Cultural Department] of the UFA Studio in Berlin in 1925, where experimental montage films such as *Ballet mécanique* (shown under the title *Images mobiles*) and René Clair and Francis Picabia's *Entr'acte* (1924) were projected alongside works of abstract animation by Viking Eggeling, Hans Richter, Walter Ruttmann and Ludwig Hirschfeld-Mack.

The desire to construct a specificity of cinematic aesthetics has often been cited to explain the vehemence with which directors sought to valorize abstract form over concrete content, defining avant-garde cinema effectively as an anti-mimetic art and severing it from the realm of referentiality. At the same time, the excitement about 'rhythm' among filmmakers and film theorists the 1920s cannot be explained by aesthetic concerns alone. Rather, as the passages from Fülöp-Miller above suggest, rhythm, considered as a primal force, also held out the promise to lend film a power to influence the body directly, by-passing rational intellect. The desire for such an affective appeal largely motivated 1920s debates on the value of 'pure' or 'absolute' film with respect to a cinema of story-telling.[13] Germaine Dulac, for example, in an article published in 1927, describes the affective force of Gance's rhythmical experiments in *La Roue* to argue that the rhythmical movement of abstract forms could affect the body of the spectator no less than the rhythms of music: 'Des lignes qui se déroulent dans leur ampleur suivant un rythme [...] peuvent-elles émouvoir, sans décor, par elles-mêmes, par le seul jeu de leur développement?' [Can lines unfolding in their fullness according to a given rhythm [...] affect the viewer's emotions by themselves, without

---

12 See Deleuze, *Cinéma I. L'Image mouvement*

13 This point is also made by Guido: 'Les exigences de dépouillement, de nudité et de pureté s'originent ici dans une même tendance culturelle, qui fait tomber de son piédestal la parole, la raison et la signification, pour privilégier l'émotion "primitive" et immédiate' (148) [The demands for reduction, nudity and purity originate in the same cultural tendency, which topples speech, reason and signification in order to privilege the 'primitive' and immediate power of emotion].

any sets, by the sheer play of their development].[14] While Dulac's call to divest film of sets and plots recalls the experiments of Fernand Léger and René Clair, her question about the emotional appeal of purely abstract forms in rhythmical movement has a more direct link with other experiments occurring across the Rhine – most notably Richter's abstract rhythmical studies *Rhythmus 21* (originally titled *Film ist Rhythmus*), *Rhythmus 23* and *Rhythmus 25*, in which Richter animated abstract geometrical shapes. Like Dulac, Richter – who, as a painter involved with the Zurich Dada movement, had long sought to create a 'universal language' of pure forms – saw the reduction of cinema to abstract optical rhythms as a means of focusing the medium on its unique element:

> Rhythmus, Tempo, Takt und der plastische Wert der einzelnen Formen sind die Elemente, die hierbei hervorträten. [...] Der neue Film beruht in [...] der Bedeutung, die die Details dem plastischen Gegenstand und seiner Bewegung verleihen, also genau in dem, was bisher ganz zufällig und unbewußt neben der Handlung, neben den Dekorationen und Schauspielern herlief.[15]

> [Rhythm, tempo, cadence and the plastic quality of individual forms are the elements that would now come to the fore. [...]. The significance of the new film resides in the details of the plastic object and its movement – that is, precisely in those elements that previously existed haphazardly and unconsciously alongside the story, the actors and the scenery.]

But, like Dulac, Richter also saw in rhythm a means of tapping into the spectator's bodily affects. In an article entitled 'Rhythm' for the American journal *The Little Review* of 1926, he described rhythm as 'the inner nature-force, through which we are bound up with the elemental nature-forces' and 'the essence of emotional expression', which 'expresses something different from thought'.[16] Later, Richter would describe rhythm as an 'unwiderstehliche[s] Naturprinzip' (57) [irresistible principle of nature]. Most importantly, he believed that

---

14   Germaine Dulac, 'Les esthétiques, les entraves, la cinégraphie intégrale' [Aesthetics, Obstacles: Integral Cinegraphie], in *Écrits sur le cinéma (1919–1937)*, ed. Prosper Hillairet (Paris: Paris Expérimental, 1994), 103. On the debates concerning abstract filmmaking in France and on Dulac in particular, see Guido 123–75.

15   Hans Richter, 'Der Gegenstand in Bewegung' [The Object in Movement], in Jeanpaul Goergen (ed.), *Hans Richter: Film ist Rhythmus* [*Hans Richter: Film is Rhythm*] (Berlin: Freunde der Deutschen Kinemathek, 2003), 42.

16   Hans Richter, 'Rhythm', in *Hans Richter: Film ist Rhythmus*, 38.

the body's susceptibility to rhythmical influences pointed the way towards a more effective kind of filmmaking, in which rhythmical movement – purified of extraneous elements such as story, character and setting – would exert an 'irresistible' effect over the spectator's affective life: 'Dieser Film hier gibt keine "Haltepunkte", an denen man in Erinnerungen umkehren könnte, man ist – ausgeliefert – zum "Fühlen" gezwungen – zum Mitgehen im Rhythmus – Atmen – Herzschlag: – . . . der durch das Auf und Ab des Vorgangs, d a s deutlich machen kann, was Fühlen und Empfinden eigentlich ist . . . ein Prozeß – B e w e g u n g ' (28) [This film offers no 'stopping points' at which one could turn back through one's memory. The viewer is – exposed – forced to 'feel' – to go along with the rhythm – breathing – heartbeat: – . . . which, in its oscillations, can make clear what it means to feel and to sense . . . a process – m o v e m e n t]. Like Fülöp-Miller's characterization of filmic rhythm as the modern avatar of an orgiastic 'primal rhythm', Dulac and Richter's insistence on the link between rhythm, sensation and affect points us back to the broader link between questions of dynamic aesthetics on the one hand and the modern understanding of the body on the other – suggesting the inextricability of two discourses that drew on the same anthropological imaginary. In what follows, I wish to examine this connection more closely, particularly as it played out among German filmmakers in the 1920s. After exploring the broader interactions between discourses on rhythm and the body and discourses on rhythm in film, I will turn to an extended reading of one film that encapsulates some of the central stakes of the rhythm debates: Fritz Lang's *Metropolis* (1927).

Rhythm and the Speed of Modern Life

It would be difficult to overlook the connection between the fascination with accelerated montage in the wake of Gance's *La Roue* and the experience of modernization in terms of accelerated rhythms. Bücher's contention that the 'tempo and duration of [the worker's] labour no longer obeys his will' led to a broad-based understanding of the experience of modern life in terms of acceleration.[17] Thus Simmel

---

17 In the sphere of work science, Bücher's arguments gave rise to a series of studies designed to weigh the benefits of accelerated tempo on the 'pleasure' of work. See for example M. K. Smith, *Rhythmus und Arbeit*; D. Awramoff, *Arbeit und Rhythmus. Der Einfluss des Rhythmus auf die Quantität und Qualität geistiger und körperlicher Arbeit, mit besonderer Berücksichtigung des rhythmischen Schreibens* [*Work and Rhythm. A Study of the Influence of Rhythm on the Quantity and Quality of*

begins his famous essay 'Die Großstädte und das Geistesleben' (1903) [The Metropolis and Mental Life] by differentiating rural and urban life in terms of tempo: the city's rapid pace, he wrote, 'stiftet [...] einen tiefen Gegensatz gegen die Kleinstadt und das Landleben, mit dem langsameren, gewohnteren, gleichmäßiger fließenden Rhythmus ihres sinnlich-geistigen Lebensbildes' (117) [sets up a profound opposition to the small town and rural setting, with the slower, more habitual and more evenly flowing rhythm of their sensual and mental life]. This sense of an increasing and increasingly uncontrollable velocity informed the imagination of many of the rhythmical gymnastics groups from the first decades of the twentieth century. Indeed, the notion of reconnecting with a slower and more 'habitual' rhythm was central to any number of the reform movements that sprang up around the turn of the century. It played a particularly prominent role in anthroposophical and theosophical thought. In his book *The Rhythm of Life: Character Building as an Aid to Health* (1907, translated into German in 1912), the theosophist Archibald Keightley broadly summarized the understanding of the rhythm problem among cultural reformers when he asked: 'Have we fallen in with the true rhythm of life? I think that we have not done so. A very large number – almost a majority – of people at the present day are sufferers in one way or another from physical, nervous or mental instability. The circumstances of their lives, in one way or another, are too much for them' (Keightley 8).[18] In part as a response to such concerns, Rudolf Steiner would develop his own system of eurhythmical gymnastics in 1912, which – in the words of his sister Marie – sought to turn modern nerves back 'auf frühere Einstellungen' [to earlier states].[19]

Mental and Physical Labour, with a Focus on Rhythmical Writing] (Leipzig: Wilhelm Engelmann, 1902).

18   Keightley's book appeared in German under the title *Das Gesundheitsproblem: Der Rhythmus des Lebens*, trans. by Therese Panizza (Berlin: Paul Raatz Verlag, 1912).

19   The phrase comes from Marie Steiner's foreword to her brother's posthumously published eurythmics lecture. The entire passage reads: 'Aber bedrohlich für unser Menschtum ist dies: Überall blökt das Radium, meckert das Grammophon, schwirrt der Film; die Maschine hat auf allen Linien gesiegt, selbst auf denen der Kunst; wo Lebendiges versucht wird, muss es schnell weichen und wird mechanisiert. [...] Es wirkt antiquarisch, aber wenn man seine modernen Nerven zurückschraubt auf frühere Einstellungen und nicht zapplig wird, wirkt es auch wohltuend' [What threatens our humanity is this: we are bombarded on all sides by the bleating of radium, the blaring of the gramophone, the whirring of film; the machine has triumphed in all domains, even that of art; wherever life attempts to thrive, it must quickly yield to mechanization. [...] This seems old-fashioned to say, but it does us good to turn our nerves back to earlier states and

As we have seen, the association of modernity with speed informed an array of avant-garde movements and experiments around the turn of the century, not least the futurist celebration of the 'new beauty of speed'.[20] Not surprisingly, it also informed the fascination with the cinema and its capacities for rapid montage. Thus Jean Epstein celebrated the cinema as a medium particularly capable of recording modernity's increased 'vitesse de penser' [speed of thought].[21] In the German context, it was above all Walter Ruttmann's 1927 film *Berlin: die Sinfonie der Großstadt* [*Berlin: the Symphony of the City*] that attempted to construct a vision of urban modernity through the motif of accelerating rhythms – an argument visible right from the film's introductory sequence. Recalling the ubiquitous association of natural rhythms with the movement of waves, Ruttmann opens the film with an establishing shot of a watery surface distinguished above all by its slowly lapping ripples. But no sooner has the film established this scene of 'natural motion' than he cuts into it with the superimposition of two abstract geometric figures, reminiscent of Richter's and Ruttmann's own abstract films, which begin to turn – in a manner recalling the pervasive discourse on continuous rotation – at an increasingly accelerated pace. In a graphic match-cut, these figures then morph into an accelerated montage sequence of a train on its way to Berlin, in which shots of furiously spinning wheels, speeding tracks and telephone lines alternate to the pace of a pounding rhythmical score by Edmund Meisel. In a film intent – like Léger's *Ballet mécanique* – to compare the movements of humans with those of machines and mechanical automata, the transition from the waves to the train offers a rudimentary narrative of modernity; modernization, in *Berlin: die Sinfonie der Großstadt,* entails the expulsion from the warm folds of Klagesian rhythm into the cold and

---

avoid becoming fidgety], M. Steiner, 'Vorwort', in Rudolf Steiner, *Eurhythmie als sichtbare Sprache. Ein Vortragszyklus vom 24. Juni bis 12. Juli 1924 im Goetheanum* [*Eurythmics as a Visible Language. A Lecture Series from 24 June to 12 July 1924 in the Goetheanum*] (Dornach, Switzerland: Philosophisch-Anthroposophischer Verlag am Goetheanum, 1927), ii. Steiner's system, with its goal of rendering visible otherwise imperceptible ethereal forces, differed from that of Jaques-Dalcroze. Nonetheless, they shared the motivation of countering the nervousness pervasive in modern life. See also A. Dubach-Donauth, *Die Grundelemente der Eurhythmie* [*The Basic Elements of Eurhythmics*] (Dornach: Philosophisch-Anthroposophischer Verlag am Goetheanum, 1928), i–xi.

20 For a good discussion of the representation of speed in modern art, see Andreas Braun, *Tempo, Tempo!*

21 Jean Epstein, 'Le cinéma et les lettres modernes' (1921) [Cinema and modern literature], *Écrits sur le cinéma*, vol. 1 (Paris : Seghers, 1974), 68.

Fig 3. Poster for Walter Ruttmann, Berlin. Die Sinfonie der Großstadt *(1927), courtesy of the Deutsche Kinemathek*

sober domain of 'Takt' – a machinic cadence that finds expression in the mass ornaments that increasingly come to dominate Ruttmann's film in the entertainment sequence towards the end (figure 3).[22]

With its fragmentation of the speeding train through rapid and abrupt cuts, Ruttmann's montage seems like an almost direct citation of Abel Gance's *La Roue*. Through such interfilmic references, *Berlin: die Sinfonie der Großstadt* suggests a vision of filmic montage as a particularly apt medium for capturing an experience of modernity as the overcoming of natural rhythms. It also lays the groundwork for a number of montage sequences that will centre on the motif of acceleration and mechanical rhythms. To take one example: at the end of the second act, in a sequence linking modern tempo to the rise

---

22 On the relation of mass ornaments to machinic rhythm, see of course Siegfried Kracauer, 'Das Ornament der Masse' (1927) [The Mass Ornament] in *Das Ornament der Masse. Essays* (Frankfurt am Main: Suhrkamp, 1963), 50–64. Anton Kaes has proposed a similar reading of this opening sequence as a condensed narrative of modernity specifically with reference to the experience of dislocation that had characterized the lives of millions of immigrants to Berlin in the early twentieth century. See Kaes, 'Leaving Home: Film, Migration and the Urban Experience', *New German Critique* 74 (1998), 179–92.

of mass communications, Ruttmann inserts an accelerated montage sequence in which female typists and telephone operators can be seen working furiously as the typewriters and switchboards begin to spin in circles. As Joachim Radkau has shown, the nervous system itself was often compared to a vast system of telephone (or telegraph) wires, and telephone operators were thought to be particularly susceptible to neurasthenia and hysteria.[23] In this sense, Ruttmann's vision of communication technologies can be read as a metaphor for the modern nervous system, overloaded by its exposure to the rapid rhythms of industrial life. As the pace of this montage sequence continues to accelerate, Ruttmann drives the point home by inserting shots of screaming monkeys and fighting dogs in a textbook example of intellectual montage. Unable to exert any self-control, the animals here function as symbols for the nervous inhabitants of the metropolis, in a manner analogous to the slaughtered cows Eisenstein inserted into the final scene of *Strike* as a stand-in for the hapless workers.

If the montage of telephone operators represents the height of acceleration during the morning shift, another key image of speed will come after the lunch break. In a sequence set off by images of the printing-press churning out newspapers,[24] Ruttmann underscores the dangers of surpassing the body's organic rhythms. In shots reminiscent of Richter's short film *Inflation* released in the same year (1927) and Simmel's *Philosophie des Geldes*, the animated word 'Geld' (Money) flies repeatedly towards the spectator in an increasingly rapid rhythmical succession. This is then followed by another sequence of symbolic montage, unfolding in an ever-increasing tempo and associating images of a gathering storm, whirling shots taken from within a moving roller coaster, and the panic-stricken eyes of a woman who looks down from a city bridge as she prepares to jump to her death.

In his reading of Ruttmann's *Berlin* film in *From Caligari to Hitler*, Siegfried Kracauer criticizes the filmmaker for what he sees as an over-indulgence in formalistic rhythmical temporal compositions that overshadow any concern with the denotative referents of the individual images.[25] As David Macrae observes, Kracauer uses the

---

23 See Joachim Radkau, *Das Zeitalter der Nervostät: Deutschland zwischen Bismarck und Hitler* [*The Era of Nervosity: Germany Between Bismarck and Hitler*] (Munich: Carl Hanser, 1998), 227, 239.

24 On the connection between the daily press and modern tempo around 1900, see Peter Fritzsche, *Reading Berlin 1900* (Cambridge: Harvard University Press, 1998), 51–87.

25 See Kracauer, *From Caligari to Hitler*, 183–87.

terms 'rhythm' and 'reality' in strict opposition, so that rhythmical formalism would signify a flight from social concerns into a kind of new objective *l'art pour l'art*.[26] Defending Ruttmann against Kracauer's critique, Macrae suggests that, rather than falling into the tired dichotomy opposing denotative content to formalistic play, the social significance of the film might be sought at the formal level itself. For Macrae, *Berlin* practises a kind of Eisensteinian 'collision and interaction of multiple layers of visual signification', producing 'a transcendental level of signification' through the combination, arrangement and juxtaposition of different elements (258). In my own reading, however, I would suggest that we look for the film's cultural-historical significance at the level of Ruttmann's *temporal* compositions and, more specifically, in his manipulation of tempo. Given the centrality of 'rhythm' as a category for German modernity's understanding of its own experience, it seems crucial to me to understand how *Berlin* comments on that experience through the use of accelerated montage. Far from a flight into pure formalism, Ruttmann's montage performs a mimesis of the very industrial tempo that had so preoccupied writers on rhythm since Bücher. While the film's rhythms might not carry any denotative meaning, they do carry a *connotative* one, gesturing towards a much broader perception of the disjuncture between organic and technological rhythms in the modern world.

In staging modernity as the overcoming of Klagesian rhythm, *Berlin: the Symphony of the City* could be read as an answer of sorts to another popular film from two years earlier that was no less preoccupied with questions of rhythm and filmic representation: Wilhelm Prager's 1925 Kulturfilm [cultural and educational film] and body-culture showcase *Wege zu Kraft und Schönheit* [*Paths to Strength and Beauty*]. Where Ruttmann's film begins with an image of flowing rhythm only to catapult the viewer into a world of accelerated, mechanized movements, *Wege zu Kraft und Schönheit* opens with a demonstration of nervous mechanization before proclaiming the restoration of a more flowing, organic rhythm through gymnastics and dance.[27] Like *Rhythm is it!*, *Wege zu Kraft und Schönheit* follows the standard documentary schema by setting up a problem and then

26 See David Macrae, 'Ruttmann, Rhythm, and "Reality": A Response to Siegfried Kracauer's Interpretation of *Berlin. The Symphony of a Great City*', in Dietrich Scheunemann (ed.), *Expressionist Film. New Perspectives* (Rochester: Camden House, 2003), 256.

27 I can offer only a cursory reading of *Wege zu Kraft und Schönheit* here. For more on the context and arguments of the film, see my article 'Imagining the Nation through the Energetic Body: the Royal Jump', 55–74.

offering solutions.[28] Indeed, before showing audiences a single image of beautiful bodies, Prager's film begins with an admonishment about the spread of nervousness,[29] followed by an extended vision of urban modernity as a neurasthenic nightmare; we see images of a bourgeois family caught in the throes of nervous convulsions and shot in a rapid and abrupt montage style reminiscent of Gance and Epstein, an impressionist collage of superimposed images of bustling city traffic and seemingly endless tracking-shots showing lines of workers trapped in oppressive Taylorist factories. As the film then transitions into the demonstrations of body culture, Prager includes an entire section on dance and rhythm under the title 'Rhythmische Gymnastik' [Rhythmical Gymnastics]. Here too we find a Klagesian subtext when Prager introduces this sequence with a shot of ocean waves and flowing wheat fields – both paradigmatic manifestations of rhythm for Klages – followed by an intertitle reading: 'Bewegungen werden schön durch ihren Rhythmus. Das ist ein Gesetz der Natur' [Movements are made beautiful by rhythm. This is a law of nature].[30] The section that follows illustrates all the most prominent schools of rhythmical dance and gymnastics, including (among others) those of Jaques-Dalcroze, Rudolf von Laban, Mary Wigman, Rudolf Bode and the Loheland School.

Many of the performers included in the 'rhythmical gymnastics' section of *Paths to Strength and Beauty* would have adhered to Klages's theories, and the film frames its presentation of eurhythmics as a whole within the Klagesian project to access the body's primal rhythmical flows. Most of the exercises shown consist of flowing bodily movements, and some performances are even staged at the edge of a lake in front of the lapping waves (figure 4). Perhaps the most ardent of Klages's supporters shown in the film was Rudolf Bode, who, as the film tells us, had devised a system for reintroducing the vital alternation of tension and relaxation into all bodily movements. As we saw in chapter 1, Bode saw his system as an effort to undo the nefarious effects of technological modernity; in his study

---

28   See Bill Nichols, *Representing Reality*, 18.

29   This section begins with an inter-title reading: 'Die Menschen heute sind nicht alle gut gebaut, nicht alle kräftig, aber sets sind sie nervös' [Not all people today are well built and strong. But they are all nervous].

30   For the description of flowing wheat fields, see Klages, *Vom Wesen des Rhythmus*, 33–34: 'Nicht nur die See bewegt sich in Wellen mit wiederum periodischem Wechsel von Steigen und Fallen, sondern nicht minder unter dem Winde der Wald, das Getreidefeld, der bewegliche Sand' [It is not only the oceans that move in waves with a periodic alternation of rising and falling but also – and no less a result of the wind – forests, wheat fields and sand].

Fig 4. Still from Wege zu Kraft und Schönheit *(1925), courtesy of the Deutsche Kinemathek*

Rhythmus und Körpererziehung (1923) [Rhythm and Bodily Education], he describes modernization bluntly as an 'Entrhythmisierungsprozeß' (33) [process of derhythmification], in which the body's rhythmical life-force had been suppressed under a disciplinary regime of technological *Takt*. Only eurhythmical gymnastics, he argued, could liberate the flow of primal rhythm. Opposed as this section of Prager's film is to the images of mechanization with which the film opens, it is clearly intended to visualize such a liberation through the motion-picture medium. In this way, it largely portends the flowing images of calisthenics and diving that Leni Riefenstahl would later produce in her account of the 1936 Berlin Olympics.[31]

Mediating the Body and Technology: Moving Images as Interface

On one level, then, both *Berlin. The Symphony of the City* and *Paths to Strength and Beauty* were really about the opposition between machinic movement and organic rhythm, even if the films opted, as it were, for different sides of the opposition. But the stakes of this opposition and of the broader discourse on rhythm extend well beyond the content of these two films to touch upon one of the central questions behind 1920s thinking about the cinema as a time-based medium. Examining writings on the cinema from the period, one is struck by the extent to which the body-cultural discourses I have been exploring here serve as a point of reference in discussions about filmic rhythm. A case in point can be seen in the figure of Sergei Eisenstein. In his writings on montage, Eisenstein characterizes 'rhythm' as a dynamic force essential 'for every art-form, and, indeed, for every kind of expression'.[32] Using the term 'rhythm' virtually synonymously with his key concept of 'conflict', he defined rhythm as the result of a tension between the organic and the technological, 'formlessness' and 'rational form' or 'Nature and Industry' (46). In poetry, he argues, echoing the poetic debates we encountered in the last chapter, this rhythmical dynamic translates into a 'conflict between the metric measure employed and the distribution of accents, over-riding this measure' (48). Analogously, Eisenstein locates the 'rhythm' of filmic montage in the dynamic conflict between the metrical regularity of shot-lengths and the distribution of movement within the individual shots. This concept of rhythm as a dynamic tension between metric and organic elements stood at the centre of Eisenstein's critique of quantitative models of rhythmical montage such as that of Pudovkin, whom he accused of harbouring an all too metrical concept of rhythm based on a 'relationship of lengths'.

In formulating his model of rhythmical montage, Eisenstein draws an explicit analogy with the debates already under way in body-cultural circles. Although Eisenstein faults Klages for the

---

31 On the place of rhythm – and Klages and Bode's theories in particular – in Riefenstahl's work, see Michael Mackenzie, 'From Athens to Berlin', 302–36.

32 Sergei Eisenstein, 'A Dialectical Approach to Film Form', in *Film Form: Essays in Film Theory*, ed. and trans. by Jay Leda (San Diego: Harcourt, 1977), 47.

latter's one-sided focus on the irrational,[33] his concept of rhythm as a struggle between the organic and the technological informing all expression clearly has affinities with Klages's notion of rhythm as a force opposed to machinic regularity and discipline in handwriting and other modes of bodily expression.[34] Accordingly, in comparing his own model of dynamic rhythm to Pudovkin's metrical concept of shot-lengths, Eisenstein looks for authority to none other than Rudolf Bode. Comparing Bode's concept of rhythmical gymnastics favourably to the quantitative muscle-training of the popular American calisthenics teacher Bess Mensendieck, Eisenstein argues that 'From this [Pudovkin's equation of rhythm and isometrical shot lengths] comes [sic] metric rather than rhythmic relationships, as opposed to one another as the mechanical-metric system of Mensendieck is to the organic-rhythmic school of Bode in matters of bodily exercise' (49). Such passages suggest the extent to which Eisenstein's notion of filmic 'conflict', while purporting to translate Marxian dialectics into filmic aesthetics, also resonated with the vitalist models of rhythm so important for the early twentieth century's understanding of the body.

In this, Eisenstein was hardly alone. While not everyone shared his dialectally informed montage theory, many 1920s film theorists did attempt to think rhythm in *opposition* to metre. As the dance critic André Levinson describes it in an article for *L'Art cinématographique* of 1927: 'D'une façon générale, l'articulation du film n'est pas symétrique; elle ne répond pas au mètre du vers qui est une pulsation régulière; ni aux bâtons de mesure qui règlent et jalonnent la musique. Elle s'évade des formules numériques' [In general, the structure of film is not symmetrical; it does not correspond to the metre of verse with its regular pulse, nor to the beats that regulate and punctuate music. It escapes all numerical formulas].[35] In Germany, a similarly non-metrical notion of rhythm can be seen in the work of Hans Richter. While a member of the Dada circle in Zurich during the war, Richter

---

33 Eisenstein states that Klages wrongly 'attributes everything in motion to the field of the "soul" and only the hindering element to "reason"' (47).

34 See for example Klages's description of handwriting: 'So sehen wir das Eigenleben des Menschen in einen beständigen Kampf mit der Macht der Schablone verwickelt' (Klage, *Ausdrucksbewegung*, 140) [Thus we see the autonomous life of the human being caught up in a constant battle with the power of the pattern]. Eisenstein sounds a similar note when he writes about speech that 'all its sap, vitality, and dynamism arise from the irregularity of the part in relation to the laws of the system as a whole' (47).

35 André Levinson, 'Pour une poétique du film', *L'Art cinématographique* 4 (1927), 65.

had developed contacts with the dance group around Rudolf von Laban and – just before he began making films with Viking Eggeling – designed sets for the dance performances of the artist and Laban dancer Sophie Taeuber. As we saw above, Richter considered rhythm the essence of emotional expression. But, like Eisenstein after him, he sought to oppose rhythm to any simple metrical determination of frame lengths, conceiving it rather – in a formulation reminiscent of Bücher and Jaques-Dalcroze – as a unifying principle: 'Rhythm', he wrote in one passage, 'is not definite, regular succession in time or space, but the unity binding all parts into a whole. […] It […] is the inner nature-force […] through which we are bound up with the elemental nature-forces' (Richter, 'Rhythm', 38). Moreover, as Malcolm Turvey has argued, Richter's *Rhythm* films are structured precisely around the interplay between established patterns of regular movement – the parallel and perpendicular movements of white geometric figures against a black background or vice versa – and the 'surprises' and 'deviations' that continually interrupt these patterns.[36]

That filmmakers would take an interest in the opposition between rhythm and metre should hardly come as a surprise. At stake in that opposition was a question of movement and time already foreshadowed in the philosophy of Bergson. As Christine Lubkoll has argued, Bergson's efforts to distinguish between analytic conceptions of time as a series of fixed points and the experience of becoming as *durée* must be seen as one of the key sources for the vitalist model of rhythm articulated by Klages, with its opposition between flowing and punctual movements.[37] Bergson, as is well known, considered the analytic sequences produced by chronophotography and early film, with their dissection of action into serialized moments, to be the very model of a spatialized conception of movement as a series of static points, whereas authentic movement consisted in the continuum of a non-quantifiable evolution within the intervals between the points.[38] More recently, Gilles Deleuze, in his exploration of the modernist 'movement image', has attempted to defend the cinema against Bergson's critique, arguing that Bergson had access only to the earliest films, shot with stationary cameras before a static

---

36 Malcolm Turvey, 'Dada Between Heaven and Hell: Abstraction and Universal Language in the *Rhythm* films of Hans Richter', *October* 105 (2003), 30.
37 See Lubkoll 87–90.
38 See Henri Bergson, *L'Évolution créatrice*, 305–15.

stage.[39] With the development of montage and mobile camera-work, subsequent filmmakers would increasingly explore the possibilities of motion pictures to represent movement as a formless flow.[40] Deleuze's distinction between a (pre-World War II) 'movement image' and a (post-WWII) 'time-image' has been the subject of some critique, and it is not my intention to take up this debate here.[41] But I do wish to recall the extent to which Deleuze saw the film of the 1920s – and particularly the avant-garde experiments in rhythmical filmmaking – as a series of eminently Bergsonian experiments: an effort to return to a primary state of pure movement or universal variation described by Bergson in *Matière et mémoire* [*Matter and Memory*].[42] For Deleuze, the cinema of the 'movement image' is almost inherently Bergsonian, tending quasi-teleologically towards the restoration of pre-subjective 'gaseous' states of pure movement.[43] In order to demonstrate this conception, it might not be by chance that Deleuze himself focuses on the predilection of experimental filmmakers for the motif of water:

---

39 Georges Didi-Huberman has argued that Bergson in fact had Marey's chronophotography in mind, and not projected motion pictures. Chronophotography, and the work of Bergson's contemporary Marey in particular, 'constituait sans doute, aux yeux de Bergson, la forme moderne par excellence de ce qu'il dénonçait comme "illusion cinématographique"' (Didi-Huberman 229) [undoubtedly constituted, from Bergson's perspective, the modern form *par excellence* of what he disparagingly called the 'cinematographic illusion'].

40 See Deleuze 12.

41 For a discussion of these critiques, see Robert Stam, *Film Theory. An Introduction* (Oxford: Blackwell, 2000), 261–62. See also Gunning, 'Loïe Fuller and the Art of Motion', 76.

42 See Deleuze, 83–104. For the discussion in Bergson, see Henri Bergson, *Matière et mémoire. Essai sur la relation du corps à l'esprit* [*Matter and memory. Essay on the relation between body and spirit*] (Paris: Presses Universitaires de France, 2008 [1896]), 11–81.

43 'Si le cinéma n'a nullement pour modèle la perception naturelle subjective, c'est parce que la mobilité de ses centres, la variabilité de ses cadrages l'amènent toujours à restaurer de vastes zones acentrées et décadrées : il tend alors à rejoindre le premier régime de l'image-mouvement, l'universelle variation, la perception totale, objective et diffuse' (94) [If the cinema in no way takes natural and subjective perception as its model, this is because the mobility of its centres, along with the variability of its framings, always lead it to restore vast zones without centre or frame: it then tends to return to the first regime of the movement image, universal variation, perception in its total, objective and diffuse state]. The teleological aspect of Deleuze's theory has been pointed out most recently by Jacques Rancière. See Rancière, *La Fable cinématographique*, 150.

[L]'eau est le milieu par excellence où l'on peut extraire le mouvement de la chose mue, ou la mobilité du mouvement lui-même : d'où l'importance optique et sonore de l'eau dans les recherches rythmiques. Ce que Gance avait commencé avec le fer, avec le chemin de fer, c'est l'élément liquide qui allait le prolonger, le transmettre et le diffuser dans toutes les directions. Jean Mitry, dans ses tentatives expérimentales, commençait avec le chemin de fer, puis passait à l'eau comme à l'image qui pouvait nous livrer plus profondément le réel comme vibration : de « Pacific 231 » à « Images pour Debussy ». Et l'œuvre documentaire de Grémillon parcourt ce mouvement, de la mécanique des solides à une mécanique des fluides, de l'industrie à son arrière-fond marin. (112–13)[44]

[Water is the quintessential milieu in which one can extract movement from the object moved or the mobility of movement itself. Hence the importance of water as a visual and auditory element in rhythmical experiments. What [Abel] Gance had begun with his images of iron and railways would be developed, transmitted and disseminated in all directions by the liquid element. In his experiments, Jean Mitry started by filming the railway (in *Pacific 231*) and then turned to water (in *Images pour Debussy*) as the image that could better capture reality as vibration. The documentary work of [Jean] Grémillon passes through the same stages, from the mechanics of solids to the mechanics of fluids, from industry to the marine element hidden underneath.]

44 Mitry (1904–88), whose experimental films *Pacific 231* (1949) and *Images pour Debussy* (1952) Deleuze mentions here, plays an important role in the history of conceiving filmic aesthetics in terms of rhythm. In his monumental *Esthétique et psychologie du cinéma* (1965) [*The Aesthetics and Psychology of Cinema*], Mitry devotes an entire chapter to the discussion of filmic rhythm in which, once again, he differentiates sharply between rhythm and metre. Citing Klages directly, Mitry shares the latter's equation of rhythm and life: 'Comme le dit Ludwig Klages, "Le rythme est un phénomène de vie général, auquel participe tout être vivant et aussi l'homme; la mesure est une création humaine; le rythme peut se manifester sous la forme la plus parfaite en l'absence complète de mesure. La mesure par contre ne peut se manifester sans la collaboration d'un rythme."' [As Ludwig Klages states, 'Rhythm is a general phenomenon of life, in which all living beings including the human participate; metre is a human creation; rhythm can manifest itself in its most perfect form in the complete absence of metre. But metre cannot manifest itself without the collaboration of rhythm'], J. Mitry, *Esthétique et psychologie du cinéma* (1965) (Paris: Cerf, 2001), 157–58. Because of this distinction, Mitry rejects the analogy of filmic rhythm to musical rhythm (which he sees as defined by regular cadence), arguing instead that filmic rhythm is akin to the free rhythms of prose poetry. Nonetheless, he retains the association of rhythm with emotion, positing that rhythm serves to lend an affective force to intellectual images, reconnecting them to the realm of dynamic movement and experiential *durée* (172–76).

According to Deleuze, then, the aim of modernist rhythmical filmmaking lay in the effort to access a realm of pure Bergsonian movement hidden beneath the habitual world of solid bodies and geometric space.

Deleuze's claims about the Bergsonian possibilities of early cinema have been echoed by other contemporary critics, most recently by Tom Gunning in his reading of Loïe Fuller's famous serpentine dances as a Bergsonian flow of uninterrupted movement.[45] Georges Didi-Huberman, for his part, has extended this effort to rehabilitate early moving-image media to include even Marey's chronophotography, particularly those images – occupying a marginal position in Marey's work – in which phantom traces blur the clear boundaries between the individual phases. For Didi-Huberman, such 'blurs' – which Marey himself considered imperfections in his effort to capture clear static moments – inscribe Bergsonian *durée* into the static photograph in the form of a visual 'traîne' [the train of a dress], which constitutes the non-quantifiable and non-dissectible trace of becoming: '[La traîne] rend visible une zone indécise du temps, ce "mouvement qui glisse dans l'intervalle"' [The train gives visual form to an ambiguous zone of time, to the 'movement that slips into the interval'].[46] In citing these arguments, my point is not to decide whether moving images grant access to the world of flowing rhythms or are bound to the world of division, seriality and *Takt*. But I do wish to emphasize the ongoing pertinence of a question about the filmic medium that I have been attempting to delineate from films and film theory in the 1920s. If that question has remained so central to our understanding of cinematic aesthetics, the reason for this might well lie precisely in the cinema's ambiguity. As an 'art of the machine', film seemed to be bound up with the tempo of modern technology and – as Walter Benjamin argued in his famous artwork essay – with the aesthetics of fragmentation.[47] However, as an 'art of motion', in Gunning's phrase,[48] the cinema's animated pictures also seemed to hold out the promise of recapturing the movement of life in its most vital aspect. In this ambiguity, the cinema seemed to embody, during the 1920s, what Christine Lubkoll has identified as the general function of rhythm in the modern imagination since Bergson: that of an interface,

45 See Gunning, 'Loïe Fuller and the Art of Motion', 86–87.
46 Didi-Huberman 245.
47 See of course Walter Benjamin, 'Das Kunstwerk im Zeitalter seiner technischen Reproduzierbarkeit' (1935) [The Work of Art in the Age of its Mechanical Reproducibility], in *Illuminationen*, 136–70.
48 See Gunning, 'Loïe Fuller and the Art of Motion'.

a 'Schaltstelle, an der Natur in Kultur übergeht, aber auch Kultur auf Natur zurückverwiesen werden kann' (Lubkoll 90) ['a switching-point at which nature is transformed into culture, but where culture can also be directed back into nature'].

If some 1920s avant-garde filmmakers sought to use the interface of the cinema to access the primal rhythms of nature, however, it is worth noting, in the light of my discussions of Ruttmann and Eisenstein above, that – especially after the demise of Expressionism and the emergence of 'New Objectivity' in Germany – many others saw the medium as a means not only of accessing primal rhythm but also of submitting it to rational control.[49] Richter, for example, often described film as a tool for harnessing the affective power of rhythm in the service of the (constructivist) intellect. As he put it in an article of 1924 entitled 'Die schlecht trainierte Seele' [The Badly Trained Soul],

> Die lebendige Kraft, die wir in dieser [rhythmischen] 'Bewegung' besitzen, […] kann […] zum Bestandteil menschlicher Macht werden – aber man müßte im Stande sein, diesen Prozeß zu beherrschen, um das Gebiet der Empfindungen ebenso unserem Urteil zugänglich zu machen, wie die anderen menschlichen Willensgebiete, aus deren Entwicklung die 'Seele' bisher ausgeschaltet blieb.[50]
>
> [The vital force that we possess in this [rhythmical] 'movement' [...] can become a tool of human power. But one must be capable of mastering this process in order to make the domain of sensations as accessible to our judgment as the other domains of the human will, from whose development the 'soul' has hitherto been excluded.]

Tapping into the power of primal rhythm – which he here identifies with the Klagesian term 'soul' – Richter thus sought to submit it, through the mechanized medium of film, to the control of the instrumental will. Writing two years after Richter, the critic Rudolf Kurz laid out a similar vision of abstract film in his famous study *Expressionismus und Film* (1926) [*Expressionism and Film*]. In a discussion of the rhythmical experiments of Richter and Eggeling, Kurz argued that such films served to tap into the elemental rhythms of organic life: 'Es ist das geistige Niveau, auf dem der Rhythmus uranfänglich durch die körperlichen Empfindungen von Puls und Herzschlag, durch die natürliche Abfolge primitivster Arbeitsleistungen

---

49 Guido makes a similar point (21, 25).

50 Hans Richter, 'Die schlecht trainierte Seele', in *Hans Richter: Film ist Rhythmus*, 28.

gleichsam biologisch enstanden sein mag.' [This is the mental stage at which primal rhythm probably first arose, as if biologically, from the bodily sensations of pulse and heartbeat, from the natural sequence of the movements of primitive labour].[51] But while reactivating such primitive rhythms, Eggeling and Richter's films sought above all to subordinate them to precise mathematical order: 'In exakt errechneten Proportionen,' he writes of Richter's *Rhythmus 21*, 'treten die Formelemente in die "Handlung" des Films. Ihr Wachstum, ihr Verschwinden, ihre Ausbreitung, ihre Verkümmerung ist jeder Willkür enthoben und erfolgt in zahlenmäßig festgelegten Tempi' (99) [The elemental forms enter into the 'action' of the film in precisely calculated proportions. The patterns by which they grow, disappear, spread or wither away are in no way arbitrary; rather they follow mathematically calculated tempi]. In this way, the medium of film could be understood as an eminently industrial apparatus, which both taps into the vital force of rhythm and also renders it calculable for productive ends: 'Das Irrationelle ist grundsätzlich ausgeschaltet: Kunst ist Organisierung der gleichen Kräfte, die im Leben wirksam sind, ausgedrückt in Verhältnissen einfachster Formen' (98) [The irrational is excluded as a matter of principle; art functions to organize the powers at work in life, expressed in relations between the simplest forms]. Such an understanding of film as industrial apparatus also informed Weimar's most celebrated filmic representation of industry: Fritz Lang's *Metropolis*.

Rhythm in *Metropolis*

On its release in 1927, *Metropolis* was widely criticized for its histrionic acting style as well as its contrived plot: the tale of Freder (son of the head of Metropolis Joh Fredersen) descending into the underground workers' city to reconcile his stern father with his subjects and humanize technology in the process was – with all its heavy-handed Christian symbolism – too reminiscent of the now bygone literature of the expressionist era.[52] But if critics panned the

51 Rudolf Kurz, *Expressionismus und Film* (Berlin: Verlag der Lichtbild-Bühne, 1926), 94.

52 Indeed, in this respect, as critics have long noted, the plot of the film borrowed directly from Georg Kaiser's expressionst play *Gas* (1918), in which a 'millionaire's son' goes among the workers in order to transform the exploitative space of the factory into a model for a new community. See for example Sol Gittleman, 'Fritz Lang's *Metropolis* and Georg Kaiser's *Gas I*: Film, Literature and the Crisis of Technology', *Der Unterrichtspraxis* 12 (1979), 27–30.

film's narrative, they almost universally praised its formal visual constructions – and particularly its choreography of mechanical movement.[53] In an article for *La gazeta literaria de Madrid* [*The Literary Gazette of Madrid*], for example, Luis Buñuel argued that *Metropolis* amounted to 'two films joined at the hip':[54] viewed as a vehicle for narrative, *Metropolis* consisted of a disappointing mixture of 'trivial, overblown, pedantic and outdatedly romantic' tropes, facile symbolism and an 'overwhelming and theatrical acting style' (106–7); but viewed as a 'plastico-photogenic' experiment, the film offered a mesmerizing vision of mechanical rhythms: 'What a fascinating symphony of movement! How the engines sing amidst wonderful transparent triumphal arches formed by electric charges! [...] [T]he rhythmic succession of wheels, of pistons, of never-yet created mechanical forms create a magnificent ode, a brand new poem for the eyes. Physics and chemistry are miraculously transformed into Rhythmics' (107). Although *Metropolis* has rarely been seen as part of the project for a rhythmical cinema, a glance at such critical responses as that of Buñuel suggests that it ought to be read at least in part within this context. After all, Lang's film focuses on the central question at stake in the broader rhythm debates: that of the limits between technology and organic life in the new context of urban and industrial technologies.

In its attempt to articulate those limits, moreover, the film employs a thoroughly Klagesian opposition. Right from its opening sequence, *Metropolis* stages industrial modernity as a regime of mechanical *Takt* in Klages's sense. After an initial montage of pistons, flywheels and gears in repetitive motion, the film zeroes in on a shot of the ten-hour work-clock that organizes the time of the city. In fact, what we see are two clocks: the first, marked with 24 hours, appears to retain some connection to the rhythms of diurnal time. Below it, however, the face of the rationalized ten-hour clock looms five times as large. By contrast to the diurnal clock, which features only the hour- and minute-hands, the ten-hour clock is distinguished by the marked presence of two rapidly flashing lights and the addition of a second-hand, which races around the clock face in a jerky, staccato movement.

---

53 If this reception seems to echo that of *La Roue* five years earlier, it is hardly fortuitous. As Guido shows, French theorists tended more and more to understand narrative as a 'pretext' for exploring movement (Guido 156).

54 Luis Buñuel, 'Metropolis', film review, reprinted in Michael Minden and Holger Bachmann (eds.), *Fritz Lang's Metropolis: Cinematic Visions of Technology and Fear* (Rochester: Camden House, 2000), 106.

The film's highlighting of both the second-hand movement and the flashing lights finds equivalents in Thea von Harbou's descriptions of clocks in her novel *Metropolis*, which repeatedly emphasize the importance of the *second*.[55] Towards the beginning of the novel, the narrator describes the giant work-clock overlooking the city from the top of the New Tower of Babel with its relentless counting of seconds: 'Freders Augen hingen an der Uhr des Neuen Turms Babel, wo die Sekunden als atmende Blitze auffunkten und wegloschen, unaufhaltsam im Kommen wie im Gehen' [Freder's eyes were fixed on the clock-face of the New Tower of Babel, where the seconds flashed on and off like breaths of lightning, relentless in their coming and going].[56] Moments later, in a description reminiscent of Lang's images of the scythed figure of death in the film, Freder finds the same clock on the wall of his father's office and imagines it as a scythe turning in a staccato circular motion:

> [Freder] stand still und blickte unablässig auf den dunklen Schädel seines Vaters und sah, wie der ungeheure Zeiger der Uhr, unaufhaltsam vorwärtsschreitend, gleich einer Sichel, einer mähenden Sense, wieder hinaufschob an der zahlenumbauschten Rundung, die Höhe überkroch und sich abermals senkte, um den vergeblichen Sensenschlag zu wiederholen. (21)[57]

> [Freder stood still and continued to stare at his father's dark skull. He watched as the monstrous clock hand, in its relentless forward motion, like a sickle or a reaping scythe, climbed back up the clock's number-laden curve, crawled over the top and sank down again, only to repeat the vain swipe of the scythe once more].

Clearly associated with Taylorization and its obsession with micromanaging the seconds of labour time, the deathly second-hand in

---

55 Conceived at the same time as the film (and as an explicit source for the latter), Harbou's novel version was published in instalments in 1925 in the journal *Illustriertes Blatt* (Frankfurt am Main). See Holger Bachmann, 'The Production and Contemporary Reception of *Metropolis*', in *Fritz Lang's Metropolis. Cinematic Visions of Technology and Fear*, 10–11.

56 Thea von Harbou, *Metropolis* (Frankfurt am Main: Ozeanische Bibliothek, 1984 [1925]), 19.

57 Harbou clearly links the clocks in the novel: 'Es war die gleiche Uhr, wie sie von der Höhe des Neuen Turms Babel, von Scheinwerfern gebadet, ihre Sekundenfunken über die große Metropolis vespritzte' (Harbou 20) [This was the same clock which, perched atop of the New Tower of Babel and bathed in spotlights, sprayed its flashes of seconds out over the great metropolis].

Fig 5. Still from Fritz Lang, Metropolis (1927), courtesy of the Deutsche Kinemathek

Metropolis also constitutes a potent metaphor for Klagesian *Takt* in its cadenced, non-flowing movement.

As the film continues, moreover, that staccato movement finds a direct echo in the choreography of working bodies. In the sequence immediately following the shot of the two clocks, the film cuts to the machine halls underground, where two geometric groups of workers, serialized by their identical uniforms, can be seen walking in different directions, the highly stylized, staccato gait of one group recalling the movement of the second-hand from the previous scene. Transforming the workers' gait from a continuous flow to a series of static snapshots, the choreography follows what Felicia MacCarren has called the aesthetics of 'the minimal gesture' in modernist machine dance.[58] Soon after these shots, we see what exactly has transformed the workers' bodies when Freder catches his first glimpse of the machine hall in the famous 'Moloch' sequence. From Freder's point of view, we observe the workers twitch back and forth like pendulums in a mechanical dance (figure 5). Through this meticulous choreography of cadenced bodily movement, *Metropolis* depicts modernization in a

---

58 See Felicia MacCarren, *Dancing Machines. Choreographies in the Age of Mechanical Reproduction* (Stanford: Stanford University Press, 2003), 11.

manner similar to that of Klages and the proponents of eurhythmical body culture. Modernization appears here as a process entailing the temporal disciplining of the body through a regime of industrial *Takt*, where the body's flowing rhythms are divided and segmented by the mechanical ticking of the industrial clock. 'Nach schmalen Sekunden gemessen', states the narrator in von Harbou's novel, 'immer den gleichen Griff auf die gleiche Sekunde, auf die gleiche Sekunde' (25) [Measured according to narrow seconds, always the same gesture at the same second, at the same second].

Indeed, the suppression of rhythm by rationalized time characterizes not only the representation of the workers' bodies in *Metropolis*, but also that of the city itself, which is repeatedly figured as a meta-body suffering under the tyranny of the intellect. While this motif of the city as body comes out most distinctly in the famous allegory of the head and the hands, it is also inscribed into the very structure and history of the city. In Harbou's novel, the narrator recounts how Fredersen originally built his city over an ancient river, which he had dammed up, but which constantly threatens to flood the city anew.[59] The novel ends with the liberation of this vital source in the form of a cathartic flood, which Harbou celebrates as a metaphor for the return of life to a rigidified modern body: 'Die Steine der Totenstadt wurden lebendig' (141) [The stones of the city of the dead came to life]. In this, the city undergoes a process directly parallel to Joh Fredersen himself. Repeatedly, the hyperintellectual head of the city is compared to a block of stone erected over an ancient spring, and the novel culminates with Maria describing Fredersen's healing process in terms of water breaking through rigid stone. 'Ach, Freder' she exlaims to Fredersen's son,

> mir war, während dein Vater hier stand, als hörte ich eine Quelle in einem Felsen rauschen. Eine Quelle mit salzschwerem Wasser und rot von Blut. Aber ich wußte auch: Wenn die Quelle stark genug ist, daß sie den Felsen durchbricht, dann wird sie süßer sein als Tau und weißer als Licht. (193)

> [Oh Freder! As your father stood here, it was as if I could hear a spring rumbling beneath the stone. The water was heavy with salt and red with blood. And I knew that if this spring gained enough strength to break through the stone, it would be sweeter than dew and whiter than light.]

---

59   See Harbou, *Metropolis*, 169.

Interestingly, the agent of this healing process in the novel appears to be the engineer Rotwang, Fredersen's ancient rival for the love of the deceased Hel, who creates the destructive robot in the image of Freder's lover Maria to destroy Fredersen's city. It is this destruction of Fredersen's work, moreover, that acts as the catalyst for his healing. In an earlier scene in the novel, Rotwang describes himself to the robot Maria by means of the same allegory of water and stone used to describe Fredersen:

> Alle Quellen des Guten sind in mir zugeschüttet. Ich glaube, sie seien tot; aber sie sind nur Lebendig-Begrabene. Mein Ich ist ein Felsen-Finsternis. Aber ich höre tief in dem traurigen Stein die Quellen rauschen. Wenn ich dem Willen trotze, der über dir und mir ist, wenn ich das Werk zerstöre, das ich nach dir schuf... Es geschähe Joh Fredersen recht, und mir wäre wohler! (129)

> [All the wellsprings of good in me have been filled up. I thought they were dead, but they have only been buried alive. My conscious self is a stony darkness. But deep within the sad stone, I can hear the sound of flowing springs. If I go against the will ruling over you and me, if I destroy the work I created in your image... It would serve Joh Fredersen right, and I would feel better!]

Thus in the novel, the destruction of technology is tantamount to the destruction of the great stones of rationality.

Harbou's allegory of the liberation from rationalization as the rediscovery of a buried spring underneath the stone recalls nothing so much as the vitalist discourse on modernization as the repression of primal rhythms. Bode, for example, repeatedly resorts to the allegory of an ancient spring covered over by blocks of stone to describe the process of 'derhythmification' of the body under the influence of modern rationalism. Conversely, he compares the liberation of the body's repressed rhythms through eurhythmical gymnastics to the unleashing of this source in the form of a vitalistic flood which would tear down all the barriers erected by the intellect in its segmentation of nature.

> Das einzige, was wir vermögen, ist, die Bahn freizumachen, falls doch noch einmal die Woge des Lebens gegen das Bollwerk des Rationalismus anrauschen sollte, es überflutend mit den Formen rhythmisch bewegten Lebens. Ob die Woge kommt, ob sie hoch genug schlagen wird, wissen wir nicht. Wir können nur hinweisen auf Symptome, die vielleicht andeuten, daß die Flut im Stiegen ist. (Bode 33)

[All we can do is clear the way in case the wave of life should rise up again to assault the fortress of rationalism, flooding it with the forms of rhythmically moving life. Whether this flood will come, whether this wave will crash with enough force, we cannot know. We can only point to symptoms which perhaps suggest that the flood is rising.]

But such a cathartic destruction of the architecture of rationality, Bode continued, would be possible only if the rhythmical source of life had not totally dried up: 'wo das Wasser des Lebens endgültig versiegt ist, schafft kein Wegräumen von Steintrümmern und Felsengeröll eine rhythmisch sprudelnde Quelle' (73) [Where the water of life has definitively run dry, no removal of stone rubble or boulders can create a spring of bubbling rhythm].

With its representation of cathartic destruction, Harbou's novel sought to stage a similar clash between vital rhythm and Fordist rationality to that of the dance reformers – right down to the 'dancing-girl' (Rotwang's robot) who leads the crowd during the destruction of the city: 'Die Masse wollte sich an der Maschine vergreifen. Ein tanzendes Mädchen führte die Masse an' (Harbou 147) [The masses wanted to attack the machine. A dancing girl led the masses forward]. The novel's obsessive preoccupation with stone and vital waters clearly also finds an echo in the famous flood sequence in the film version of *Metropolis*. Most specifically, the film recalls Harbou's allegory of the buried spring in the many images of water smashing through the geometric stone buildings of the underground city (figure 6). But while the film retains Harbou's critique of rationality, it largely plays down the positive connotations of the flood to present the unleashing of vital forces more specifically as a source of danger. Like the novel, the film draws a direct parallel between the images of flooding water and the movement of the workers in revolt as they tear down every barrier on their unstoppable flow towards the machine rooms.[60] As has been pointed out before, moreover, this formless flowing mass is unmistakably coded as feminine, marked as it is by the presence of the workers' wives, who appear in this scene for the first time in the film. If this characterization of the masses as a feminine flood takes up a longstanding tradition of gendered fantasies about the unruly masses stretching back to the origins of

---

60 In the novel, Harbou repeatedly emphasizes the flowing, watery quality of the masses: 'Vor der strömenden, grölenden Masse her tanzte ein Mädchen. […] Die Masse teilte sich. Ein breiter Strom goß sich brodelnd hinab in die Gänge der Tiefbahn' (143) [A girl was dancing in front of the streaming, bellowing masses. […] The masses parted. A wide stream flowed bubbling down into the shafts of the underground railway].

Fig 6. Still from Fritz Lang, Metropolis *(1927), courtesy of the Deutsche Kinemathek*

modern crowd psychology in nineteenth-century thinkers such as Gustave Le Bon,[61] it also recalls the understanding of primal rhythm by reformers like Bode, who championed the rhythms of nature as a feminine, fluid element opposed to the hyper-masculine activity of rational segmentation. For Bode, modern men had become – like Fredersen in *Metropolis* – nothing but intellect: 'Der "moderne" Mann ist in der Tat einseitig intellektuell gerichtet, aber dieser Sieg des Intellekts in ihm hat zur Voraussetzung eine Schwächung seiner seelisch-rhythmischen Kräfte' (Bode 68) [Modern men are in fact completely given over to the intellect, but this victory of the intellect within them entails a weakening of the rhythmical powers of their souls]. This is, of course, not to make Bode's philosophy into any paradoxical sort of feminism. On the contrary, he explicitly attacks the figure of the 'new woman', who, he argues, suppresses women's 'motherly' calling by imitating the already overly-intellectualized

---

61 See Lutz Musner, 'Stadt. Masse. Weib: Metropolenwandel, Massenphobie und Misogynie im Fin-de-Siècle' [City, Masses, Woman: Transformations of the Metropolis, Fear of the Masses and Misogyny in the Fin de Siècle] in Günther Hödl, Fritz Mayrhofer and Ferdinand Opll (eds.), *Frauen in der Stadt* [*Women in the City*] (Linz: Österreichische Arbeitskreis für Stadtgeschichtsforschung, 2003), 63–83.

modern man.[62] Bode clearly understood rhythm – in opposition to the will, the intellect or 'Geist' (spirit) – as a 'feminine' element, but one that ran counter to the codes of femininity informing the Weimar figure of the new woman: one closer to the world of 'nature' and able to 'heal' an overly rationalized society. Both the novel and film versions of *Metropolis* code the flood similarly as a manifestation of a feminized nature: but where the novel presents the feminine flood of rhythm as a healing element, the film presents it as a force no less threatening than the rigid *Takt* it opposes. The screen version of *Metropolis*, that is, displays the greatest anxiety precisely before the natural, formless and 'feminine' rhythm championed by Klages and Bode.

And yet, the film does attempt to imagine a productive relation between the two poles: according to the central motto of the film, it is the *heart* that ought to mediate between the intellect and the body. Certainly the topos of the mediating heart in *Metropolis* functions on one level as a metaphor for the cinema itself, which Lang largely understood – under the influence of Béla Balázs – as a forum for mediating linguistic, social and cultural barriers through the establishment of a universal language of gestures and expressions. We first encounter the figure of the mediating heart in Maria's catacomb sermon on the Tower of Babel, which offers an allegory of *Metropolis* itself in its call for mediation between the classes, and which is presented as a kind of film within the film. Indeed, as other critics have pointed out, Babel was often invoked in the wake of the

---

62 'Nimmt die Sturmkraft der Seele ab, so erliegt der Mann dem Intellekt, d.h. es entstehen jene Typen, die heute die Großstädte bevölkern und in deren instinktlosen Dummheiten und deren Nachahmung unsere "Emanzipierten" das Heil der Seele erblicken. Nimmt andererseits im Weibe die Materie, die Stromschwere der Seele ab, so stirbt die instinktkräftige Mütterlichkeit, und das Weib erliegt gleichfalls dem Intellekt. Es enstehen jene Typen, wie sie gleichfalls nur die zivilisierte Großstadt hervorbringt, weibliche Gestalten, die ohne Muttersehnsucht dem Männlichen nachstreben, ohne aber die fehlende weibliche Stromschwere durch männliche Bildkraft ersetzen zu können, Zwittergebilde und Zeichen einer sinkenden Art' (69) [As the storm-power of the soul diminishes, men succumb to the intellect. This gives rise to those types that populate cities today. Our 'emancipated' women see their salvation in the imitation of such men with their stupidity and lack of instinct. On the other hand, as the material flows of the soul diminish in women, their instinct for motherliness dies out and they also succumb to the intellect. This gives rise to those types which, once again, can only be brought forth by the civilized city: female figures with no desire for motherhood, who strive for masculinity but cannot replace their missing feminine flows with masculine creative force, hybrid forms and signs of a declining species].

Great War to describe the condition that film's universal language would help to overcome. As Balázs described it in the introduction to *Der sichtbare Mensch* (1924) [*Visible Man*], 'Andererseits scheint uns gerade die Filmkunst eine Erlösung von dem babelschen Fluch zu versprechen. Denn auf der Leinwand der Kinos aller Länder entwickelt sich jetzt *die erste internationale Sprache*: die der Mienen und Gebärden' [Film art appears to promise an overcoming of the curse of Babel. For on the screens of all cinemas of all countries, *the first international language* is developing: the language of gestures and facial expressions].[63] As Lang himself put it in an article of 1926, published just before the release of *Metropolis*:

> Werden wir uns doch klar darüber: Der Film ist der Rhapsode des 20. Jahrhunderts. Er kann aber viel mehr noch für die Menschheit werden: Der Wanderprediger, der zu Millionen spricht. Durch die stumme Beredtsamkeit seiner bewegten Bilder, deren Sprache unter allen Breitengraden gleich gut verstanden wird, kann der Film ein redlich Teil dazu beitragen, das Chaos wieder gutzumachen, das seit dem Turmbau zu Babel die Völker daran hindert, sich so zu sehen, wie sie wirklich sind.[64]

> [Let there be no mistake: film is the rhapsodist of the twentieth century. But it could be much more for humanity; it could be the travelling preacher who speaks to millions. With the silent eloquence of its moving images, whose language is equally comprehensible in all latitudes, film can make a genuine contribution to overcoming the chaos that has prevented peoples from seeing each other as they really are ever since the Tower of Babel.]

In what follows, however, I want to suggest that *Metropolis* also attempts to imagine moving images as another form of mediation: namely as a forum for mediating between technological and organic rhythms: film as a *Schaltstelle*, in Lubkoll's terms, between nature and culture. It is *this* mediating function, I will argue, that finds its objective correlative in the film in the figure of the pulsating heart.

To see this, we need to look more closely at the web of heart imagery recurring throughout the film, starting with the famous 'heart-machine' at the centre of the city's technological apparatus.

63   Béla Balázs, *Der sichtbare Mensch oder die Kultur des Films* [*Visible Man or the Culture of Film*] (Frankfurt am Main: Suhrkamp, 2001), 22. For an extended reading of the Babel motif in early cinema, see Miriam Hansen, *Babel and Babylon: Spectatorship in American Silent Film* (Cambridge: Harvard University Press, 2005).

64   Fritz Lang, 'Ausblick auf Morgen. Zum Pariser Kongress' [Looking Towards the Future: On the Paris Congress], *Lichtbild-Bühne* 19:229 (25 Sep 1926), 9–10.

In her novel, Harbou describes the heart-machine as a pumping mechanism, audible throughout the underground city as an intermittent 'Pulsschlag' (beating pulse), which keeps the danger of flooding in check by continually pumping away the excess water building up beneath the city.

> Gewiß war, daß in der unterirdischen Arbeiterstadt das Pochen dieses Pumpwerks als ein leiser, nie unterbrochener Pulsschlag ständig zu hören war, wenn man den Kopf an eine Mauer legte – und daß, wenn dieser Pulsschlag einmal schwieg, kein anderes Deuten möglich war, als daß die Pumpen standen und dann stieg der Strom. (155)

> [It was certain that, if one laid one's head against the walls of the underground workers' city, one could always hear the beating of this pumping mechanism as a faint, uninterrupted pulse – and it was also certain that if this beating pulse ever went silent, there was no other possible explanation than that the pumps had stood still and the flood was rising.][65]

Thus mediating between technology and the forces of nature – the city and the primal spring over which it was built – the 'heart machine' at the centre of Fredersen's city can be seen to embody a certain fantasy of cinematic movement as a constructivist machine for ordering the rhythms of nature.

This interpretation becomes even more plausible when one considers the design for the heart-machine in *Metropolis*. As Standish Lawder long ago observed, the appearance of Lang's heart-machine, with its circular form featuring groups of four hooked lines on the outer edges (figure 7) makes an unmistakable reference to an earlier work of rhythmical filmmaking: the 1923 film *L'Inhumaine* [*The Inhuman Woman*] by Marcel L'Herbier. In L'Herbier's film – in lavish sets designed by Fernand Léger – a similar design adorns the centrepiece of the laboratory of the engineer Einar Norsen, a machine that can, as Einer explains in one sequence, 'ranimer les mouvements

---

65 The depiction of the heart in terms of a pumping mechanism in fact forms something of a leitmotif in the novel. In a description of Maria being pursued by Rotwang, for example, the narrator states: 'Wie ein Pumpwerk hörte sie ihr Herz, immer schneller, immer dröhnender' (65) [She heard her heart beating like a pumping station, faster and more thunderously with every beat]. In his own reading of the film, Tom Gunning sees the function of the city in a similar light as the periodic diffusion of excess energy and reads the disaster sequences – the Moloch scene and the revolt at the end – as manifestations of the same mechanism of 'energy release' rather than interruptions of it. See Tom Gunning, *The Films of Fritz Lang. Allegories of Vision and Modernity* (London: British Film Institute, 2000), 63.

Fig 7. Still from Fritz Lang, Metropolis (1927), courtesy of the Deutsche Kinemathek

du cœur' [reanimate the movements of the heart]. L'Herbier's film tells the story of the opera singer and *femme fatale* Claire Lescot, whose ruthlessness towards her male suitors is matched only by her penchant for 'primitive' sexuality. Throughout the early part of the film, Claire can be seen giving eccentric soirées, in which black performers dressed in tribal attire entertain her with rhythmical dances, filmed in chaotic accelerated montage sequences. What Claire's suitors share is the desire to bring her sexuality under control and tame the 'inhuman' woman with her exotic rhythms. It is the engineer, Einar, who wins the contest, and his 'heart machine' plays a key role in the process. First, Einar invents a proto-radio device, which allows Claire's concerts to be transmitted instantly anywhere in the world, thus rendering her effectively immobile. ('Ici', he tells Claire in his laboratory, 'quelque chose va vous faire renoncer au voyage' [There is something here that will make you give up your travels]). Then, when Claire nearly dies after being poisoned by another jealous suitor, Einar sets his laboratory into motion and – in a final montage sequence unwinding in furious acceleration – uses his machine to reanimate Claire's heart. As Richard Abel has argued, L'Herbier's audiences would clearly have understood the engineer's machine as a metaphor for the cinema in its capacity to preserve or reanimate life.⁶⁶ But I would add that this reanimation of the heart's pulse also embodied a fantasy – once again played out in gendered terms – of subjecting the rhythms of nature to the order of male technology. Einar not only resuscitates Claire's heart, he also controls the dangerous rhythms – we see him literally struggling to make it through the montage sequence at the end – embodied in Claire's primitivist soirées with their rapid montage. Receiving an artificial electric heartbeat, Claire thus becomes a metaphor of the cinema's power to impose temporal order over life.

Coming back to *Metropolis*, the heart-machine, in its capacity as a regulator of the dangerous flow of primal rhythm, is matched perhaps only by the 'good' Maria's catacomb sermon – a sermon on the need for a mediating heart – by which she continually defuses the workers' desire for revolt. But as anyone who has dealt with *Metropolis* at any length knows, this 'good Maria' is never far from her wicked double – or to borrow the terms generally applied to the film, the virgin is never far from the vamp.⁶⁷ It should come as no surprise, then, to see the robot Maria represented as a nightmarish double of the orderly 'heart machine'. Accordingly, at the climactic moment of Rotwang's transformation of the robot, Lang superimposes the image of a pulsing heart onto the mechanical creature's chest, whose rhythmical movement sends vital currents soaring through its body. The suggestion here, I think, is that Rotwang has endowed his creation not only with Maria's external appearance, but also – as Andreas Huyssen points out – with her sexual life force.⁶⁸ The image of the pulsing heart follows almost directly upon shots of Rotwang's glass tubes and flasks, which appear to fill with Maria's blood as he effects the transformation.

In many ways, Rotwang's experiment also recalls the resuscitation of Claire in *L'Inhumaine*, and both the engineer Rotwang and L'Herbier's engineer could be seen as stand-ins for the filmic artist. But in fact, the 'cinema' that Rotwang creates with his construction of the robot is the opposite of that of Einar Norsen. Whereas Einar uses technological rhythms to transform an uncontrollable female sexuality into an obedient machine, Rotwang's experiment, by

---

66 Richard Abel, *French Cinema. The First Wave 1915–1929* (Princeton: Princeton University Press, 1984), 393.

67 The 'virgin' and 'vamp' dichotomy has a long history in feminist scholarship. The terms were first applied to *Metropolis* by Andreas Huyssen. See Huyssen, 'The Vamp and the Machine: Technology and Sexuality in Fritz Lang's *Metropolis*.' *New German Critique* 24–25 (Autumn 1981–Winter 1982): 221–37.

68 See Huyssen, 235.

Fig 8. Still from Fritz Lang, Metropolis *(1927), courtesy of the Deutsche Kinemathek*

infusing the robot with the life-force of organic rhythm, transforms what was a thoroughly obedient machine – the *Maschinenmensch,* which was to be the perfect worker of the future and which the audience saw following Rotwang's every command in an earlier scene – into an agent of uncontrollable sexual chaos. In this sense, Rotwang also creates a precise counterpart to the controlling heart-machine at the centre of Fredersen's industrial city. And it is hardly a coincidence that the 'false' Maria will lead the flood of raging workers on a rampage to destroy that same heart-machine.

In parallel to this attack, the false Maria also institutes an alternative rhythmical spectacle with her famous erotic dance at Yoshiwara's. In a scene reminiscent of Claire Lescot's sexualized soirées in *L'Inhumaine,* Maria arrives atop a giant pedestal held up by a circle of nearly-nude black male figures clad in 'primitivist' tribal attire (figure 8). Maria's subsequent Josephine Baker-style dance – which Lang's editing stages as an ever accelerating rhythmical frenzy – sends her male audience into convulsions, causing them to lose all self-control and attack one another before the stage. In terms of its effects upon its audience, Maria's erotic spectacle recalls the belief, widespread in the early twentieth century, that violent or erotic representations in the cinema could provoke an atavistic regression in spectators. Indeed,

Lang specifically constructs Maria's dance as an example of what contemporaries called 'Schaulust' [the pleasure of looking], which was understood to reside in the pleasure of atavistic regression before the screen.[69] Through editing, close-ups and superimposition, Lang gradually reduces Maria's spectators to a collage of lustful eyes. Through this emphasis on the staring eyes, Lang presents the male audience not so much as voyeuristic – in the sense of a distanced, controlling gaze – but rather as mesmerized, Maria's rhythmical spectacle causing them to *lose* all self-control.[70]

This cinema of rhythmical contagion stands diametrically opposed to the good heart-machine and it must, like the rebellious Claire Lescot in *L'Inhumaine*, be brought under control at the end of the film. As Siegfried Kracauer recognized, this exorcism occurs not only through the burning of the bad Maria, but also through the re-ordering of the mass flood into a perfectly geometric mass ornament. The crowd's unified and disciplined movement in the final handshake scene seems to suggest that the 'heart-machine – mediating between the body and the intellect, nature and technology, rhythm and metre – has once again assumed the function of imposing order over life's formless flows.

Given the complex history of the rhythm debates and the wide range of positions they encompassed, there is room, I think, to question Kracauer's hasty reading of such formations as premonitions of Nazism.[71] Rather than reading these moments as premonitions of things to come, we might, I would reiterate in closing, see them as moments that look *back* to a certain conception of the cinema, one

69 See especially Walter Serner, 'Kino und Schaulust' [Cinema and the Pleasure of Looking], *Die Schaubühne* 9 (1913), 807–11.

70 Janet Ward has also emphasized this point, arguing that the collage of eyes represents not a mastering male gaze, but rather a moment of loss of control – one signalled also by the many eye-like shapes that seem to look back at the audience from Maria's stage. See Ward, '*Metropolis* and the Technosexual Woman of German Modernity', in Katharina von Ankum (ed.), *Women in the Metropolis. Gender and Modernity in Weimar Culture* (Berkeley: University of California Press, 1997), 131–32.

71 See Kracauer, *From Caligari to Hitler*, 164: 'The pictorial structure of the final scene confirms the analogy between the industrialist and Goebbels. If in this scene the heart really triumphed over tyrannical power, its triumph would dispose of the all-devouring decorative scheme that in the rest of *Metropolis* marks the industrialist's claim to omnipotence'. Subsequent criticism has largely followed Kracauer's lead. See Huyssen, 'The Vamp and the Machine', 236–37. Of course, the opposite reading of this final sequence might be just as apt. After all, it was the champions of primal rhythm such as Bode who would go on to take leading roles in the Nazi administration.

embodied by L'Herbier's rhythmical heart-machine and whose imaginary power consisted in subordinating the rhythms of nature to mechanical order. Such an imposition of order defined a filmic imaginary shared by experimental and narrative filmmakers alike in the 1920s, who largely saw the cinema, in Guido's description, as an 'outil de canalisation et de contrôle du mouvement' [a tool for channelling and controlling movement]. As we will see in the next chapter, this project also stood at the heart of another domain of filmic practice often overlooked in Weimar histories: advertising.

4. The Compulsory Power of Resonance: Rhythm, Attention and the Weimar Advertising Film

> Was am Fließband den Rhythmus der Produktion bestimmt,
> liegt beim Film dem der Rezeption zugrunde.[1]
>
> [What determines the rhythm of production on the conveyor-belt
> forms the basis of the rhythm of reception of film.]

Synergies of Film and Advertising in the 1920s

If the concern with rhythmical aesthetics united the abstract films of Richter and Ruttmann with popular films such as *Metropolis*, this concern was hardly limited to those genres. Rhythmical filmmaking also played a key role in another domain of modern filmmaking rarely discussed in histories of Weimar cinema: that of advertising. Although 'lebende Plakate' [living posters] had existed alongside other short formats since the very earliest years of cinema and helped pave the way for the propaganda industry that arose during WWI, filmic advertising only developed into a fully-fledged and profitable industry with the onset of the Weimar Republic.[2] Whereas the pre-war

---

1   Walter Benjamin, 'Über einige Motive bei Baudelaire' [On some Motifs in Baudelaire] (1939)

2   On the history of advertising film before 1918, see Ingrid Westbrock, *Der Werbefilm. Ein Beitrag zur Entwicklungsgeschichte des Genres vom Stummfilm zum frühen Tonfilm* [*The Advertising Film. A Contribution to the History of the Genre From Silent to Early Sound Film*] (Hildesheim: Georg Olms, 1983), 30–44; Günter Ägde, *Flimmernde Versprechen. Geschichte des deutschen Werbefilms im Kino seit 1897* [*Flickering Promises. History of German Advertising Films for the Cinema Since 1897*] (Berlin: Verlag das Neue Berlin, 1998), 1–72. According to Westbrock and Ägde, the first verifiable advertising film in German was *Bade zu Hause* (1896) [*Bathe at Home*], an advertisement for 'Schaukelwellenbäder' [rocking bathtubs] made in Oskar Messter's Berlin studio and shown in the Berlin Apollo Theater as part

years were dominated in Germany above all by the pioneering work of Oskar Messter and Julius Pinschewer, by the end of the 1920s, no fewer than 86 advertising film agencies were operating in Germany alone.³ In its Weimar phase, moreover, the history of advertising film is inextricably bound up with that of the avant-garde. Filmmakers such as Hans Richter, Walter Ruttmann, Lotte Reiniger and Guido Seeber all worked closely with advertising companies, in particular Pinschewer's 'Werbefilm GmbH', and found in the advertisement film not only a source of income but also, and much more crucially, a favourable field for aesthetic and technological innovation: a space in which techniques of graphic experimentation, forms of alternative editing, and the use of sound and colour were tried out before they moved into mainstream film.⁴ Indeed, in films such as Ruttmann's *Der Sieger* (1922) [*The Victor*] for Excelsior tyres or Reiniger's *Das Geheimnis der Marquise* (1922) [*The Marquise's Secret*] for Nivea facecream, one can identify the same forms and movements employed in these filmmakers' abstract work from the same period.⁵

In this chapter, I want to consider how this synergy between avantgarde film and the science of advertising functioned particularly around the question of rhythm. As I will demonstrate, far from a mere formalist aesthetic principle, rhythm constituted a point of interface where experimental film aesthetics and advertising theory intersected – both of them drawing on the body of knowledge arising from Bücher's study to investigate the effects of visual rhythms on spectators and consumers. Following an initial discussion of rhythm in Weimar advertising theory, I shall offer a close analysis of one of the most fascinating films of the genre: Julius Pinschewer and Guido

---

of a variety show in 1896 and 1897 (Westbrock 31; Ägde 9–11). See also Annika Schoemann, *Der deutsche Animationsfilm von den Anfängen bis zur Gegenwart 1909–2001* [*German Animation Film From its Beginnings to the Present*] (Sankt Augustin: Gardez!, 2003), 90.

3   See Westbrock, 62.

4   On this point, see esp. Westbrock, *Der Werbefilm*, 102–03. Pinschewer, who began making advertisement films in the 1910s, made over 100 of them during the 1920s. For more on Pinschewer's career, see Jeanpaul Goergen, 'Julius Pinschewer: A Trade-mark Cinema, in Thomas Elsaesser (ed.), *A Second Life. German Cinema's First Decades* (Amsterdam: Amsterdam University Press, 1996), 168–74.

5   On the formal parallels between Ruttmann's abstract films and his advertisement films, see Westbrock, 53. This subject is also discussed in Harold Putsch and Martin Loiperdinger's documentary *Film ist Rhythmus. Werbefilm und Avantgarde* (1991) [*Film is Rhythm. Advertising Film and Avant-Garde*].

Seeber's advertisement for the 'Kipho' (Kino und Photo) exhibition of 1925 in Berlin.[6]

If one wishes to gauge the interest in rhythmical filmmaking among advertising theorists by the mid-1920s, a good place to start is an article published in 1926 by the advertising psychologist Käthe Kurtzig in the prominent work-science journal *Industrielle Psychotechnik* [*Industrial Psychotechnics*]. In it, Kurtzig argues that film offers a particularly apt medium for product advertising, not only on account of its inherent 'Bewegung, Abwechslung und Zerstreuung' [movement, variety and distraction], but also because the cinema has a unique ability to captivate spectators' visual attention: 'Vor allem aber hat [der Film] den unschätzbaren Vorzug, den Blick nicht erst auf sich lenken zu müssen. [...] Jedermann, der vor der Leinwand sitzt, muß zwangsläufig alles, was ihm von dort entgegentritt, sehen' [Above all, film has the invaluable advantage of not having to compete for the audience's attention. [...] Everyone sitting in front of the screen is compelled to see whatever it sends their way].[7] This compulsive viewing situation made it imperative that advertising films produce pleasure, and Kurtzig's article, accordingly, sets out to catalogue the strategies for doing so. Specifically, she distinguishes four methods of pleasing the cinema's captive audience. Comical advertisements sought to win over consumers through light humour; the 'Trickfilm' ['trick film'] sought to impress them by means of animation and special effects. The Scherenschnittfilm [silhouette film], which Kurtzig saw as particularly appropriate for women's products (the category is illustrated with images from Lotte Reiniger's ad *Die Barcarole* (1924) [*The Barcarole*] for Mauxion pralines), sought to attract consumers through the grace and elegance of its ethereal aesthetic presentation.[8] And finally Kurtzig described what she called the newest type of advertising film: 'der absolute Film' (311) [the absolute film]. Illustrated with an image from Walter Ruttmann's *Der Aufstieg* (1926) [*The Ascent*] (figure 1), in which Ruttmann employed the abstract vocabulary familiar from his *Opus* films to advertise the Düsseldorf 'Gesolei' exhibition on Health (<u>Ge</u>sundheit), Social Aid (<u>So</u>zialfürsorge) and body culture (<u>Lei</u>besübung), Kurtzig's

---

6 The film can be found under various titles, including *Film, Du musst zur Kipho*, and simply *Kipho*. The latter title will be used throughout this chapter.

7 Käthe Kurtzig, 'Die Arten des Werbefilms' [Types of Advertising Film], *Industrielle Psychotechnik* 3:10 (1926), 310–11

8 As Westbrock points out, the 'Scherenschnittfilm' – literally 'scissor-cut film' – was the only genre in which women filmmakers (most prominently Lotte Reiniger) could establish themselves as directors (48).

Fig 1. Walter Ruttmann, Der Aufstieg *(1926), still from Käthe Kurtzig, 'Arten des Werbefilms' (*Industrielle Psychotechnik, *1926)*

notion of the absolute advertising film clearly derives its name from the concept of the 'absolute' film recently introduced in the famous Berlin *soirée* of the same name of 1925, in which works of Ruttmann, Richter, Fernand Léger and others were shown together in an evening of rhythmical filmmaking. Like its avant-garde homologues, the absolute advertising film functioned above all through the power of rhythm, which Kurtzig believed uniquely capable of affecting spectators viscerally:

> Der absolute Film [...] bringt in seiner Durchführung keine geschlossene Handlung, sondern versucht, durch das Bewegungsspiel von Ornamenten und Figuren einen gedanklichen Inhalt sichtbar zum Ausdruck zu bringen; er wirkt vor allem durch die rhythmische Kraft der Bewegung, die den Zuschauer zum Mitschwingen bringt und ihn die Vorgänge auf der Leinwand nicht nur sehen und verstehen, sondern erleben läßt. (314)

> [The absolute film [...] does not present any rounded storylines but attempts to offer the visual expression of an ideational content through the abstract movement of ornaments and figures; it functions above all through the rhythmical power of movement, which awakens a resonating movement in the spectators, causing them not only to see and understand the images on the screen but to feel them.]

Unlike all the other forms of pleasure mentioned by Kurtzig, 'rhythm' thus elicited a direct bodily response to the moving image.

Kurtzig's description of the power of rhythm in absolute advertising recalls nothing so much as the language used by filmmakers themselves to describe abstract filmmaking. As we saw in the last chapter, Richter insisted again and again on the quasi-hypnotic effect of abstract rhythm on spectators. As he describes it in his 1929 study *Filmgegner von heute – Filmfreunde von morgen* [*Opponents of Film Today – Friends of Film Tomorrow*]: 'Nur wenige Regisseure [ahnen] etwas von der Notwendigkeit des Rhythmus. Und von seiner Kraft: seiner Unwiderstehlichkeit' [Few directors have any idea of the necessity of rhythm. Of its power: its irresistible attraction].[9] Richter was also well aware of the connection between this 'irresistible' quality of rhythm and Bücher's theories of work. As he explained in another passage from the same text, citing standard examples from Bücher's *Arbeit und Rhythmus*: 'Die Kraft des Rhythmus ist erwiesen. Der Takt des Marsches belebt den Schritt. Schiffer erleichtern sich das Rudern durch rhythmischen Gesang. Drescher, Schmiede, Straßenpflasterer vollziehen ihr einförmiges Klopfen im Rhythmus' (Richter, *Filmgegner*, 93) [The power of rhythm has been amply demonstrated. Rhythmical marching animates the feet. Oarsmen use rhythmical singing to lighten their task. Blacksmiths, threshers and road-pavers all perform their monotonous pounding in rhythm].[10]

9   Richter, *Filmgegner von heute – Filmfreunde von morgen* (Berlin: Hermann Reckendorf, 1929), 34.

10   Richter's examples are all direct echoes of Bücher and constitute the standard examples cited in rhythm discussions derived from the latter's work (see Bücher, *Arbeit und Rhythmus*, 21–25). For example, the educational theorist Gustav Klar, in a discussion of the use of rhythm in education, explained: '[D]urch den Rhythmus [wird] in die körperlichen Betätigung, die Arbeit im ursprünglichen Sinne, ein Moment der Erleichterung und Beschleunigung hineingetragen: man denke an das Dreschen, Rammen, Rudern, den Gleichschritt einer marschierenden Gruppe – Tatsachen, auf deren arbeitsökonomische Bedeutung Karl Bücher in seinem wertvollen Buche, "Arbeit und Rhythmus" mit Recht aufmerksam macht' (Klar 4) [Rhythm facilitates and accelerates bodily activity, i.e. labour in the original sense: one need only think of the activities of threshing, piling, rowing and the synchronized marching of groups. Karl Bücher noted these phenomena in his excellent book *Arbeit und Rhythmus*]. In Richter, the above passage is accompanied by a series of film stills demonstrating the derivation of filmic rhythm from the rhythms of labour. The first shows a group of street-pavers pounding the cobblestones rhythmically (a motif that also figured heavily in Walter Ruttmann's *Melodie der Welt* [*Melody of the World*] of 1929). This is followed by images becoming progressively more abstract: an animated tie from Man Ray's *Emak Bakia*, a spinning spiral form from Ruttmann's *Opus 1924*, and finally abstract geometrical shapes from Richter's *Rhythmus 1921* and Eggeling's

That the model of rhythm in Kurtzig's writing on the 'absolute advertising film' was derived from the same domain as Richter's is suggested by the location of Kurtzig's article in *Industrielle Psychotechnik*, which frequently published articles dealing with the questions of rhythm and work raised by Bücher's study. Articles such as Heinrich Reinhardt's 'Rhythmus und Arbeitsleistung' [Rhythm and Labour Efficiency] of 1926 or Erich Kupke's 'Mensch und Arbeitsrhythmus' [Man and the Rhythm of Work] of 1933 drew directly on Bücher's theories to discuss the use of rhythm as a means of increasing productivity by increasing the bodily pleasure of workers. Indeed, almost all publications in psychotechnics included sections on rhythm and its potential for increasing bodily pleasure and efficiency.

More significantly, Kurtzig's article coincides with a broader discovery of rhythm by theorists of advertising in the mid-1920s. Although earlier works of advertising occasionally commented on the use of metred verse to facilitate the memory or the efficacy of repetition, such works did not include discussions of rhythm in itself as a source of pleasure or efficacy.[11] This would change, however, over the course of the 1920s.[12] In particular, Kurtzig's claim that the rhythmical advertisement film brings spectators into 'resonance' [Mitschwingen] with its own abstract movements finds a direct corollary in one of the most widely-discussed works of advertising theory from the time: *Rhythmus und Resonanz als ökonomisches Prinzip in der Reklame* (1926) [*Rhythm and Resonance as Economic Principles*

Symphonie diagonale. The images are accompanied by a continuous caption linking them all under a project of rationalizing rhythm: 'Der Rhythmus wirkt gleichsam als Naturprinzip unwiderstehlich – Er kann einen sich drehenden Kragen zu einem lebendigen Wesen machen, – einer reinen Bewegung Eindringlichkeit verleihen, – reinen Formen durch die Kraft seiner Ordnung Sinn geben' (93–95) [Rhythm exerts an irresistible attraction like a principle of nature – it can turn a spinning tie into a living being, endow a pure movement with penetrating force, and lend meaning to pure forms through its ordering power].

11 See for example Christoph von Hartungen, *Psychologie der Reklame* [*Psychology of Advertising*] (Stuttgart: C.E. Poeschel, 1921), 73; Theodor König, *Reklamepsychologie* [*Advertising Psychology*], 2nd edn (Munich: R. Oldenbourg, 1924), 189.

12 The increasing engagement of advertising theorists with advertising film can be gauged in the pages of *Die Reklame*, the official organ of the Weimar 'Association of Advertising Experts' and the most prominent advertising journal of the period. Only a few isolated articles on film advertising can be found in issues of *Die Reklame* in the first half of the 1920s, whereas after 1925 such discussions become more frequent, culminating in the special issue entitled *Der Werbefilm* in June 1927.

of Advertising] by the head of the Hamburg Phönix rubber factory, Fritz Pauli. Reacting to the explosion of print advertisements, posters and animated electric signs increasingly fighting for consumers' attention in the Weimar years, Pauli proposed the precise rhythmical calibration of advertising as the most effective way to reach potential buyers. Like many psychotechnicians and advertising psychologists, Pauli saw the concentration of attention as a mode of labour entirely analogous to physical work, and he accordingly drew on theories of work science to rationalize the consumer's mental labour. Specifically, in a direct adaptation of Bücher, Pauli argued that the rhythmization of visual impressions could optimize consumers' psychic pleasure and thus the 'productivity' of their attention:

> Diese Überlegungen, die aufgezeigten praktischen Beispiele und die Untersuchungen *Büchers* auf dem Gebiet der rhythmischen Gestaltung der physischen Arbeit berechtigen mich nunmehr, für Anwendungen und weitere Forschungen auf dem Gebiete der Werbeschwingungen folgenden Leitsatz aufzustellen: Aperiodische Arbeit wirkt unlustvoll und schnell ermüdend im Gegensatz zu periodischer Arbeit, die durch Resonanzzwang eine rhythmische Gestaltung der *motorischen* Komplexe bewirkt. Das Aufnehmen von werblichen Darbietungen ist eine Arbeitsleistung der Angebotsempfänger. Aperiodische oder nicht abgestimmte zusammengesetzte Werbemittel wirken [...] unlustvoll und schnell ermüdend, im Gegensatz zu periodischen oder abgestimmten Werbesystemen, die durch Resonanzzwang eine rhythmische Gestaltung der *psychischen* Komplexe wirke.[13]

> [These observations, along with the examples given here and *Bücher's* investigations into the rhythmical forms of physical labour, lead me to propose the following guiding principle for further research and practical applications in the area of advertising rhythms: Aperiodic labour produces displeasure and rapid fatigue. Periodic work, on the other hand, brings about a rhythmical organisation of the *motor* complexes through the compulsory power of resonance. The reception of advertising presentations, similarly, is an act of labour on the part of the consumer. Aperiodic, rhythmically dissonant and badly coordinated advertising materials produce [...] sensations of displeasure and fatigue. Periodic and well-tuned advertising systems, on the other hand, bring about a rhythmical organization of *psychic* complexes through the compulsory power of resonance.]

Key to understanding the goals of Pauli's system is the term 'Resonanzzwang' [compulsory power of resonance] in the above-

---

13 Fritz Pauli, *Rhythmus und Resonanz als ökonomisches Prinzip in der Reklame* (Berlin: Verband Deutscher Reklamefachleute, 1926), 39.

cited passage, which recurs like a leitmotif throughout his study.[14] Just as the individual body attunes itself quasi-automatically to the collective rhythms of labour, so the spectator, Pauli believed, is calibrated psychically to the tempo of rhythmical displays. Not unlike Hans Richter, Pauli thought that this rhythm could be harnessed as an irresistible force, binding the spectator hypnotically to the image on display. Accordingly, he sought to create 'periodic' advertising through dynamic visual presentations on posters, animated electric signs, rhythmical radio advertisements, and – not least – film (figure 2).

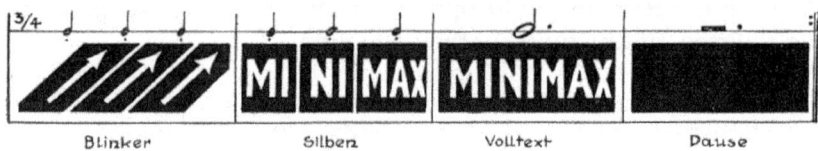

Fig 2. Sketch for an electric light advertisement for Minimax fire extinguishers, from Fritz Pauli, Rhythmus und Resonanz als ökonomisches Prinzip in der Reklame *(1926)*

If Pauli's notion of a 'compulsory' visual rhythm looks back to Bücher, however, the term *Resonanz* itself has a more immediate reference in an oft-cited theory of mechanical oscillation proposed by the engineer Heinrich Schieferstein in an article of 1922 that formed part of the German reception of Fordism. Schieferstein had argued that the cranks, levers and gears of an oscillating mechanical system could themselves be made more elastic and efficient when synchronized to a common periodic frequency or 'resonance' appropriate to them.[15] Once again making the analogy from physical to mental labour, Pauli adapted Schieferstein's model to imagine the consumer's nervous system and mental apparatus as a system of intertwined factory gears, which could be made to spin more efficiently when tuned to a common frequency by precisely timed rhythmical impressions:

> [Wir] müssen uns die Sinneswerkzeuge Augen und Ohren als stetig kreisende, exakt geschnittene Zahnrädchen vorstellen, als herausragende Teile des gedanklichen Apparates. In diese Zahnrädchen können nun von außen kommende Kräfte gut oder

14   See, for example, pp. 27, 33, 35.

15   See Heinrich von Schieferstein, 'Die Ausnützung mechanischer Schwingungen im Maschinenbau' [The Uses of Mechanical Oscillations in Engineering]. *Bayerisches Industrie- und Gewerbeblatt* 111:19 (1 October 1925), 117–23, 125–29. For Pauli's citation of Schieferstein, see Pauli, *Rhythmus und Resonanz*, 13.

schlecht eingreifen. Sind diese Eindrücke ungleichmäßig und unreguliert, so gibt es ein Knirschen und Rasseln, wie bei einem alten Autogetriebe, und der feine gedankliche Apparat zuckt vor diesen Übertragungen zurück (Unlust) oder kommt bald zum Stillstand (Ermüdung). Wir erreichen aber eine glatte Übertragung der Kräfte, wenn wir im richtigen Tempo und richtiger Zahnung spielend in diese Zahnrädchen eingreifen. (37)[16]

[We must imagine the sensory organs of the eye and the ear as continuously rotating and precisely measured cogwheels, as protruding parts of a mental apparatus. External forces can affect the operation of these gears negatively or positively. If the impressions are uneven and irregular, the result will be the kind of grating and rattling one hears in an old car factory, and the delicate mental apparatus will instinctively resist such transferences (displeasure) or come to a standstill (exhaustion). But we can attain a smooth transference of energy if we tap into these gears while playing in a correct tempo and with correct cogging.]

Through rhythmical advertising, spectators' attention could be attuned, as it were, to the rhythms of the product display.[17] It was this power of resonance over the psyche that Pauli dubbed *Resonanzzwang* and likened to hypnosis: 'Ein solcher Rhythmus wirkt hypnotisierend und hinterläßt einen unauslöschlichen Eindruck ohne üble Begleitempfindungen; denn jeder stimmt sich sofort auf diese Lichter- und Silbenresonanz ab' (Pauli, *Rhythmus und Resonanz*, 18) [Such a rhythm functions hypnotically to leave an inextinguishable

16   See also p.14: 'Wenn, wie uns nunmehr bekannt, Rhythmus und Resonanz in physischer und technischer Beziehung Mittel zur Leistungssteigerung bzw. Aufwandsverminderung sind, so sind sie es auch in psychischer Beziehung' [If, as we now know, rhythm and resonance provide a means of increasing productivity and decreasing effort in the body and in technology, they also function this way in the psychological sphere]. Pauli's representation of the mental apparatus as a system of gears finds an echo, for example, in the illustrations accompanying Fritz Kahn's biology textbook *Das Leben des Menschen* [The Life of the Human Being], released in five volumes from 1926 to 1931. A fold-out poster entitled 'Der Mensch als Industriepalast' [The Human Being as Industrial Palace] showed the human body as a giant factory system with gears, pipes, levers, belts and workers. See Cornelius Borck, 'Communicating the Modern Body: Fritz Kahn's Popular Images of Human Physiology as an Industrialized World', *Canadian Journal of Communication* 32:3 (2007), www.cjc-online.ca/index.php/journal/article/view/1876 [accessed 20 July 2011]. Such representations clearly also informed Lang's city-body allegory in *Metropolis*.

17   A few sentences later, Pauli refers to rhythm as a 'Übersetzungsgetriebe' [translational mechanism] designed to attune the buyer's thoughts to the seller's intentions (37).

impression with no unpleasant side effects; for every consumer is immediately calibrated to the resonance of these lights and syllables].

Pauli's notion of hypnotic rhythmical advertising suggests a more complex picture of the relation between advertising and modernity in the 1920s than recent scholarship on Weimar visual culture has suggested. In her study of Weimar advertising, Janet Ward has argued that advertising theorists and practitioners sought to break through the stimulus shield of blasé city-dwellers via Benjaminian shocks.[18] But while much Weimar advertising did function via abrupt or jarring stimuli, Pauli's model of rhythmical advertising clearly adopts a different strategy. In contradistinction to the shock, with its effort to bypass the well-worn paths of psychic habit, rhythm functions by cultivating those very paths. As Pauli describes it:

> Läuft nun [...] der gleiche Vorgang ein zweites Mal ab, so trifft er sozusagen auf gebahnte Wege, auf die Spuren des vorabgelaufenen Vorganges, in welchen er reibungsloser also mit weniger Anstrengung zum Bewußtsein gelangt. Widerholen sich jetzt diese Vorgänge in zeitgleichen Abständen, so ist erst recht für die Aufnahme dieser Zeitgestalten der Boden vorbereitet, und die Darbietungen werden immer hemmungsloser und leichter aufgenommen. (38)

> [Now, if the same phenomenon is repeated, it meets with well-worn paths, with the tracks of the previous phenomenon, through which it reaches consciousness with less resistance and less effort. If these phenomena are now repeated at regular intervals, the groundwork has really been laid for the reception of such temporal forms, and the presentations will be accepted much more easily and uninhibitedly.]

Far from shocking viewers via sudden impressions, Pauli sought to hypnotize viewers through the use of precisely calibrated mechanical repetition. Through rhythm, he explained, the consumer 'wird zu einem Teil des Schwingsystems' (22) [becomes part of the oscillating system].[19]

18 Janet Ward, *Weimar Surfaces. Urban Visual Culture in 1920s Germany* (Berkeley: UC Press, 2001), 123: 'Outdoor ads of the German 1920s took the apparently ingenuous, literal form of surface decoration: but they strategically aimed, via the techniques of montage stimulation and desire simulation, to break through the stimulus shield of the indifferent or distracted passer-by, and so remold the urban mass consciousness in their own image'.

19 Beyond its relation to the Fordist-inspired notions of mechanical resonance, the vocabulary of 'Schwingungen' and 'Mitschwingen' employed by theorists such as Pauli and Kurtzig also recalls the discourse around dance and dance spectatorship in the 1920s. An article from the journal *Die Tanz-Gemeinschaft* from 1929, for example, used the term 'Zusammenschwingen' to describe

Nor does this viewpoint represent an isolated margin of Weimar advertising theory. Indeed, the resonance of Pauli's efforts to adapt rhythm theory for advertising can be gauged by the unprecedented reception it received among Weimar's foremost advertising industry association, the Verband deutscher Reklamefachleute [Association of German Advertising Practitioners] (VdR). It was the VdR that published Pauli's richly illustrated book in 1926, shortly after printing a glowing review of his lectures on rhythm in its journal *Die Reklame* [*Advertising*], the foremost periodical of advertising theory in Germany at the time. In the review, in addition to commenting on the ability of rhythm to bring about a 'Rationalisierung der Reklame' [rationalization of advertising] through the systematic reduction of the consumer's psychic energy, the author celebrated in particular the possibilities of using rhythm to produce bodily pleasure in consumers:

> Der Kampf der Werbefachleute besteht in der Hauptsache in der Bewältigung der Frage, wie Werbemittel zu gestalten sind, die das Unlustgefühl des Beschauers aus sich heraus überwinden. Das System Pauli benutzt psychische Komplexe im Menschen, um die Aufnahme der Werbung lustvoll zu gestalten. Die Erkenntnis der Gesetzmäßigkeit, mit der Menschen auf rhythmisch gestaltete bzw. verbundene optische und akustische Eindrücke reagieren, ermöglicht die gesetzmäßgie Gestaltung der Werbemittel. Dies vor allem ist Neuland, geahnt bisher nur in der Anwendung des Werbeverses.[20]

> [The struggle of advertising practitioners consists above all in trying to find ways of organizing advertising materials so that they overcome the spectator's sense of displeasure simply by themselves. The Pauli system uses people's psychic complexes in order to make the reception of advertising pleasurable. Studying the regularity with which people react to rhythmically ordered or combined optical and acoustic impressions helps us to arrange the advertising materials

---

the participation of audiences in the movement of dance. See Maria Grevelli, 'Tänzertum und Menschlichkeit', in *Die Tanz-Gemeinschaft* 3 (1929), 4. In its more ritualized manifestations, this notion of collective oscillation would clearly have an influence on Nazism. On this point, see Lucia Ruprecht, 'Ambivalent Agency. Gestural Performances of Hands in Weimar Dance and Film', in *Moving Bodies, Moving Pictures: Dance in Early German Cinema*, special issue of *Seminar*, ed. Michael Cowan and Barbara Hales, 46:4 (2010), 262.

20   F. G., 'Rhythmus und Resonanz als ökonomisches Prinzip in der Reklame' [Rhythm and Resonance as Economic Principles in Advertising], *Die Reklame* 19 (1926), 513. A similarly positive review of Pauli's lectures by Christian Kupferberg was attached to the book as a preface.

accordingly. This, above all, is a new territory, only faintly presaged in the use of verse in advertising up to now.]

Shortly after this review, Pauli himself contributed articles to *Die Reklame* on film advertisement and the calibration of auditory and visual impressions in electric advertising, and the journal reprinted his discussion of the rhythmical film from *Rhythmus und Resonanz* the following year.[21]

It hardly seems a coincidence that this 'discovery' of the power of rhythm by Germany's most prominent advertising association goes hand in hand with its discovery of filmic advertising as an object of research. Looking through the issues of *Die Reklame* from the 1920s, one will find only scattered reflections on the role of film in advertising before 1925, accompanied by the occasional advertisement by film producers themselves. The interest in film rises dramatically, however, after 1925, culminating in a lengthy special issue entitled *Der Werbefilm* [*Advertising Film*] in June 1927 with articles by Pinschewer, Kurtzig and several other practitioners and theorists, as well as the excerpt from Pauli's study on the rhythmical film. If the discovery of rhythm and film occurred simultaneously during this period, one might say, this is because advertising was itself largely being rethought as a time-based affair (involving several time-based media). This is not to say that previous spatial categories for thinking about advertising – layout, colour, font, contrast, etc. – disappeared, but they now existed alongside temporal concerns, concerns with the order, regularity and temporality of impressions received *in movement*.

This reconfiguration of advertising theory also coincided with the new push, among 1920s avant-garde filmmakers, to reconfigure film itself as an art of movement rather than story-telling. And if the two spheres could overlap in the 1920s, this is, at least in part, because both looked towards the same concept of rhythm as a means of captivating the spectators' attention. This concept informed much of the avant-garde work in advertising throughout the 1920s. This included not only Ruttmann's advertising films such as *Der Sieger* (1922), *Das Wunder* (1922) [*The Miracle*], *Das wiedergefundene Paradies* (1925) [*Paradise Regained*], *Spiel der Wellen* (1926) [*Play of the Waves*] or *Der Aufstieg* (1926) [*The Ascent*], all of which directly recycled

---

21 See Fritz Pauli, 'Das Problem des Werbefilms' [The Problem of the Advertising Film], *Die Reklame* 19 (1926), 616–17 and 'Tönende Lichtreklame' [Light Advertisements with Sound], *Die Reklame* 20 (1927), 302. The excerpt from Pauli's study on the rhythmical film was reprinted as 'Der rhythmische Film' [The Rhythmical Film], *Die Reklame* 20 (1927), 441.

forms and rhythmical movements from Ruttmann's *Opus* films, but also the work of other artists such as Richter himself. In Richter's *Zweigroschenzauber* (1929) [*Two Pence Magic*] for the Kölner Illustrierte Zeitung, for example, the act of newspaper-reading is presented not in terms of any rational transmission or reception of information but rather as an embodied and eminently pleasurable rhythmical experience: using associative montage set to a steady rhythm, the film links a series of disparate images into a rhythmical visual dance.

This reduction of content to rhythm in advertisement found perhaps its ultimate incarnation in the work of Oskar Fischinger, who went further than anyone else in synchronizing the rhythms of the soundtrack with the visual rhythms and vice versa.[22] Whereas Ruttmann's 'absolute advertising films' in fact retained a good deal of figurative images, many of Fischinger's advertising films virtually abandon recognizable objects altogether, to reduce the advertisement to the pure pleasure of audio-visual rhythms. In Fischinger's film *Kreise* (1933) [*Circles*], which consists of hundreds of animated, colourful circles moving ecstatically to the rhythms of Wagner's *Tannhäuser*, the suggestive force of the audio-visual rhythm has been so emancipated from any informational content that the product could be exchanged at random. Made in 1933 for the advertising agency *Tolirag*, Kreise originally ended with the pun 'Alle Kreise erfaßt Tolirag' [Tolirag reaches all [social] circles]. But, as Ingrid Westbrock recounts, the film was so successful with audiences that Fischinger later sold it to other companies, such as the Dutch chocolate manufacturer Van Houten, who could plug in their own sentence at the end.[23]

Kipho

One could say much more about the development of advertising film in the work of Richter, Ruttmann and Fischinger, particularly as regards the use of colour and sound. But in the space I have left in this chapter, I wish to look back at another advertising film

---

22 It is perhaps a measure of the distance between the pre- and post-war avant-garde filmmakers that this effort to synchronize image and sound would be the object of the greatest criticism in discussions of Fischinger in the 1960s and 1970s. Birgit Hein, for example, described Fischinger's famous *Komposition in Blau* (1935) [Composition in Blue] as 'eine Blauklotzrevue [...], die in der sklavischen Abhähngikeit vom Ton manchmal lächerlich wirkt' [a chorus line, which often appears ridiculous in its slavish dependence on the music'], Birgit Hein, *Film im Untergrund* [*Underground Film*] (Frankfurt am Main: Ullstein, 1971), 50.

23 See Westbrock, 75.

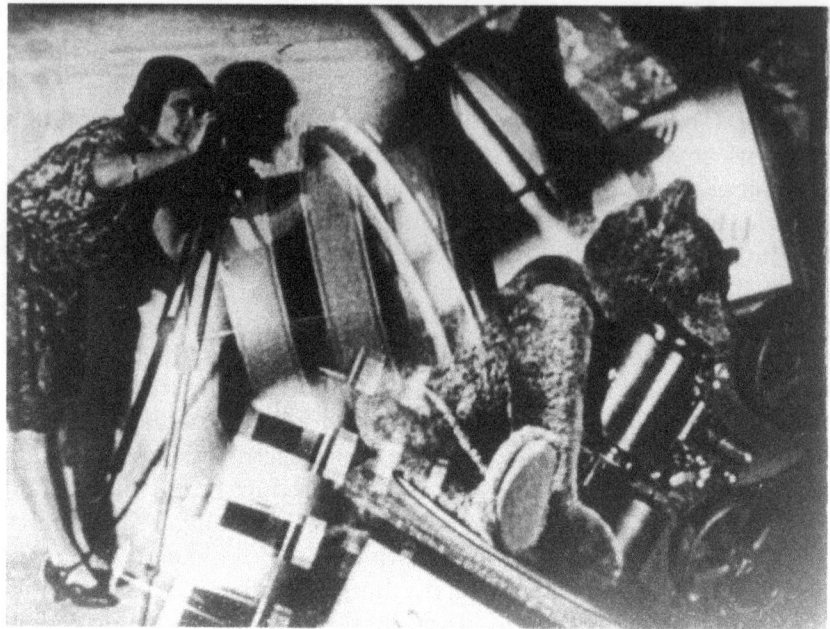

Fig 3. Still from Julius Pinschewer and Guido Seeber, Kipho *(1925), courtesy of the Deutsche Kinemathek*

which, coinciding with the industry's discovery of rhythm, very much embodied the project of rhythmical advertising as it was articulated in writings like Pauli's: namely the short film *Kipho* made by Guido Seeber for Pinschewer's advertising company in 1925 (figure 3).[24] *Kipho* has often been heralded as a landmark work in the early history of experimental cinema; Standish Lawder, for example, praised the film's dazzling array of techniques such as split-screens, superimposition, fast and slow motion, animation,

24 Seeber, who had dazzled audiences with his animation films in the 1910s and with his special effects sequences in such classics as *Der Student von Prag* (1913) [*The Student of Prague*], *Der Golem* (1914/1920) [*The Golem*] and *Lebende Buddhas* (1924) [*Living Buddhas*], was also an inventor, creating among other things the 'Seeberophon' an apparatus for projecting sound films, in 1900. Although a household name in the 1910s and 1920s, Seeber has largely fallen into obscurity today. A few notable exceptions include a catalogue published by the Stiftung Deutsche Kinemathek for the 100th anniversary of his birth under the title *Das wandernde Bild* [*The Wandering Image*] (Berlin: Elefanten-Press, 1979) and Helmut Sontag, *Sidi: eine Hommage an den Kameramann und Filmpionier Guido Seeber* [*Sidi: A Homage to the Cameraman and Film Pioneer Guido Seeber*] (Hannover: Kronsberg-Verlag, 1986). As part of the 100th anniversary series, the Deutsches Filmmuseum in Frankfurt also published facsimile prints of Seeber's writings from the 1920s.

backward movement and found footage as 'the most advanced artistic vocabulary of its day', ranking *Kipho* alongside the works of Hans Richter, Fernand Léger, Germaine Dulac or Walter Ruttmann (Lawder 180–81).[25] But to date, no film historian has engaged in any extensive way with the context in which the film was made: namely as an advertisement for the Berlin 'Kipho' exhibition of the German film and photography industries, which ran in the largest German cinemas during the weeks leading up to the exhibition from 1 to 23 September 1925 (the exhibition itself running from 23 September to 10 October).[26] As I hope to show in what follows, this context is crucial for understanding the film's formal strategies and aesthetic vocabulary, in particular its multilayered use of rhythm.

The Kipho exhibition was something of a paradoxical venture. Coming at the end of 1925, the show was designed to bolster the image of a German film industry that had, two years after the stabilization of the German Reichsmark, fallen into a deep financial crisis. Under the leadership of Erich Pommer, the Ufa studio had developed an unprofitable director-centred system which, unlike the Hollywood studio system, relied heavily relied heavily on the exportation of artistic films such as Robert Wiene's expressionist showcase *Das Cabinet des Dr. Caligari* (1920) [*The Cabinet of Dr. Caligari*] and on high-budget blockbusters such as Fritz Lang's *Nibelungen* saga (1924).[27] Against this backdrop, the Kipho exhibition represented above all an effort to drum up support among the public, investors and – especially – the government for an industry teetering on the verge of bankruptcy.[28] In the short term, organizers and contributors aimed

25 Lawder demonstrates the particular influence of Léger and Murphey's *Ballet mécanique* (1924) on *Kipho*.

26 A full programme of the Kipho exhibition was reprinted in the Berlin trade journal *Der Film*. See 'Das neueste der Woche: das Programm der Kipho' [The Latest News of the Week: The Programme of the Kipho Exhibition], *Der Film* 10:38 (1925), 27. For evidence of the Kipho film's screening in German cinemas, see 'Aus dem Programm der Kipho' [From the Programme of the Kipho Exhibition], *Lichtbildbühne* 159 (1925), 13: '[Die] Aufführung des Kipho-Werbe-Films [läuft] von Anfang September ab in den größten deutschen Film-Theatren als Werbung für die Ausstellung' [Starting at the beginning of September, the Kipho film will be playing in the largest German cinemas as an advertisement for the exhibition].

27 On this point, see Thomas Elsaesser, *Weimar Cinema and After: Germany's Historical Imaginary* (London: Routledge, 2000), 116–24.

28 Only two months after the Kipho exhibition, Ufa signed the infamous Parufamet agreement with Paramount and MGM, whereby the failing German company agreed to open up its cinemas to a greater quota of American imports in exchange for a loan of over $4,000,000. Although the move brought much-needed cash into the system, it ultimately further exacerbated Ufa's financial

to ease the recently reinstated censorship measures and reduce the so-called 'Lustbarkeitssteuer' [entertainment tax].[29] More generally, however, what they sought, in the words of E. H. Correll, director of the Phoebus film company, was 'Anerkennung' [recognition] of the importance of the German film industry as a national industry among others, one which was suffering under Weimar tax-codes and the lack of protectionist measures against foreign competition.[30] Again and again in the articles on the exhibition published in the film trade journals, one encounters sentiments such as the following from Gustav Kühn, editor of *Der Film*:

> Wenn ein Regierungsmitglied oder ein Reichstagsabgeordneter mit sehenden Augen diese Ausstellung durchwandert, dann muß er die innige Verbundenheit der deutschen Filmindustrie mit dem gesamten deutschen Wirtschaftskörper überhaupt erkennen und vornehmlich die kulturelle und wirtschaftliche Großmachtstellung, die der Film innehat.[31]

> [If members of government or parliament stroll through this exhibition with open eyes, they cannot help but recognize the deep bonds linking the German film industry to the entire German

problems. In concluding the agreement, the German company virtually lost control of its domestic cinemas and made few inroads into American markets in return.

29 These are the two most common issues mentioned in the answers to a survey organized and published by the editors of *Der Film*, in which the heads of Germany's production companies discussed their understanding of the goals and aspirations of the Kipho exhibition. See 'Unsere Kipho-Enquete' [Our Kipho Survey], *Der Film* 10:39 (1925), 38.

30 See 'Unsere Kipho-Enquete', 38. According to one writer on the Kipho, American films accounted for 97% of film production worldwide and 65% of the films shown in Germany at the time of the Kipho exhibition. See 'Die Eröffnung der "Kipho"' [The Opening of the Kipho], *Der Film* 10:39 (1925), 33.

31 Gustav Kühn, 'Wir begrüßen die Kipho' [We Welcome the Kipho], introductory statement, *Der Film* 10:39 (27. September 1925), 1. One could cite any number of similar passages. See, for example, the statement of the director of Gloria-Film in the above-mentioned survey: 'Wenn der Kapitalist aus der Ausstellung den gleichen Eindruck mit nach Hause nehmen würde, so würde er sich der Tatsache nicht mehr verschließen können, daß auch die Filmherstellung eine *Industrie* und keine Spielerei, eine auf sorgfältigster *Kalkulation* basierende und keine ins Blaue hinein kapitalvergeudende Wirtschaft ist' ('Unsere Kipho-Enquete', 40) [If business people were to take away the same impression from the exhibition, they would no longer be able to ignore the fact that film production is also an *industry* and no mere child's play. It is an economic affair, based on the most diligent *calculations*, in which we do not simply throw money around right and left].

economy and, in particular, the great cultural and economic power that film can wield.]

In this spirit, the exhibition, which attracted over 100,000 visitors during its week-long run, sought to showcase all branches of the film industry, with displays ranging from production companies such as Ufa to manufacturers of celluloid, lights and projectors – as well as exhibitions on the history and economics of the German film industry, and even a model studio where audiences could watch directors and stars at work.[32] In a sign of the organizers' patriotic aims, the exhibition also featured rotating screenings of recent German blockbusters as well as other attractions such as the sensational display of the giant dragon from Fritz Lang's *Nibelungen* film. Moreover, the exhibition was followed in November by the 'Deutsche Filmwoche' [German Film Week], in which German cinemas were asked to play only German films for an entire week.[33]

Pinschewer, who had founded the Vaterländischer Filmvertrieb [Patriotic Film Company] for the production of propaganda films during the WWII, was no stranger to patriotic causes, and the *Kipho* film largely reflected the exhibitors' aims.[34] In a series of rotating visual collages, the film depicts self-reflexively the making of a film; in the process, it offers what Seeber would later describe as a 'Querschnitt' [cross-section] of the film industry, showcasing in particular many of the very industry domains on display at the Kipho exhibition, such as lighting, sets, make-up and film-developing.[35] Moreover, the film

---

32 For a more detailed account of the displays at the Kipho exhibition, see E. U, 'Kunst und Geschäftsregisseure' [Artistic and Entrepreneurial Directors], *Der Kinematograph* 971 (1925), 23–24; Aros, 'Die Woche der Kipho' [The Kipho Week], *Kinematograph* 971 (1925), 1–2; 'Quer durch die "Kipho"' [A Look Through the Kipho]', *Der Film* 10:40 (1925), 23. For a detailed list of all exhibitors at the exhibition, see 'Was wird aus der Kipho?' [What Will Become of the Kipho?] *Der Kinematograph* 952 (1925), 16.

33 See 'Die Kundgebung des deutschen Films' [The Rally for German Film]. *Der Film* 10:38 (1925), 28; Albert Schneider, 'Der deutsche Film und die Öffentlichkeit' [German Film and the Public], *Der Film* 10:39 (1925), 41

34 See Goergen, 'Julius Pinschewer'; André Amsler, '*Wer dem Werbefilm verfällt, ist verloren für die Welt.' Das Werk von Julius Pinschewer 1883–1961* [*Whoever succumbs to the Advertisement Film is Lost to the World*] (Zürich: Chronos Verlag, 1997), 9–14.

35 Guido Seeber, *Der Trickfilm in seinen grundsätzlichen Möglichkeiten* [*The Trick Film in its Fundamental Possibilities*], reprint (Frankfurt am Main: Deutsches Filmmuseum, 1979), 244. Indeed, the film's self-reflexive dimension reproduced one of the principles of the exhibition. As one journalist described it, the model film studios offered visitors precisely such a 'cross-section' through the process

can be read specifically as a kind of 'defence and illustration' of the *German* film industry. *Kipho* is perhaps most famous today for its notably early use of 'found footage' from narrative films, particularly the closing sequence, in which we see a hand literally transform the famous sentence from Wiene's *Caligari* 'Du musst Caligari werden' [You must become Caligari] before our eyes into an advertisement for the exhibition: 'Du musst zur Kipho!' [You must go to the Kipho] (figures 4a and b). But it can hardly be by chance that the footage cited in *Kipho* derives almost exclusively from popular and highly acclaimed German films such as *Caligari*, F. W. Murnau's *Der letzte Mann* (1924) [*The Last Laugh*] and even Prager's *Wege zu Kraft und Schönheit*. Indeed, these were largely the same films screened throughout the exhibition in the 4000-seat cinema.[36]

If the depiction of film production in Seeber and Pinschewer's advertisement film is meant to underscore the productivity of the German film industry generally, it does so, as I will show below, through its formal use of rhythm. As Seeber would later explain in his book *Der Trickfilm in seinen grundsätzlichen Möglichkeiten* (1927) [*The Trick Film in its Fundamental Possibilities*], *Kipho* is designed formally as a kind of rhythmically evolving collage achieved entirely in-camera rather than through the kind of post-production editing employed by Abel Gance; developing the masking technique he first used for Doppelgänger films such as *Der Student von Prag* (1913) [*The Student of Prague*], Seeber divided the screen into several visual fields – painstakingly shot one at a time – in which images and a black screen alternate in rhythms measured out by the number of camera cranks (241–51) (figure 5). The result is a highly coordinated system

of film production: 'Es werden Regisseure, Architekten, Operateure und der ganze Stab vor den Augen des Publikums arbeiten, dem dann [...] klar werden wird, was eigentlich zur Herstellung eines Filmes alles nötig ist. [...] Das Publikum wird dann verstehen, daß es nicht Spiel ist, sondern harte und für viele unerträgliche Arbeit, welche die höchsten Ansprüche an Leistungsfähigkeit und Ausdauer stellt'. [Directors, set designers, camera operators and the entire film crew go to work right in front of visitors, who now perceive clearly how much is involved in the production of a film. Visitors now understand that this is no game but hard and often intolerable work, which demands the utmost productivity and perserverance]. 'Das moderne Filmatelier' [The Modern Film Studio], *Der Film* 10:39 (1925), 52.

36 See 'Quer durch die Kipho', 23: 'Die Spitzenleistungen deutscher Produktion, u. a. "Die Nibelungen", "Der letzte Mann", "Wege zu Kraft und Schönheit", "Liebe und Trompetenblasen," "Blitzzug der Liebe" usw. werden hier allabendlich geboten' [Top-rate German productions, such as *The Nibelungen, The Last Laugh, Paths to Strength and Beauty, Love and Trumpets, Lightning Love* and others, are shown here every evening].

 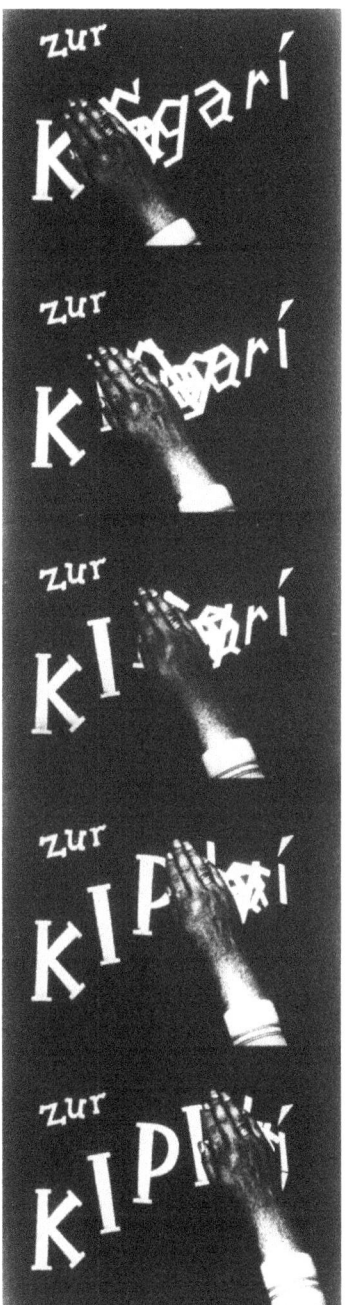

Fig 4a & b. Stills from Kipho *(1925), courtesy of the Deutsche Kinemathek*

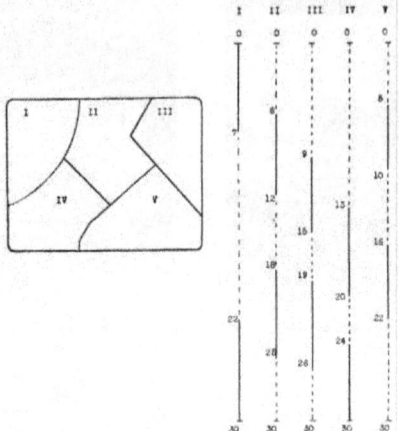

Fig 5. Guido Seeber, chart illustrating in-camera montage technique, from Der Trickfilm in seinen grundsätzlichen Möglichkeiten *(1927)*

of visual counterpoint, in which multiple fields of images alternate at precise rhythmical intervals.

Such a system can be read in purely formalist terms, and Seeber himself linked his rhythmical experiments in *Kipho* to the new trend in 'absolute' filmmaking represented by Léger, René Clair and Ruttmann, calling in particular for filmmakers to trade in narrative scripts for rhythmical 'Partituren' [scores] (241, 244). Like many experimental filmmakers and critics in the 1920s, moreover, Seeber seems to conceive this opposition to narrative cinema historically in terms of a return to the cinema's origins as a medium of visual attractions.[37] Such a realignment of cinema with attractions is suggested, in particular, by a plethora of images of early motion-picture technology – much of which could also be seen in a model of an 'Urkino' [primitive cinema] constructed by Seeber for the exhibition – including chronophotographic sequences, zoetropes, praxinoscopes and magic lanterns (figure 6).[38] Such optical toys, all shown spinning in frenetic rotation, suggest a vision of cinema as an

[37] On the avant-garde's romanticization of early (non-narrative) cinema, see of course Tom Gunning, 'The Cinema of Attractions: Early Film, its Spectator and the Avant-garde', in *Early Cinema: Space, Frame, Narrative*, ed. Thomas Elsaesser (London: BFI, 1989), 56–62. Such nostalgia for early cinema was alive and well in 1920s Germany. See for example Carlo Mierendorff, *Hätte ich das Kino! [If I Only Had the Cinema!]* (Berlin: Erich Reiß, 1920).

[38] For a detailed description of Seeber's display, see especially 'Bericht von der "Kipho"', *Lichtbildbühne* 189 (1925), 12–13.

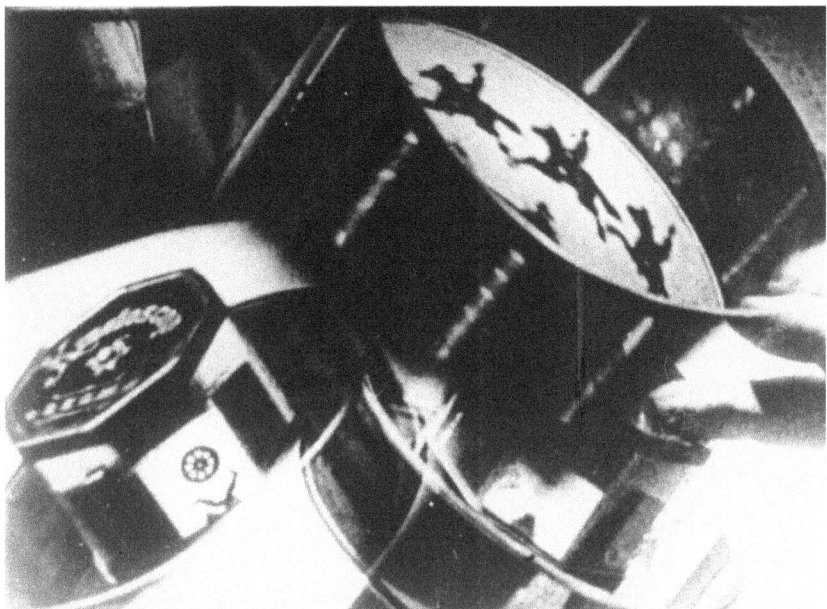

Fig 6. Still from Kipho *(1925), courtesy of the Deutsche Kinemathek*

'art of motion' rather than an art of story-telling; more specifically, they establish a pattern of *circular* motion that will be echoed through the film in the many paradigmatic images of the film industry as a system of spinning camera-cranks, projection gears and film reels (figure 7). As André Gaudreault and Nicolas Dulac have pointed out, circular motion stood at the heart of early attractions cinema and constituted its specific, machinic temporality in opposition to the linear unfolding of narrative.[39] Like other avant-garde works such as Léger's *Ballet mécanique* (1924), with its famous loop of the washing woman endlessly climbing the stairs, *Kipho* is structured around a series of mechanical loops reminiscent of the temporal structure of optical toys and early cinema. Indeed, this project is encapsulated paradigmatically in the image of a generic 'Drehbuch' [film script] now rotating on its axis rather than advancing along a narrative trajectory. For speakers of German, Seeber's visual pun would have

---

39 See Nicolas Dulac and André Gaudreault, 'Circularity and Repetition at the Heart of the Attraction: Optical Toys and the Emergence of a New Cultural Series', in Wanda Strauven (ed.), *The Cinema of Attractions Reloaded* (Amsterdam: Amsterdam University Press, 2006), 227–44: 'If, as Paul Ricœur remarks, "time becomes human to the extent that it is articulated through a narrative mode", the temporality of optical toys is closer to that of the machine; it is more mechanical than anything else' (228).

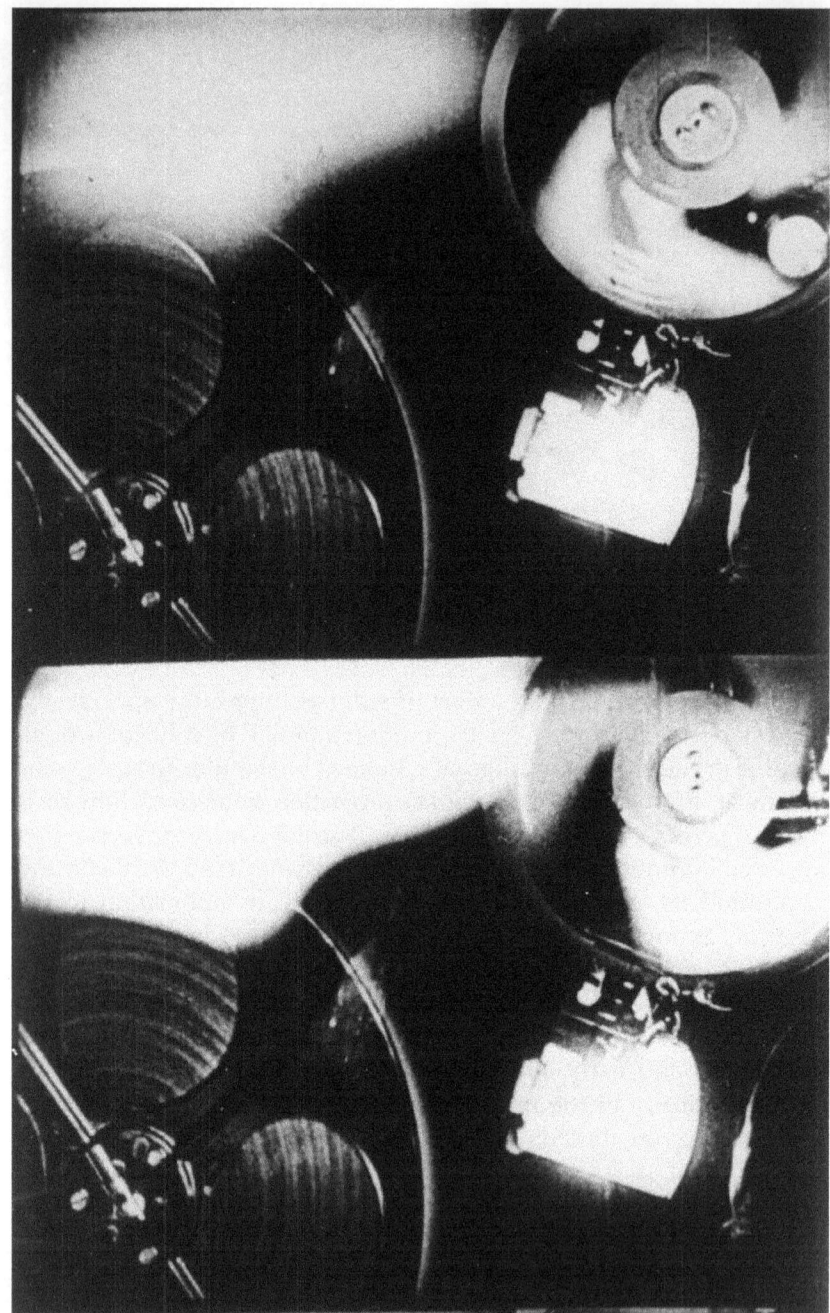

Fig 7. Still from Kipho (1925), courtesy of the Deutsche Kinemathek

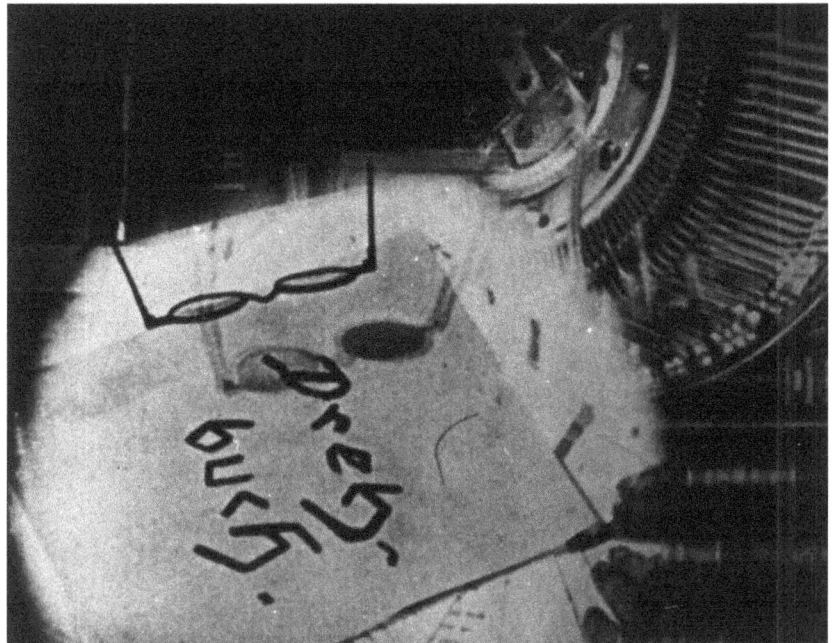

Fig 8. Still from Kipho *(1925), courtesy of the Deutsche Kinemathek*

been unmistakable, the German term 'drehen' signifying both to 'rotate' and to 'make a film' [einen film drehen] (figure 8).

But if the privileging of circular motion in *Kipho* recalls early cinema, it also recalls the temporality of machinic rhythms generally. As we have seen, Bücher saw continuous rotation as the central criterion differentiating the traditional rhythms of labour – dictated as they were by the alternation of periods of intensity with periods of rest – from machinic rhythms, which eliminated the 'idle backstroke' [toten Rückgang] of human limbs.[40] More than staging the production of a film, *Kipho* stages, in miniature, precisely this narrative of rhythm and its transformation in the industrial age. Early in the film, we see a number of images of hands engaged in distinct back-and-forth movements as they perform various tasks such as hammering, sawing or wiping in the preparation of the film sets. But these working bodies are soon absorbed into the frenetic spinning of the filmic apparatus via the hand operating the camera crank (figure 9). Through this progression from back-and-forth to circular movement, *Kipho* recalls Bücher's diagnosis of modernity, even as it playfully reverses Bücher's evaluation. Where Bücher lamented the

40 See my discussion of Bücher in chapter 1, pp. 22–29

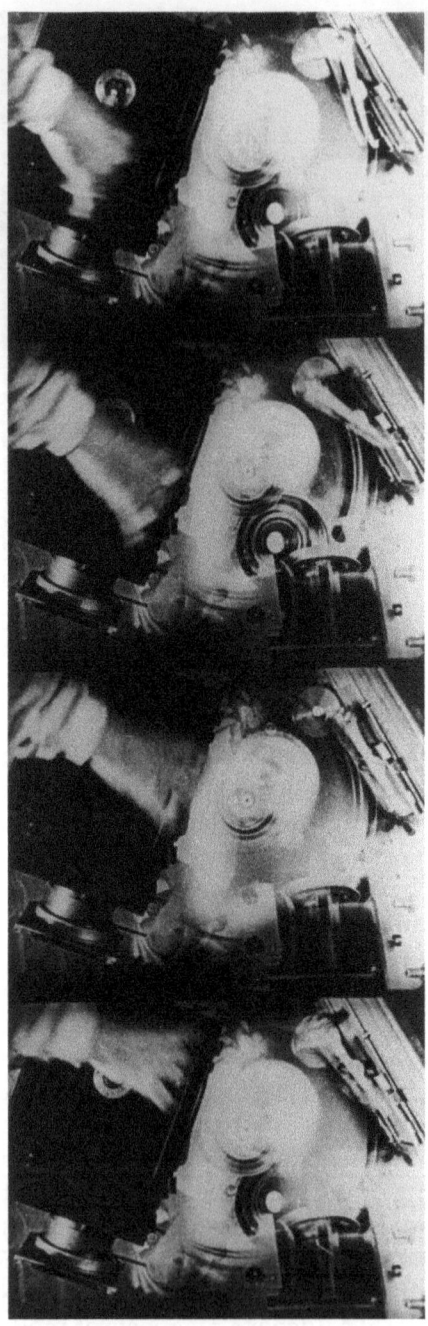

Fig 9. Still from Kipho *(1925), courtesy of the Deutsche Kinemathek*

Technology's Pulse

Fig 10a & b. Stills from Kipho *(1925), courtesy of the Deutsche Kinemathek*

loss of the poetry of work, *Kipho* calls for a new poetry of machines, a mechanized poetry dictated by the crank of the film-camera.

Indeed, this relation describes not only the film's treatment of working bodies but also its very formal operations as a compilation film, which continually lifts the footage it borrows out of its original diegetic context to absorb it into the film's mechanical loops. A case in point can be seen in Seeber's adaptation of a shot of the Wigman dancers from the rhythmical gymnastics section of Prager's *Wege zu Kraft und Schönheit*. As we saw above, Prager's film introduced this section with a citation from Klages, and the Wigman dancers were meant to illustrate the reintroduction of natural rhythms into a mechanized epoch. But in appropriating the footage, Seeber turns this argument on its head, now refashioning the circle of dancers into one circular mechanical loop among others. Like the marching feet of soldiers or the repetitive jump shown on the zoetrope, Wigman's dancers are absorbed by Pinschewer's film into an endless array of spinning gears, cranks and film rolls (figures 10 a and b).

If this gesture of mechanizing natural rhythms recalls Hans Richter's view of film as a medium for submitting the force of rhythm to human control, it also depicts the filmic medium as part of a broader logic of industrial technology. In this way, the film looks forward to such prominent avant-garde works as Ruttmann's *Berlin* film or Dziga Vertov's *Chelovek s kinoapparatom* (1929) [*Man with a Movie Camera*], which similarly displayed the cutters, projectionists and cameramen contributing to film production as part of a vast and coordinated industrial apparatus (Vertov employs many of the same comparisons between the camera crank and the rotation of machinery). More importantly, this portrayal of film as a productive industrial apparatus conformed to the broader objective of the Kipho exhibition, which was to promote the film industry *as* a national industry rather than an artform. As one reporter described it in a review of the exhibition for the most prominent industry journal *Der Kinematograph*:

> Nichts wird die Zwiespältigkeit des kinematographischen Problems besser beweisen als die Kipho, die zum ersten Mal die Entwicklung des Lichtspiels an Hand historischen Materials erkennen läßt. [...] Diese Krise [der Filmindustrie] rührt letzen Endes daher, daß das industrielle Problem des Filmes vor der Kunst vergessen wurde; der Wille zur Kunst hat die finanziellen Möglichkeiten untergraben! [...] Die Pioniere und die ersten Geschäftsleute der Kinematographie haben, das beweist die Kipho, den Film von der industriellen Seite angepackt; die Kunst kam für sie erst in zweiter Linie.[41]
> [Nothing will demonstrate the conflicting aspects of the cinematic problem better than the Kipho exhibition which for the first time shows us the development of the cinema by means of historical material. [...] The crisis of the film industry stems, in the last analysis, from the fact that the industrial side of film has been forgotten underneath a preoccupation with art; the will to art has undercut the cinema's financial possibilities. [...] The Kipho exhibition demonstrates that the pioneers and first entrepreneurs of the cinema saw it as an industrial affair; for them art was only a secondary consideration.]

In a thinly veiled critique of the Pommer system, this observer sees the real potential of the cinema not in art but rather in financial profit. From this perspective, the effort to return to film's origins was not simply an aesthetic gesture but also, and above all, a way of articulating a vision of the cinema's calling: that of a national industry. Against this backdrop, the machinic rhythms of the *Kipho* film, with its coordinated system of cranks, reels and gears, should be seen as an effort to reimagine the German cinema as a productive industrial apparatus, which absorbs the hand of the artist into its productive

---

41 E. U., 'Kunst und Geschäftsregisseure', 23. The writer goes on to call for an end to the cultivation of artistic films designed for export and the encouragement of profit-minded directors ('Geschäftsregisseure') in the American style.

resonance. Through his complex visual collages, Seeber sought to refashion a wasteful industry into the very image of industrial productivity, an apparatus as efficient as a Fordist factory.

But it would be a mistake to see Seeber's cultivation of machinic rhythms only as a representational strategy; for that rhythm was also meant to fulfil a specific function with respect to the film's status as an *advertising film*. Indeed, it is perhaps no coincidence that Fritz Pauli himself used stills of various mechanical loops from the *Kipho* film to illustrate his article 'Das Problem des Werbefilms' [The Problem of the Advertisement Film] published in *Die Reklame* in 1926.[42] For in the many images of spinning camera cranks, reels and platters, *Kipho* offered a perfect image of Pauli's theory of rhythmical spectatorship. Just as these spinning flywheels absorb the working bodies shown *in* the film into their circular motion, so they were also meant to absorb the spectators *of* the film, via the eye and the nervous system, into their frequency, propelling them into the Kipho exhibition.

Such a performative effect of rhythmical advertising finds its most salient expression, in the film, in the much celebrated transformation of the footage from *Caligari*. Whereas in Wiene's film the original injunction 'Du musst Caligari werden' emanated from an ancient book to overcome the psychiatrist (compelling him to imitate the 17th-century charlatan Caligari), Seeber's transformed sentence, 'Du musst zur Kipho!', now emanates from the film itself to command spectators into the Kipho exhibition. As such, it not only demonstrates the 'transformative power of montage' in found-footage films,[43] but also encapsulates the very compulsory-hypnotic power – the 'Resonanzzwang' – that Pauli attributed to rhythmical advertising, and indeed the influence that the *Kipho* film itself was supposed to exert over spectators' captivated attention.

Significantly, the famous sentence 'Du musst Caligari werden' had already formed the centrepiece of a well-known advertising campaign: in the weeks preceding the premiere of *Das Cabinet des Dr. Caligari* in February 1920, hundreds of posters containing the still enigmatic injunction appeared in cinema journals and in the public spaces of Berlin, positioning viewers as the objects of the same hypnotic command that befalls Wiene's psychiatrist (figure 11). As Stephan Andriopoulos has suggested, this hypnotic injunction in *Caligari* can largely be read as a metaphor for the filmic medium itself in its more sinister incarnations in the early twentieth-

---

42 See Pauli, 'Das Problem des Werbefilms', 616.

43 William C. Wees, *Recycled Images. The Art and Politics of Found Footage Films* (New York: Anthology Film Archives, 1993), 13–14.

Fig 11. Poster for Das Cabinet des Doktor Caligari, *from* Der Kinematograph *(1920)*

Fig 12. Poster for Kipho *exhibition, from* Der Film *(August 1925)*

century imagination: throughout the 1910s, neurologists and child psychologists had warned of the dangerous suggestive influence of the cinema over youthful or uneducated spectators, who – not unlike Wiene's psychiatrist or the somnambulist Cesare – might be compelled to commit the kinds of violent crimes suggested to them by popular crime films.[44] Through its poster campaign, *Caligari* thus sought to titillate potential viewers with the pleasures and dangers of filmic regression.

In citing the Caligari injunction, Pinschewer and Seeber clearly sought to perform a similar positioning of viewers as the objects of a hypnotic media effect; indeed, like the makers of *Caligari*, they cited the sentence not only in the ending of *Kipho*, but also in print advertisements placed in the pages of journals such as *Der Kinematograph* and *Der Film* (figure 12) But if *Kipho* takes over the association of film and hypnosis from *Caligari*, it turns the value of that hypnosis on its head. In *Kipho*, far from representing an occult or fantastic force, hypnosis now appears as *a process entirely amenable to rational control* and designed to induce the maximum efficiency of consumer attention. Rather than titillating spectators with the pleasures of psychic regression, *Kipho* now promises to make spectators into productive consumers. In so doing, the film depicts the German film industry as an eminently Fordist system, one which treats consumption as part of the productive cycle and leisure as an extension of work.[45] In Pauli's words, 'der Angebotsempfänger [...] [wird] selbst zu einem Teil des Schwingsystems' (Pauli, *Rhythmus und Resonanz*, 22) [The consumer becomes part of the oscillating system]. Visualized in miniature in the spinning loops that dominate the film, such a circular logic is specifically suggested by the titles at the end of the film; unfurling from an imaginary film reel, they promise to insert exhibition goers into the film industry itself by

---

44 See Stefan Andriopoulos, *Possessed: Hypnotic Crimes, Corporate Fiction and the Invention of the Cinema*, trans. by Peter Jensen and Stefan Andriopoulos (Chicago: University of Chicago Press, 2008), 91–128.

45 Ford famously believed that higher wages would make workers contribute more productively to the welfare of national business through increased consumption. As he described it in his autobiography, *My Life and Work* (1923): 'If we can distribute high wages, then that money is going to be spent and it will serve to make storekeepers and distributors and manufacturers and workers in other lines more prosperous and their prosperity will be reflected in our sales. Country-wide high wages spell country-wide prosperity'. Henry Ford, *My Life and Work* (London: William Heinemann, 1923) 124–25. Ford's autobiography was translated into German in 1923 under the title *Mein Leben und Werk*, and the first German Ford factory was opened in 1925 in Berlin.

means of sample film-shots, beauty and screen aptitude tests and a make-up contest (all interactive attractions that did indeed form a key part of the exhibition).[46] Lifting *Caligari's* hypnotic injunction from its context in Germany's most famous expressionist film, then, *Kipho* refashions that hypnosis into the lynchpin of a Fordist feedback loop, where spectatorship and consumption are treated as no less vital components of the rhythms of work (more specifically of the film industry) than the hand-movements on the conveyer belt or the camera-crank.

Media in Motion

If the thematization of a rationalized hypnosis via rhythm in *Kipho* specifically recalls Pauli's theory of rhythmical advertising, it also forms part of a general reflection on the broader transformations of media and aesthetics in the industrial age. In the final section of this chapter, I want to reconsider the broader implications of *Kipho's* rhythmical aesthetic for the history of mass media in the early twentieth century. In showcasing various components of the film industry, *Kipho* repeatedly presents the celluloid medium as one of a number of mechanized mass media, including not only photography but also the audio media of phonograph and telephone, as well as the ubiquitous typewriter. All these media appear to be defined less in terms of their capacity for transmitting meaning than in terms of their psychic effects on receivers. One can see this emphasis most specifically in the film's treatment of writing. The first thematization of writing comes in the form of a collage, in which a set of hands performing what appear to be graphology tests can be seen next to a set of hands operating a typewriter at a furious tempo, suggesting a mechanization of writing that will be repeated in the many images of typists in Ruttmann's *Berlin: die Sinfonie der Großstadt* and Vertov's *Man With a Movie Camera* (Figure 13).[47] After this shot, the film increasingly

---

46 As one writer for the *Lichtbildbühne* explained, during the first days of the exhibition, 30 people were selected to appear in short film recordings. The latter were then screened before exhibition audiences, who voted on the contestants' beauty and screen aptitude. See 'Aus dem Programm der Kipho', 13. Such contests offer a quite literal example of Benjamin's observation that film had turned audiences into 'experts', authorized to evaluate the spectacle before them. See Benjamin, 'Das Kunstwerk im Zeitalter seiner technischen Reproduzierbarket', 154–60.

47 The handwriting, consisting mostly of wavy lines, specifically recalls Klages's discussion of rhythmical handwriting in his *Ausdrucksbewegung und*

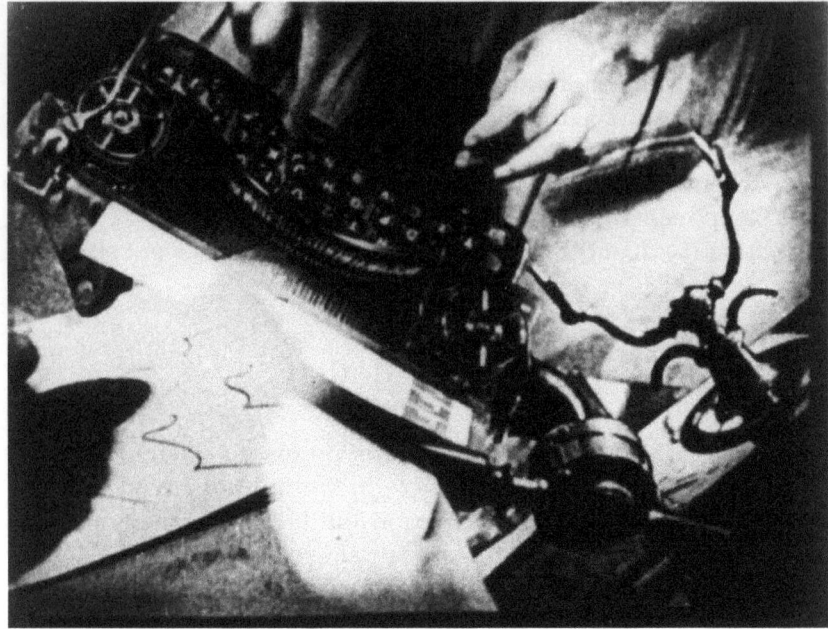

Fig 13. Still from Kipho *(1925), courtesy of the Deutsche Kinemathek*

features images of typographical script set into mechanical rhythms, a motif culminating in the animated citation from *Caligari*. Finally, the film ends with a set of animated texts in superimposition; as messages unwind on an imaginary film reel in the foreground, a background loop continues to rotate the words 'Kino', 'Photo' and 'Kipho' in mechanical succession. If this background text points to a dynamization of photography signalled by the neologism 'Kipho', it also demonstrates, in its very form, a dynamization of texts and titles, which appear throughout *Kipho* in rhythmical blinks, dances and loops on the screen.

Here, too, the rhythmization of words and letters in *Kipho* finds a counterpart in Pauli's arguments about textuality in advertising. For Pauli, the advertisement text was anything but a transparent medium serving to transmit information rationally; rather, cut into isolated

Gestaltungskraft where – in a foreshadowing of the wave discussion in *Vom Wesen des Rhythmus* – he posited wavy, curved lines as one of the distinguishing features of a rhythmical handwriting. In his description of Nietzsche, for example, Klages explains: 'Trotz größter Leserlichkeit hat sie [...] einen perlenden Rhythmus, der die Schärfen zahlreicher Winkel spielend einverleibt' (Klages, *Ausdrucksbewegung*, 141) [Despite its high degree of legibility, Nietzsche's handwriting possesses [...] a sprightly rhythm that playfully integrates the hard edges of numerous angles].

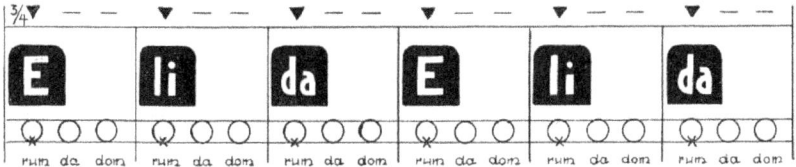

Fig 14. Sketch for a traffic advertisement (for Elida cosmetics), from Fritz Pauli, Rhythmus und Resonanz als ökonomisches Prinzip in der Reklame (1926)

syllables and introduced at rhythmical intervals, the text took on a performative function, serving to capture the consumer's attention. Pauli proposed all sorts of ways to place text into rhythmical motion, such as kinetic illuminated advertisements, animated films and even coordinated traffic advertisements in which billboards containing isolated syllables would be placed at rhythmical intervals along traffic routes. The illustration for one such advertisement shows how to dissolve the brand name Elida (a German cosmetics producer) into isolated syllables whose timed appearance could then be coordinated with the regular rattling of the rolling train to form a rhythm in 3/4 time ('rum da dom, rum da dom', etc.) (Pauli 21) (figure 14). Although it is perhaps fortuitous that Pauli's example of the regular rattling of the train recalls Klages's theorization of rhythm and *Takt*, the differences between the two treatments are nonetheless instructive: where Klages sought at all costs to overcome the segmenting divisions produced by the acoustic bumping and focus on the continuous movement of the train, Pauli takes his cue precisely from this acoustic segmentation to divide words, like products in a Fordist factory, into their constituent syllables. In proposing such a dissolution of text into isolated fragments, Pauli was in fact only codifying advertising practices already heavily in use by the mid-1920s; Fritz Giese, for example, saw electric advertising as one of the prime examples of the machinic rhythms of the modern metropolis: 'Der Text, das Bild, die Reklame wird rhythmisch zerlegt geboten, nicht auf einmal gegeben. Stück um Stück, wie im Trickfilm, erscheint das Ganze aus Teilen, aber diese Teile erfassen wir besser, wenn die Abfolge in gleichen Phasen verläuft' (Giese, *Girlkultur*, 23) [The text, the image, the advertisement are not presented all at once, but rhythmically dissected. Bit by bit, the whole is created out of parts as in an animated film, but we can grasp these parts better if their succession proceeds at equal intervals].

For readers of Friedrich Kittler, such a 'dissection' of text into a series of fragmentary syllables will surely recall the new paradigm of textuality ca. 1900, where the generation of random syllables in psychological performance tests via tachistoscopes and mnemometers had displaced the model of reading as an internal hermeneutic process.[48] In the 1920s, this type of performance test found its logical application in the realm of advertising and advertising psychology.[49] Walter Benjamin, for one, recognized the transformation of textuality implied by the rise of advertising when he remarked, in *Einbahnstrasse* (1928) [*One Way Street*]:

> Die Schrift, die im gedruckten Buch ein Asyl gefunden hatte, [...] wird unerbittlich von Reklamen auf die Strasse hinausgezerrt [...]. Ehe der Zeitgenosse dazu kommt, ein Buch aufzuschlagen, ist über seine Augen ein so dichtes Gestöber von wandelbaren, farbigen, streitenden Lettern niedergegangen, dass die Chancen seines Eindringens in die archaische Stille des Buches gering geworden sind.[50]
>
> [Writing, which had found refuge in the printed book [...], is now dragged mercilessly out into the street by advertisements. [...] Before a contemporary individual even opens a book, his eyes have been exposed to such a blizzard of changeable, colourful and conflicting letters that he has very little chance of penetrating the book's archaic stillness.]

As Benjamin's description of the blizzard of moving letters suggests, the fragmentation of words in advertising went a step beyond the nineteenth-century memory tests discussed by Kittler in the pervasiveness of the kinetic element. In this observation, moreover, Benjamin was hardly alone; much of Benjamin's interest in advertising was stimulated by the constructivist phase of the Bauhaus represented especially by László Moholy-Nagy.[51] The latter's typographical, or

---

48   See Kittler, *Aufschreibesysteme*, 219 [*Discourse Networks* 214]: 'Der Sieg der Psychophysik ist ein Paradigmenwechsel. Statt der klassischen Frage, was Leute können könnten, wenn sie gebildet und liebevoll genug gebildet würden, taucht das Rätsel auf, was sie immer schon können, wenn Automatismen nur einzeln und gründlich getestet werden' [The victory of psychophysics is a paradigm shift. Instead of the classical question of what people would be capable of if they were adequately and affectionately 'cultivated', one asks what people have always been capable of when autonomic functions are individually and thoroughly tested]. Tachistiscopes and mnemometers are devices for psychological testing via the controlled presentation of stimuli.

49   See Frederic J. Schwarz, 'The Eye of the Expert: Walter Benjamin and the Avant Garde', *Art History* 24:3 (2001), 401–44.

50   Walter Benjamin, *Einbahnstrasse* (1928) (Frankfurt am Main: Suhrkamp, 1955), 141–42.

51   On the connection between Benjamin and Moholy-Nagy, see Schwarz, 'The Eye of the Expert', 406–08.

'typophoto', experiments in his film-sketch *Dynamik der Großstadt* [*Dynamics of the City*], for example, attempted to reproduce the new conditions of reading on the commercial street – above all the rapid intake of signs and letters in movement – in book form. In his book *Malerei, Fotografie, Film* (1927) [*Painting, Photography, Film*], Moholy-Nagy described his typophoto film sketch specifically as an effort to undo the linearity of typography and approximate to the rhythmical and simultaneous temporality of film and advertising: 'Jede Zeit hat ihre eigene optische Einstellung. Unsere Zeit: die des Films, der Lichtreklame, der Simultanität sinnlich wahrnehmbarer Ereignisse. Sie hat für uns eine neue, sich ständig weiter entwickelnde Schaffensbasis auch in der Typografie hervorgebracht' [Each era has its own unique optical configuration. The optical configuration of our era is that of film, electric advertisements and the simultaneity of perceptible phenomena. This configuration has given us a new basis for artistic production in the realm of typography as well].[52] Moholy-Nagy's mention of electric light advertisement here is not fortuitous; as Frederic J. Schwarz has suggested, in their effort to dynamize typography and textuality, the artists at the Bauhaus took commercial advertising as their central model and offered courses in advertising psychology and psychotechnics.[53]

With its dancing and blinking letters, *Kipho* can be read, among other things, as an experiment in the dynamization of typography similar to those of Mohology-Nagy. In this sense, Pinschewer and Seeber might have found yet another reason to turn to the citation from *Caligari*. For the text of that hypnotic injunction was itself already characterized precisely by its dynamic presentation, writing itself in animated letters before the protagonist's captivated gaze. In *Kipho*, this kinetic presentation now takes on a specifically rhythmical quality when the Caligari injunction is dissected into individual words that blink across the screen.

Indeed, *all* the titles shown in *Kipho* appear in rhythmical form, flashing, dancing or unwinding before spectators' eyes. Seeber

---

52 László Moholy-Nagy, *Malerei, Fotografie, Film,* Neue Bauhausbücher (Berlin: Gebr. Mann, 1986), 37. Moholy-Nagy's description of modernity's 'optical configuration' as characterized by simultaneity once again links his experiments to the notion of the cross-section film and the aesthetics of simultaneity. Seeber, in fact, knew Moholy-Nagy's work well and described his *Dynamik der Großstadt* as a model script for the non-linear, 'cross-section' aesthetics he sought to develop in films like *Kipho* (Seeber, *Der Trickfilm,* 244).

53 See Schwarz, 414–15. When he left the Bauhaus, Moholy-Nagy himself opened a private practice as a designer of advertising posters and books (Schwarz 428, 430).

clearly recognized the links between such a dynamization of text in film and electric advertising, as he himself compared the two in a lengthy discussion of methods for creating animated titles and text in *Der Trickfilm*.[54] In this context, Seeber mentions not only the 'Wanderschrift' [scrolling text] used in electric light advertisements, but also self-writing texts (of the type used in *Caligari*), texts that grow and shrink, and one type of animated text specifically used for the closing title showing the word 'Kipho' in the *Kipho* film:

> Man kann eine große Reihe von Hilfsmitteln dazu verwenden, Titel wirkungsvoll entstehen zu lassen. Wir weisen z.B. darauf hin, daß man eine Titelzeile der Länge nach in der Mitte durchgeschnitten und zunächst kurze Zeit beide Hälften gegenläufig bewegt hat, so daß der Zuschauer im ersten Augenblick nicht in der Lage ist, die Buchstaben zu entziffern. Erst bei Stillstand und richtiger Gegenüberstellung jeder der beiden Schriftzeilen gelingt es dem Zuschauer, den Text zu lesen. (171)

> [One can employ a wide array of means to make titles appear in a striking manner. We can, for example, point to an instance in which a title was cut in half lengthwise and both halves made to move back and forth in opposite directions for a short time, so that at first the spectators could not make out the letters. Only after the two halves of the text come to a standstill in the correct positioning with respect to one another is the spectator able to read the text.]

In the context of this dynamization of typography, the paradigmatic image of the spinning 'Drehbuch' in *Kipho* also acquires another level of meaning. Framed between a stack of books and more typewriters in furious movement, the spinning book connotes not only a desire to revive pre-narrative cinema, but also an argument about the filmic medium in relation to the book. Far from reproducing the hermeneutic operations of silent reading, the cinema would represent the culmination of a process entailing the kineticization of communications media already under way in the early twentieth century. As such, the film suggests, cinema would represent the paradigm of media development in an era in which media are understood not in terms of their capacity to facilitate internalized meaning, but in terms of their performative effects on viewers' attention. Like the letters in the tachistoscope, Seeber wanted *all* the images in *Kipho* to exist at the edge of comprehensibility, attaining what he described as 'die Grenze der kurzen Zeit der Sichtbarkeit, innerhalb der das Auge das Gezeigte noch identifizieren und erfassen

---

54 See Seeber 162–78.

kann' (248) [the shortest possible interval of visibility during which the eye can still identify and grasp the content presented].

The media-theoretical argument contained in *Kipho* also overlaps with a new rationalized understanding of aesthetics in the mid-1920s, which helped to make the very phenomenon of the 'absolute advertising film' possible. As Frederic Schwarz has argued, the preoccupation with advertising and typography among the avant-garde underlay an effort to redefine the artist as a professional expert in matters of graphic layout at a time of increasing competition from mass advertising.[55] As such, the engagement of artists with advertising formed part of a wider reconfiguration of aesthetics in the age of New Objectivity, a move away from models of genius and artistic inspiration toward an image of the artist as technical expert. While this process finds perhaps its best-known expression in the work of constructivist artists and the Bauhaus, it also can also be clearly seen in the realm of film advertisement, where artists such as Ruttmann, Reiniger and Seeber saw no contradiction in placing abstract film in the service of advertising psychology.[56]

Against the backdrop of the artist's transformation into an expert in matters of graphic design and presentation, beauty was understood not as something ineffable, and certainly not as an autonomous realm free of material interests, but rather as the result of entirely rational calculations. As Pauli described it, in the age of consumerism, the beauty of artistic creation was being displaced by a new form of beauty: the beauty of speed to be sure, but above all the beauty of precise calculations:

> *Die Kunst hört eben dort auf, wo die Gesetzmäßigkeit beginnt.* Beide Wege führen zur Schönheit oder, was dasselbe bedeutet, zur vollendeten Zweckmäßigkeit. Nur daß der Weg über die Kunst der tausend Stimmungen und Imponderabilien der unterworfene, daher unzuverlässigere ist, während der gesetzmäßige Weg sicher zum erstrebten Ziel führt. Dieser Weg ist deshalb der kürzeste und somit rationellste. (Pauli, *Rhythmus und Resonanz*, 29)

55   See also Ward, *Weimar Surfaces*, 136–40.

56   For his part, Seeber seems not to have sensed the slightest contradiction in the use of abstract film for advertising. As he explained in *Der Trickfilm*: 'Auch der Rekamefilm hat sich bis zu einem gewissen Grade dieser Ausdrucksform bedient und ein durchaus gelungener Versuch war der von der Fa. Pinschewer in Berlin gezeigte "Kipho-Film", dessen technische Ausführung s. Zt. dem Verfasser übertragen war' (244) [Advertising film has also made use of this expressive form to a certain extent. A successful attempt in this direction was the *Kipho* film produced by the Pinschewer Company in Berlin, for the technical execution of which I was responsible].

[*Art stops where the conformity to rules and laws begins.* Both paths lead to beauty or – what amounts to the same thing – to absolute purposiveness. Yet the path through art, because it depends on a thousand imprecise sentiments and imponderable forces, is unreliable, whereas the rule-bound path is sure to lead to the desired goal. This path is therefore the shortest and hence the most rational.]

Such a rational path to beauty, Pauli argued, found its most paradigmatic expression in the advertising poster, and it hardly seems a coincidence if Pauli's posters recall the artworks of Futurism and Viennese Kinetismus (figure 15). Indeed, Pauli argued that such

Fig 15. *Model for advertising poster, from Fritz Pauli,* Rhythmus und Resonanz als ökonomisches Prinzip in der Reklame *(1926)*

rhythmized presentations marked the general thrust of all avant-garde art:

> Man sieht doch auch hier [in der Graphik] überall längst das Ringen nach dem Ausdruck in dieser Richtung. Kubismus, Impressionismus, Expressionismus und wie die 'Ismen' alle heißen, sind Etappen auf dem Wege, dessen Ziel die Gebrauchsgraphik für ein Gebiet der Reklame im Rhythmus und der Resonanzwirkung vielleicht erreichen kann. (30)

> [In graphic design, too, one sees an omnipresent struggle for expression of this sort. Cubism, Impressionism, Expressionism and all the other 'isms' are really stages in a development whose goal can perhaps be reached by practical graphic design in its use of rhythm and resonance for advertising.]

While Pauli's own grasp of avant-garde art movements may well appear reductive, his interpretation of recent developments in art was not entirely incomprehensible. As is well known, many of the artists associated with Italian Futurism, French Cubism or Viennese Kinetismus had long been undertaking rhythmical compositions similar to those proposed by Pauli. In the context of the late 1920s, it was easy to see these movements as so many precursors to the rational experiments with image and text layouts in advertising.

At the end of his study, Pauli called upon graphic artists to 'combine beauty with efficacy' [das Schöne mit dem Wirksamen [...] vereinigen], a sentiment that recalls not only the programme of the Bauhaus, but also the many collaborations in the realm of film advertising. As a concrete collaboration between an artist and an advertising specialist, *Kipho* offers a prime example of such an aesthetic programme and performs a similar gesture of rationalizing the aesthetic process in the interest of efficiency. Integrating the Wigman dancers from *Wege zu Kraft und Schönheit* into its machinic movement, the film transforms the organic rhythms of expressionist dance into something repetitive and calculable.

Expanding on this observation, I would summarize my argument, in closing, by stating that the basic operation of the *Kipho* film consists in such a rationalization of the irrational, be it the ritualized movement of the Wigman dancers or the occult hypnosis of *Caligari*. But this is also the basic gesture of the constructivist approach to rhythm in the 1920s. According to Pauli, the medical sciences had never really succeeded in explaining the uncanny attraction of rhythm for modern viewers.[57] But if it was not explicable, the hope was that rhythm might be controllable, a power to be harnessed in the service of both physiological and psychological productivity. Like Pauli, avant-garde filmmakers from Richter to Ruttmann largely adhered to this fantasy of controlling rhythm and understood film as a medium for doing so. Perhaps no filmic sequence is more indicative of this project than the citation and subversion of *Caligari* in the *Kipho* film. Where *Caligari* titillated viewers with the prospect of succumbing, like the psychiatrist, to the forces of a medium understood as occult, *Kipho* promised to insert viewers into a decidedly machinic temporality, training them in productive consumption. Commanding viewers to go to the exhibition of the German film industry, *Kipho* also promised to make viewers a part of that industry through a feedback loop that inserted consumption into a productive cycle. Far from Karl Bücher's lament about the end of poetry, then, *Kipho*'s rhythmical collages suggested a new kind of visual poetry for a thoroughly mechanized age, one that saw the artist as expert, the consumer as producer and the spectator as a productive worker in the national film industry.

---

57 'Welche Bewandtnis es nun mit dem Rhythmus an sich, mit dem Phänomen des Resonanzzwanges, der rhythmischen Gestaltung der motorischen und seelischen Komplexe eigentlich hat, dafür ist sowohl die psychologische als auch die physiologische Wissenschaft uns eine fest umrissene Erklärung noch schuldig geblieben' (Pauli, *Rhythmus und Resonanz*, 35) [Both the pychological nor physiological sciences have failed to provide us with a clearly defined explanation of rhythm, the phenomenon of compulsory resonance or the rhythmical form of motor and psychological complexes].

5. Surviving the Rhythms of America: Jazz and the Fantasy of Technological Mastery

[D]ie Betonung und Verherrlichung des *Rhythmus*, die ein Charakteristikum unserer Zeit geworden ist, [findet] auch in der musikalischen Betätigung seine Auswirkung. Wer die Tagesliteratur aufmerksam verfolgt, der wird beobachten, dass das Wort 'Rhythmus' viel öfter Anwendung findet, als in früheren Zeiten. Die Großstadt hebt die Gewaltigkeit ihres Rhythmus hervor, und das Turnen von Anno dazumal wurde vielfach durch die mit Musik begleiteten 'rhythmischen Bewegungen' verdrängt.[1]

[The cultivation and celebration of *rhythm*, which has become a characteristic of our time, has also had an impact on musical performance. Anyone who pays attention to the daily press can observe that the word 'rhythm' is used much more frequently today than it used to be. The city imposes its immense rhythm; the ancient art of 'gymnastics' has largely been replaced by 'rhythmical' movement to the accompaniment of music.]

Rhythm and the Primitive in Early Twentieth-Century Musicology

Although I mentioned the importance of composers such as Hans von Bülow and Igor Stravinsky in chapter 1, the last three chapters, with their focus on lyric poetry and the moving image, have neglected any extended discussion of the medium that served as the most dominant reference-point for modernity's other rhythmical experiments: music. Bücher's *Arbeit und Rhythmus* began, after all, as a study of primitive work-songs, and musicology was one of the foremost domains in which German modernity's rhythmical imaginary was forged. As we have seen, moreover, composers and musicologists such as Jaques-

---

1 Artur Iger, 'Jazz Industrie' (1926) [Jazz Industry]

Dalcroze and Stravinsky very much saw their endeavours as aiming to revive 'primitive' rhythms – particularly polyrhythms – within a Bücherian anthropological framework. This framework would continue to inform musicology well into the 1920s. To offer only one example, in a 1925 article entitled 'Primitive und moderne Musik' [Primitive and Modern Music] for the Prague journal *Der Auftakt* – one of the Weimar Republic's vanguard musicology journals – the music historian Erwin Felber claimed that despite the increasing 'Ausrottung' [eradication] of indigenous culture under colonial rule, one could still observe primitive forms of organic, rhythmical communal life among Bushmen, Papuans or Samoans: '[I]hr musikalisches Leben bewegt sich im Gegensatz zum Abendland, in dem die Musik vielfach eine Angelegenheit der Gebildeten, gewissermaßen einer Kaste ist, in der Sphäre des "Erlebens": Singen und Tanzen gehört zu den täglichen Bedürfnissen wie Essen oder Schlafen und begleitet alle wichtigen Vorgänge und Zeremonien' [By contrast to the Occident, where music has to a great extent been relegated to the elite caste of the educated, their musical life occupies the sphere of 'experience'; singing and dancing, which accompany all important events and ceremonies, are daily needs on a par with eating or sleeping].[2] For Felber, as for many other musicologists, evidence of such a holistic integration of music and daily life in primitive cultures could be found in the presence of polyrhythms: 'da gibt es eine schier unerschöpfliche Mannigfaltigkeit des Rhythmus in immer neuen Variationen und Kombinationen des Gleichzeitigen bis zur Polyrhythmik des Schlagwerks hin' (309) [one observes there a truly inexhaustible variety of rhythm, occurring simultaneously in endless variations and combinations down to polyrhythmical percussion performances].

Like so much of the anthropologically inflected musicology of the time, Felber's fetishization of rhythm as the mark of unsullied 'primitive' cultures participated in a widespread projection of European desires onto other peoples.[3] Moreover, that projection depended upon a particular modern dialectic of collecting, where the value of displays of 'primitivity' was predicated on the very disappearance of indigenous ways of life that European researchers lamented.[4] Indeed, Felber may have have gained much of his

2   Erwin Felber, 'Primitive und moderne Musik' [Primitive and Modern Music], *Der Auftakt* 5 (1925), 307.

3   On this point, see Kofi Agawu, 'The Invention of "African Rhythm"', *Journal of the American Musicological Society* 48:3 (1995), 380–95.

4   On this point see, for example, Assenka Oksiloff, *Picturing the Primitive. Visual Culture, Ethnography, and Early German Cinema* (NY: Palgrave, 2001), 61; on the

knowledge about primitive rhythm in the same way that Bücher had – through the many 'Völkerschauen' [human ethnographic displays] exhibited in European cities in the late nineteenth and early twentieth centuries.[5] One of the principal attractions of such displays was precisely the performance of rhythms in song and dance. Thus the Viennese writer Peter Altenberg, in his literary reworking of the exhibition of an Ashanti village from 1896, depicted his characters' initial approach to the display as an acoustic anticipation of contact with primitive rhythm: 'Sie gingen weiter. Man hörte das Geräusch von eisernen Castagnetten, dumpfen Holztrommeln, Messingringen. Sie kamen zu dem Tanzplatze der Aschanti."Syncopierte Rhythmen" sagte der Hofmeister, "hört ihr?! Tàdă tădádă dădà tădádă – – – "' [They continued. They heard the noise of iron castanets, muted woodblocks, brass rings. They arrived at the dancing arena of the Ashanti. 'Syncopated rhythms', the teacher said. 'Can you hear them?! Tàdă tădádă dădà tădádă – – – '].[6]

In the decades between Altenberg's sketches and Felber's musicology, such nineteenth-century displays were increasingly

---

imbrications of musicology and colonialism in Germany, see Vanessa Agnew, 'The Colonialist Beginnings of Comparative Musicology', in Eric Ames, Marcia Klotz and Lora Wildentahl (eds.), *Germany's Colonial Pasts* (Lincoln: University of Nebraska Press, 2005), 41–61.

5   On human displays, see especially Werner Michael Schwarz, *Anthropologischer Spektakel. Zur Schaustellung 'exotischer' Menschen in Wien 1870–1910* [*Anthropological Spectacle: Displaying 'Exotic' People in Vienna 1870–1910*] (Vienna: Turia und Kant, 2001).

6   Peter Altenberg, *Aschantee* (1896), in Kristin Kopp and Werner Michael Schwarz (eds.), *Aschantee. Afrika und Wien um 1900* [*Ashanti. Africa and Vienna around 1900*] (Wien: Löcker, 2008), 8. Four years later, in his *Philosophie des Geldes* (1900), Simmel would translate Altenberg's observation back into the scientific mode: '[A]uch in der Musik [ist] das rhythmische Element das zuerst ausgeprägte und gerade auf ihren primitivsten Stufen äußerst hervortretende. Ein Missionär ist in Aschanti bei der wirren Disharmonie der dortigen Musik von dem wunderbaren Takthalten der Musiker überrascht' (554) [In music, as well, rhythm is the first element to be developed and the most prominent element at the primitive stage. A missionary in Ashanti, after hearing the confusing disharmony of the local music, is surprised by the incredible talent of the musicians when it comes to maintaining the beat]. To a greater extent than Simmel, Altenberg seems to have been aware of the curious parallels undermining any effort to differentiate 'modern' and 'primitive' societies according to rhythm. As the passage continues, the children who are present with their schoolmaster begin to compare the rhythms of the Ashantee music to the rhythms of threshers and of a train. The Hofmeister agrees, adding: 'Mache nur nicht gleich solche Abgründe zwischen uns und ihnen' (9) [Don't be so quick to create a chasm between us and them].

eclipsed by a growing archive of phonograph and moving-image recordings, in which songs and dances were stored and collected as visible and audible evidence of a 'lost' world of rhythmical life.[7] The presence of such mechanical media can be felt throughout early twentieth-century debates about rhythm and culture. Even Ludwig Klages has recourse to the audible evidence of sound recordings in order to 'demonstrate' the fundamental incompatibility between the modern and primitive experience of rhythm:

> Besonders das Berliner 'Psychologisches Institut' läßt seit Jahrzehnten in allen Ländern der Erde, wo irgend noch leidlich ursprüngliche Stämme zu finden sind, von den Tanzgesängen und sonstigen Liedern der Primitiven durch einen ganzen Stab fachmännisch geschulter Forscher die genauesten Tonbilder aufnehmen. [...] Wir [...] schenken nur dem einen Umstand Beachtung, daß die Forscher in nicht wenigen Fällen auf eine taktmäßige Gliederung der Melodien schlechtweg verzichten mußten, in den übrigen aber ihr nur durch nahezu unablässigen Wechsel metrischer Gruppen von teilweise uns kaum noch auffaßbarer Umfänglichkeiten genügen konnten. (Klages, *Vom Wesen des Rhythmus*, 50–51)

> [In particular, the Berlin Psychological Institut has, for the past few decades, sent out an army of expert researchers into all corners of the earth where more or less unsullied tribes can still be found, in order to make the most precise audio recordings of the dance songs and other chants of primitive peoples. [...] We restrict our observations here to the fact that, in many cases, these researchers could not locate any metrical structure in the melodies, and other songs could only be transcribed through a nearly constant alternation of measures, some of them too complex for our grasp.]

The fact that Klages would cite 'precise' mechanical media as evidence for a world free from all technological precision underscores once again the paradox of modernity's infatuation with 'primitive' rhythms, which were only accessible through the lens of

---

7 On the role of phonograph recordings in ethnomusicology, see Eric Ames, 'The Sound of Evolution', *Modernism/modernity* 10:2 (2003), 297–325; for evidence of ethnographers' interest in filming 'primitive' dances, see Oksiloff, *Picturing the Primitive*, 43–69. While many of these recordings were made during colonial expeditions such as the 'Südsee-Expedition' financed by the Hamburg Museum of Ethnology from 1908 to 1910, others were made in Europe in the Völkerschauen. During the Great War, scientists also found another source of subjects: prison camps for soldiers from India and North Africa. In his exceptional documentary *The Half Moon Files* (2007), Philip Scheffner examines the immense sound archive (Berliner Lautarchiv) that resulted from one of the largest of these projects, in which Wilhelm Doegen made some 1650 phonograph voice-recordings, as well as several films, of soldiers interned in Wünsdorf.

technology. But this paradox contained another: archival recordings – as well as live ethnographic displays – interacted with scientific knowledge about exotic peoples in a kind of mutually reinforcing loop, where discourses about 'primitivity' both informed how non-European cultures were represented and relied on the same media representations for visible and audible evidence.

Jazz Rhythm Between the Primitive and the Modern

Certainly, this extensive discourse on rhythm and primitivity informed the new emphasis on rhythm and the downplaying of harmonics in modern music after 1900 by composers such as Stravinsky.[8] By the 1920s, however, it exerted its most decisive influence on the German reception and adaptation of American jazz. Indeed, perhaps no other topic was as central to the discourse on jazz as that of rhythm. Writing for the Austrian musicology journal *Musikblätter des Anbruch* in 1925, the composer Alexander Jemnitz spoke for many when he explained: 'Der Jazz bedeutet [...] nicht allein Emanzipation des Rhythmus von der Melodie, sondern zugleich auch Suprematie des ersteren über die letztere' [Jazz does not only entail [...] the emancipation of rhythm from melody, but asserts the supremacy of the former over the latter].[9] Jemnitz's contention that jazz marked the definitive triumph of rhythm over melody in modern music would find dozens of echoes in the Weimar literature on jazz. For example, in a lengthy study from 1927 entitled *Jazz: eine musikalische Zeitfrage* [*Jazz: A Musical Question of Our Time*], the cultural critic Paul Bernhard described how jazz syncopation had brought about an 'unchaining' of rhythm from its captivity within the monotonous regularity of waltzes and polkas: '[Im Jazz] tritt als gleichwertiger Faktor, lebendig und motivbildend, der Rhythmus hervor. Die bisher in Melodie und

---

8   Indeed, Felber saw this new tendency as a genuine resurgence of rhythmical vitality in a tired European society: 'Die abendländische Melodie, die sich seit Jahrhunderten auf harmonischer Grundlage weiter entwickelt hat, stirbt dahin. [...] Doch zugleich wird die Vielfältigkeit des Rhythmus [...] wieder lebendig' (311) [Western melody, which has developed for centuries on the base of harmonics, is dying out. [...] But at the same time, rhythm in all its variety is [...] coming back to life]. The model for such a rhythmical renaissance, he argued, lay precisely in the disappearing cultures of exotic peoples with their 'ursprüngliches Gefühlsleben' (311) [primitive sensibility].

9   Alexander Jemnitz, 'Der Jazz als Form und Inhalt' [Jazz as Form and Content], *Musikblätter des Anbruch* 7 (1925), 195.

Harmonie allein enthaltenen musikalischen Spannungen werden vermehrt durch die noch wirksameren des entfesselten Rhythmus' [In jazz, rhythm comes to the fore as an equal partner in a lively and motivating way. The musical energies formerly contained only in the melody and harmony are now increased by the more effective energies of unchained rhythm].[10] Not surprisingly, many observers attributed the predominance of rhythm in jazz to presumed 'primitive' dispositions of black musicians. Jemnitz, for example, spoke for many when he related the kind of syncopation that fascinated contemporary observers to the other meaning of the term 'Synkope' established by anthropologists: the trance-like states attained by 'primitive' communities during religious rites, which 'cancel out the [conscious] self underlying all individual responsibility'.[11] Other writers frequently compared the rhythms of jazz to the 'primitive' drum signals studied by ethnologists and displayed in ethnographic exhibitions.[12] Playing on such primitive associations, an anonymous

10 Paul Bernhard, *Jazz: eine musikalische Zeitfrage* (Munich: Delphin-Verlag, 1927), 47. The list of citations could go on and on. In his introduction to a special issue of *Der Auftakt* on jazz in 1926, Dr. A. Simon opens the discussion with the following statement: 'Der Jazz ist vor allem eine Erneuerung des rhythmischen Gefühls in uns, eine Aufstachelung der Dynamik und ein Monument des Optimismus in der Musik' [Jazz is above all the renewal of rhythmical feeling within us, an increase in dynamics and a moment of optimism in music], A. Simon, 'Jazz', *Der Auftakt* 6 (1926), 211.

11 The full passage reads: 'Seine jungderbe, zum erlösend nivellierenden Gesellschaftstanz hinreissende – von einem überreizten Nachkriegsgeschlecht gerade um dieses narkotischen, das Ich aller persönlichen Verantwortlichkeit gleichsam enthebenden, weil alle Nervenstränge in gleichschwebender Temperatur schwingenden Zaubers willen begehrte – Synkope' (Jemnitz, 195–6) [Its robust syncopation, which entrances people into the levelling and salvational act of social dance, which is desired by a post-war generation precisely on account of its narcotic magic — a magic that seems to cancel out the self underlying all individual responsibility because it makes all nerve-cords vibrate to the same temperature]. Jemnitz was hardly the only one to make this connection. As Paul Bernhard explained: 'Das Hauptmerkmal der neuen Tanzmusik liegt im Rhythmus, und zwar in einer rhythmischen Form, die den natürlichen rhythmischen Ablauf hemmt oder unterbricht, nämlich der Synkope. Dieses Wortes eigentlich Bedeutung ist "Ohnmacht", "plötzliche Entkräftigung"' (Bernhard, 34) [The central characteristic of the new dance lies in rhythm, specifically in a rhythmical form that stops or interrupts the natural rhythmical procession, namely syncopation. The actual meaning of this word is unconsciousness, sudden loss of strength].

12 Thus in the article cited above, Erwin Felber claimed, once again alluding to von Bülow: 'Im Anfange war der Rhythmus. Das spürt man so recht in den überkomplizierten primitiven Trommelrhythmen, welche in der Südsee als Signalsprache in noch viel realerem Sinne als die Tonsprache Verständigungs-

article in *Der Auftakt* entitled 'Primitivismus' even mused satirically that the perfect jazz instrument would be a contraption designed to emit various animal sounds. Recalling the recent fad for synaesthetic colour organs whose keys activated various tinted electric lights, the writer proposed a 'Tierorgel' [animal organ] whose keys would set off electric wires attached to tails of cats and dogs, thus provoking a symphony of howls, growls and moans.[13]

It would be a mistake, however, to reduce the discourse on rhythm in jazz reception to tropes of primitivity. On the contrary, what made jazz rhythm such a fascinating topic for 1920s observers – and what marks its real affinity with the other discussions of rhythm that I have been tracing in earlier chapters – was the way in which it could be coded simultaneously as the most primitive and the most *modern* of musical phenomena. Writing for *Der Auftakt* in 1922, for example, Max Brod described the preponderance of the rhythmical element in jazz dance in terms evoking not African jungles or tropical islands but rather assembly lines and iron architecture:

> Dabei ist die harmonische Revolte durchaus nicht das Wesentliche der neuen Tänze. Ebenso wenig wie ihre Melodie. [...] Aber gerade diese Unwesentlichkeit der Melodie lässt den *Rhythmus* des Shimmy mit geradezu ungeheuerlicher Energie hervortreten. Diesen ruhelosen, unermüdlichen Rhythmus, [...] dieses eiserne Maschinenwerk von Rhythmus, über das Melodie nur wie eine dünne durchsichtige Seidenhaut gespannt ist. Die Schönheit des Shimmy liegt (wie etwa bei einem Flugzeug, wie bei so vielen Erzeugnissen hochgespannter moderner Fabrikstechnik) nicht in irgendwelchem Schmuck, sondern in der exakten brennheiss-nützlichen Konstruktion. Fabrikgeräusche klingen in die Jazzband-Musik, hölzernes und stählernes Geklapper, die undefinierbare Ton-Explosion der Autohuppe, das Gepolter fremdartiger Glocken und Trommelautomaten, das Einstürzen alter Wände, Demolierungslust und gesund misstönendes Hurragebrüll.[14]

> [The essential innovation of these dances lies neither in their harmonic revolution nor in their melody. [...] But precisely this insignificance of the melody allows the rhythm of the shimmy to shine forth with unbelievable energy. This restless, tireless rhythm [...] is like iron machinery, over which the melody is stretched like a transparent silk sheet. The beauty of the shimmy (like that of aeroplanes and so many products of high-power factory technology) lies not in any external

mittel sind' (311) [In the beginning was rhythm. One can sense this well in the highly complex primitive drum rhythms, which are still used in the South Seas as a means of communication to a much greater extent than verbal language].

13 'Primitivismus', *Der Auftakt* 5 (1925): 50.
14 Max Brod, 'Shimmy und Foxtrott', *Der Auftakt* 2 (1922), 257.

decoration but in the precise, red-hot and functional construction. In jazz music one hears the sounds of factory noise, the rattling of wood and steel, the indefinable cacophony of car horns, the beating of automatic drums and fantastic bells, the collapsing of old walls, a desire for demolition and healthy strident cries of jubilation.]

Drawing on functionalist discourses, Brod's futurist reading of the shimmy associates jazz rhythm not with ancient rites but with the 'tireless' and 'restless' rhythms of factory technology that fascinated Engelke. Cultivating such rhythms, Brod suggested, jazz would herald a transition in modern soundscapes comparable to the transformation of urban habitats in European capitals: the demolition of 'ornamental' music and the erection of bold new iron forms.

Reading through Weimar music journals such as *Der Auftakt, Der Anbruch* and *Melos*, one is immediately struck by the coexistence of these two interpretations of jazz rhythm as the simultaneous embodiment of the primitive and of the technologically modern, a revival of ecstatic rites and the aesthetic equivalent of industrial production and urban planning.[15] In the introduction to one of the most popular treatises on jazz of the 1920s, *Das Jazz-Buch* [*The Jazz Book*], Alfred Baresel summarizes this ambiguous view of jazz rhythm succinctly: 'Der Jazz-Rhythmus [...] ist elementar und raffiniert zugleich und entspricht aufs Haar unserer modernen "Seelenhaltung"' [Jazz rhythm [...] is at once primitive and sophisticated, conforming precisely to our modern 'state of mind'].[16] And if one turns to fictional representations of jazz, the stakes are similar. In the so-called 'Zeitoper' [opera of the times] – a Weimar

---

15   Cornelius Partsch also points out the repetitive double-valence of jazz reception: 'Die Ahnung, dass man es beim Jazzerlebnis mit einem gleichzeitig brandmodernen und uralten Phänomen zu tun hat, suggeriert eine Formulierung [Heinz] Pollacks, der von "futuristischen Negertönen" spricht' [The feeling that the experience of jazz is at once ultramodern and very ancient is suggested by a formulation from Heinz Pollack when the latter speaks of 'futurist Negro music'], Cornelius Partsch, *Schräge Töne. Jazz und Unterhaltungsmusik in der Kultur der Weimarer Republik* [*Oblique Tones. Jazz and Popular Music in the Culture of the Weimar Republic*] (Stuttgart: Metzler, 2000), 85–87.

16   Alfred Baresel, *Das Jazz-Buch*, 4th edn (Berlin: Julius Heinrich Zimmermann, 1926), 5. Similarly, the poet Yvan Goll spoke for many when he described Josephine Baker's *Revue nègre*, in a now famous text on Weimar jazz, as 'die Verquickung von "letzter" und "erster" Kunst' [the combination of the 'newest' and 'oldest' art]. Yvan Goll, 'Die Neger erobern Europa' (1926) [The Negroes Conquer Europe] in Anton Kaes (ed.), *Weimarer Republik. Manifeste und Dokumente zur deutschen Literatur. 1918–1933* [*The Weimar Republic: Manifestos and Documents on German Literature*] (Stuttgart: Metzler, 1983), 257.

genre that frequently staged the confrontation between popular American and traditional European musical forms – jazz and its representatives were invested with the same mix of primitive and modernist associations. To take the best-known example, and indeed the most popular opera of the entire decade, Ernst Krenek's 1927 opera *Jonny spielt auf* [*Jonny Strikes up the Band*] recycled primitivist tropes familiar from cabaret and popular music in its construction of the hypersexual black musician Jonny (figure 1).[17] But Krenek's Jonny, coming from America rather than Africa (as earlier 'Jonny' figures had), also displays a distinct mastery over the technological world of trains, cars, telephones and radios, and this in explicit opposition to the European composer Max with whom Jonny is constantly juxtaposed in the opera.[18] Such bifurcating representations of the jazz musician, recalling as they do the ambivalent logic of stereotypes, should alert us right away – if this is still necessary – to the projective quality of Weimar's jazz imaginary.[19] Indeed, it is not difficult to see

17 On the tradition of 'Jonny' figures in German popular music, see Alan Lareau, 'Jonny's Jazz: From *Kabarett* to Krenek', in: *Jazz and the Germans: Essays on the Influence of 'Hot' American Idioms on twentieth-century Germanic Music*, ed. Michael Budds (Hilsdale, NY: Pendragon, 2002), 19–61.

18 On the Americanist associations with Krenek's figure, see Wolfgang Fichna, '"Die Überfahrt beginnt": schwarze Körper und Amerikanismus in Ernst Kreneks Zeitoper *Jonny spielt auf*', in Cowan and Sicks (eds.), *Leibhaftige Moderne*, 292–304. Contemporary reviewers also remarked on the importance of technology in Krenek's characterization of Jonny and his music. Thus in a review of the opera's premiere in Leipzig, a reviewer for *Der Auftakt* explained: 'Der Jazz ist ihm [Krenek] hier ebenso wie rasende Autos, Lokomotiven, Lautsprecher und physisch entfesselte Frauen Mittel und Theaterrequisit zur Kennzeichnung der Welt Jonnys, des Jazzbandgeigers, der "neuen Sachlichkeit" in Schwarz, die über die Problematik beschwerter Menschen, über alle Errungenschaften einer überlieferten europäischen Kultur triumphiert. Dieses Stück, das das moderne Leben in seinen sinfälligen Erscheinungsformen auf die Opernbühne stellt, das Autos rasen läßt und Eisenbahnunfälle *ad oculos* demonstriert, ist in seiner tieferen Bedeutung eine Auseinandersetzung zwischen gestrigem und heutigem Menschentum' [For Krenek, jazz is – no less than speeding cars, locomotives, loudspeakers and physically promiscuous women – a prop and a means of characterizing the world of Jonny, the jazzband violinist; he is the figure of 'New Objectivity' in black, who triumphs over the problems of aggrieved people, over all conquests of traditional European culture. This drama, which brings the characteristic phenomena of modern life onto the opera stage, showing us speeding cars and demonstrating train accidents before our eyes, is, at a deeper level, a conflict between the humanity of yesterday and that of today], review of 'Jonny spielt auf', *Der Auftakt* 7 (1927), 43.

19 According to J. Bradford Robinson, that discourse was in fact – at least in the first half of the 1920s – based on almost no actual contact with African-American music. See Robinson, 'Jazz Reception in Weimar Germany: In Search of a Shimmy

the

Fig 1. Jonny spielt auf, *cover page for piano score (1926)*

similarities to projections about 'Americanism' and American culture generally in the 1920s, phenomena associated both with technological modernization and with a perceived regression in European culture.[20]

The field of projections and cultural associations surrounding jazz reception has garnered a great deal of scholarly attention up to now from music and cultural historians. Looking over the growing body of scholarship on Weimar jazz reception, one can, I think, broadly differentiate three principal areas of enquiry. First, and perhaps

Figure', in Bryan Gillam (ed.), *Music and Performance during the Weimar Republic* (Cambridge University Press, 1994), 107–34.

20 On the background of Americanism in the German-speaking world, see Deniz Göktürk, *Künstler, Cowboys und Ingenieure... Kultur- und mediengeschichtliche Studien zu deutschen Amerika-Texten, 1912–1920* [*Artists, Cowboys and Engineers... Cultural and Media-Historial Studies of German Texts about America*] (München: Fink, 1998); on European fears of primitivization, see in particular Michael Cowan, 'Americanism, Popular Culture and the Primitive around 1900: Johannes V. Jensen's *Madame d'Ora (1904)*', *Orbis Litterarum* 60:2 (2005), 109–32.

in an effort to salvage 1920s jazz from Theodor Adorno's critiques of the 1930s, much of the scholarship of the 1980s and 1990s was concerned largely with charting the European careers of American jazz musicians such as Sam Wooding and the Chocolate Kiddies, as well as the adoption of jazz aesthetics by European composers such as Hindemith, Krenek and Kurt Weill, particularly in the 'Zeitoper' genre.[21] At the same time, in the wake of Sander Gilman's work, cultural and literary historians have devoted an increasing amount of attention to representations of primitivity in jazz reception, showing how Weimar's infatuation with jazz served as a forum for fears of racial difference.[22] Currently, however, jazz research appears to have entered into a third wave, as it were, in which researchers have begun to focus more on the technological associations of jazz reception to examine how jazz discourse activated and responded to other questions of modernity, in particular efforts to comprehend the transformations of experience wrought by industrialization and urbanization. In one of the most recent studies on the topic, for example, Jonathan Wipplinger argues that that jazz replicated Benjaminian shocks in the acoustic register, thus resonating 'with the aural experience of the urban metropolis'.[23]

Building on such work, my discussion here will pose a similar set of questions, while specifically examining how the infatuation with jazz rhythm drew on the broader rhythmical imaginary I have traced in the earlier chapters, in particular as it related to Fordism and Americanism. In so doing, I make no claim to be the first to remark on the importance of rhythm in German jazz reception.[24] But I do hope that this reading can offer a more precise understanding of the historical questions underlying the particular Weimar fantasy of mastering rhythm through jazz, as well as a more complex view

---

21 See Susan Cook, *Opera for a New Republic: The Zeitopern of Krenek, Weill, and Hindemith* (Ann Arbor: U. M. I. Research Press, 1988), 1–7; 10–26; 77–114.

22 See Marc Weiner, 'Urwaldmusik and the Borders of German Identity: Jazz in Literature of the Weimar Republic', *German Quarterly* 64:4 (1991), 475–87; Alan Lareau, 'Jonny's Jazz'.

23 Jonathan Wipplinger, 'The Aural Shock of Modernity: Weimar's Experience of Jazz', *The Germanic Review* 82:4 (2007), 301. Similarly, Theodore Rippey reads jazz, along with Siegfried Kracauer, as the 'reflection [...] of the fundamental historical situation' of an era characterized by the increasing predominance of mass culture. Theodore F. Rippey, 'Rationalization, Race, and the Weimar Response to Jazz', *German Life and Letters* 60:1 (2007), 90.

24 See for example Susan Cook, 'Jazz as Deliverance: The Reception and Institution of American Jazz during the Weimar Republic', *American Music* 7:1 (1989), 38.

of the ways in which tropes of the primitive and the modern were intertwined in Weimar jazz reception. Unlike the figure of the Bushman or the Papuan, the rhythmical 'jazz man' did not function in the Weimar imagination as the elegiac embodiment of a dying culture. Rather, occupying a more complex space at the intersection of primitivity and modernity, this figure came to serve as a model for navigating the divide between organic and technological rhythms, and more broadly between tradition and a modernity understood so acutely as an Americanization of German culture: a model of survival in a world increasingly structured by technological rhythms. In this way, jazz music and jazz dance functioned, in the Weimar imagination, as rhythmical media in the sense outlined in my earlier chapters – forums for mediating between traditional and modern temporal experience.

Jazz Dance and the 'Education' in Modern Rhythms

In perhaps the most thorough study to date of Weimar culture's infatuation with jazz, Cornelius Partsch distinguishes two phases of 1920s jazz reception that mirror Weimar cultural history generally: the first period, coinciding with the stormy political and economic years of the early 1920s, used jazz as a forum for abreacting the affects and traumas of war, revolution and hyperinflation. The second – beginning with the economic stabilization of the mid-20s and dominated by symphonic jazz on the model of the Paul Whiteman orchestra – witnessed the transition to a new interpretation of jazz as the musical expression of Fordist rationality.[25] But as useful as Partsch's schema is in describing a general trajectory of jazz reception during the Weimar years, it is important to recognize that the rationalist understanding of rhythm informing an interpretation like Brod's hardly began in the mid-decade but had appeared already in 1922; as I have shown in earlier chapters, such an interpretation was made possible by a longstanding association between rhythm and productivity that stretches back to Bücher.[26] If the eurhythmics of Klages, Bode and Rudolf Steiner sought to counter such rationalist notions of rhythm, this was, as we have seen by now, only one

25 See Partsch 55–141.

26 Partsch describes Brod's text as a precocious premonition of later interpretations, 'die Wendung zu mehr Sachlichkeit vorwegnehmend' (64) [anticipating the turn towards objectivity].

possible position, opposed by a powerful rationalist tendency that sought to harness rhythm for industrial productivity.

Jazz, for its part, was increasingly associated with this latter tendency. Indeed, Brod's functionalist interpretation of jazz found dozens of echoes in the musicological literature of the 1920s, which constantly related jazz music to industrial technology and mechanical media such as film. As the Heidelberg musicologist Manfred Bukofzer described it in an article for the journal *Melos*, '[Der Jazz] ist ein Spiegel, in dem Sport, Technik und Film reflektiert werden' [Jazz is a mirror in which technology, sports and film find their reflection].[27] Expounding on the link between jazz and film, Bukofzer argued that only jazz, with its emphasis on fast-paced rhythms, could keep up with the accelerated mechanical tempo of the filmstrip:

> Kein Zufall, dass Film und Jazz zu gleicher Zeit auftauchen. Die auf dem harmonischen Prinzip beruhende Musik kann der Geschwindigkeit des Films nicht folgen, da dessen Rhythmus schneller wechselt als die logische Steigerung der klassischen Musik. Der Jazz als bloß rhythmischer Begleiter, der sich dem Film sofort dynamisch anpassen kann, ist scheinbar die ideale Filmmusik.
>
> [It is no coincidence that film and jazz emerged at the same time. Music that relies on harmonic principles cannot keep pace with the tempo of film, since filmic rhythm alternates more quickly than the logical crescendos of classical music. As a purely rhythmical accompaniment, which can adapt itself dynamically to film, jazz is the ideal film music.]

Alongside the articles on jazz music proper, moreover, the musicology journals included frequent writings on mechanical music, and jazz was indeed a familiar and oft-used subject for makers of mechanical instruments and automata.[28] *Der Auftakt* devoted an entire issue to the topic in 1926 under the title *Musik und Maschine*

---

27   Manfred Bukofzer, 'Soziologie des Jazz' [Sociology of Jazz], *Melos* 8 (1929), 390.

28   One popular orchestrion of the 1920s, the Piano-Accordion-Jazz produced by the Seybold company in Strasbourg, included a mechanical drumset, an automatic accordion and a player piano, which played in sync with one another. Several models of the Piano-Accordion-Jazz also featured black and white players as automata. For images, see the online gallery at www.boite-accordeon.com/galerie3.html [accessed 20 July 2011]. Manufacturers of advertising automata also latched onto the theme. The company Roullet & Decamps, for example, constructed a life-sized animated replica of a jazz trio for shop windows in the early 1920s. A working model can be seen in the Musée de l'automate in Souillac, France.

[*Music and Machine*], just before another special issue devoted to jazz which appeared in the same year.[29] Finally, scattered throughout these discussions of musical idioms and instruments, musicology journals also featured several theoretical discussions of rhythm, work and productivity; for example, in a 1923 article from *Der Auftakt* entitled 'Die Lustquellen des Rhythmus' [The Sources of Rhythmical Pleasure], the musicologist Paul Nettl walked readers through the theories of Bücher, Spencer and others to explain the link between rhythm, energy and pleasure.[30] Similarly, readers of jazz handbooks could learn all about Bücher's theories; Alfred Baresel cited Bücher's arguments about rhythm and labour directly in a discussion of jazz rhythm in the second edition of his *Jazzbuch*, writing:

> Regelmäßigkeit erleichtert die Arbeit: zu beobachten bei den Steinklopfern, welche ihre Hämmer abwechselnd in gleichmäßigen zeitlichen Abständen klopfend auf die Steine fallen lassen; der gleichmäßige Schritt, das Zusammenfassen aller marschierenden Beine im hörbaren, von der Musik veranlaßten oder begleiteten 'Gleichschritt', bringt die ermüdete Truppe schnell vorwärts; die Öde des Maschinensaals wird erträglicher durch die Gleichmäßigkeit des Maschinenstampfens. [...] Der Rhythmus erleichtert die Arbeit, weil er den Aufwand an dazu nötiger Willensenergie wesentlich einschränkt. (Karl Bücher, 'Arbeit und Rhythmus').[31]

> [Regularity makes work easier. One can observe this in quarry workers who alternate the blows of their hammers at regular temporal intervals. The synchronized step of troops, when all the legs audibly fall together to the accompaniment of the music, allows the tired troops to move forward more quickly. The regularity of pumping machines makes working in the dismal machine-hall more endurable [...] Rhythm makes work easier because it reduces the amount of volitional energy necessary to complete a task.]

---

29 The articles in the special issue themselves pointed to the overlap between strictly mechanical music (pneumatic pianos, dynamophones, barrel organs, etc.) and the integration of new mechanical rhythms into jazz and modern music. Thus one writer, commenting on a performance of George Antheil's *Aeroplane Sonata* in Berlin, described the rhythmical pounding on the piano as follows: 'Dieser Rhythmus war so erschütternd, so aufpeitschend, so neuartig, daß wenige ihm standhielten' [This rhythm was so overwhelming, so violent that few people could withstand it], H. H. Stuckenschmidt, 'Aeroplansonate' [Aeroplane Sonata], *Der Auftakt* 6 (1926), 179.

30 See Paul Nettl, 'Die Lustquellen des Rhythmus' [The Sources of Rhythmical Pleasure], *Der Auftakt* 3 (1923), 244–48.

31 Alfred Baresel, *Das neue Jazz-Buch* [*The New Jazz Book*] (Leipzig: Wilhelm Zimmermann, 1929), 19–20.

Technology's Pulse

Fig 2. Jazz on the assembly line. Image from Fritz Giese, Methoden der Wirtschaftspsychologie *(1927)*

Like Hans Richter in the area of film or Jaques-Dalcroze in the area of gymnastics, Baresel saw in Bücher's theories of rhythm and labour direct scientific evidence for the beneficial effects of jazz rhythm on the bodies of listeners.

Indeed, as Baresel's discussion suggests, jazz rhythm was understood not only as an aesthetic reflection of the productive rhythms of work but also as a *stimulus* to productivity. This, I think, helps to explain the curious experiments of Weimar work scientists such as Fritz Giese, who could boast, in a 1927 textbook, of the ability of jazz to boost pleasure and productivity on the assembly line (figure 2).[32] It is only against the backdrop of this discourse on jazz rhythm and productivity that one comprehends the full resonance of Fritz Pauli's contention that jazz rhythm literally optimized the bodily performance of the dancers by increasing energy efficiency:

> Einen flotten One-step haben wir nach den Synkopen der Jazz-Kapelle absolviert. Wir genießen die befreiende Sensation und bemerken aber auch an allerhand inneren und äußeren Anzeichen, daß wir eigentlich eine recht erhebliche körperliche Leistung vollbracht haben. Wir spürten es nicht, während wir tanzten; denn *unsere Bewegungen waren in Resonanz* zu den Takten der Musik, *gesteuert im Wechselfeld des Rhythmus*. Auf irgendeine Weise wurde unser Kraftaufwand vermindert, und im weiteren Kräfteausgleich mit unserem Tanzpartner vollbrachten wir eine Leistung, die in ungleichmäßigen

---

32 The caption reads: 'Die nachstehenden Photos zeigen eine Aufnahme, bei der sichtlich unter Einfluß einer Jazzkapelle die Gesichter bei der Arbeit konzentriert verweilen. Ähnlich günstig wirken auf Frauen Märsche älteren Stils' [In the following photographs, the faces remain visibly concentrated on their work under the influence of a jazz band. Traditional marches have a similarly beneficial effect on women], Fritz Giese, *Methoden der Wirtschaftspsychologie* [*Methods of Economic Psychology*] (Berlin, Wien: Urban und Schwarzenberg, 1927), 460.

Bewegungen ausgeführt wir kaum hätten bewältigen können. (Pauli, *Rhythmus und Resonanz*, 8)

[We executed a quick one-step to the syncopated rhythms of the jazz band. As we enjoy the liberating sensation, all sorts of inner and outer signs indicate that we have achieved a significant bodily feat. We didn't feel it while we were dancing; for *our movements were in resonance* with the beat of the music, *conforming to the alternations of the rhythm*. Somehow, our energy expenditure was diminished and we achieved, in an exchange of energy with our partner, a peformance that we could not have pulled off in irregular movements.]

If Pauli's imaginary readers did not notice the extent of their performance while dancing, this is, as he understood it, because they were not thinking about their bodies at all, the conscious expenditure of energy having been replaced by the automatizing power of rhythm. Such descriptions offer a more precise understanding of the Weimar concept of 'Gebrauchsmusik': if jazz music was 'useful', this was not only because it took a secondary role as an accompaniment to dance but also because it was thought to exert a direct stimulating effect on the listener's (and ideally dancer's) body, promising an increase in energy, productivity and activity. Thus Bukofzer, in a discussion of the concept of Gebrauchsmusik, argued that jazz had put an end to the model of listening as passive and disinterested aesthetic contemplation: 'Dieser Passivität macht der Jazz ein Ende. Offensichtlich ist der Tänzer zugleich ein Hörer von höchster Aktivität' (Bukofzer 388) [Jazz has put an end to this passivity. The dancer is obviously the most active of listeners].[33]

---

33   Bukofzer's article also offers a good illustration of the way in which jazz conformed to the Kittlerian model of physiological-materialist aesthetics. Again and again, Bukofzer characterizes the transition from classical music to jazz as a movement away from spiritualized or profound 'Bedeutung' [meaning] towards a surface play of material signifiers: 'Da den Jazzinstrumenten nichts "Bedeutungsmäßiges" anhaftet, sind sie nur Zeugen der Materialfreudigkeit. Wenn nun Paul Bekker als Kriterium der neuen Musik den Wandel "von der Betonung des Bedeutungsmäßigen der Kunst zur Betonung des Materialwerts der Kunst" erkennt, so dürfte daraus hervorgehen, daß sich der Jazz organisch in die Tendenzen der neuen Musik einpasst. [...] Abkehr von allem Bedeutungsmäßigen und Spiel mit dem Material zeigt sich in fast erschreckender Konsequenz in der Verjazzung klassischer Stücke' (388-89) [Since jazz instruments have no inherent connection to the 'meaningful', they merely bear witness to a joy in materiality. When Paul Bekker posits the transition 'from the emphasis on the meaningful in art to an emphasis on the material value of art' as a criterion of modern music, we can deduce from this that jazz corresponds organically to the tendencies of modern music. [...] The turn away from all meaningfulness and the

The association between jazz rhythm, rationalization and energy helps to explain, I think, the vehemence with which proponents of natural rhythm such as Isadora Duncan and Klages rejected any association with jazz. Writing in 1927, Duncan insisted that a true revival of 'American' rhythm would be modelled on the wave-like 'undulation' of the Rocky Mountains rather than 'the sensual tilting of Jazz rhythm' (Duncan 47). Beyond racist stereotypes of lasciviousness, what bothered eurhythmical theorists about jazz was its imagined proximity to the rhythms of technology. Thus Marie Steiner, in a preface to a posthumous edition of her husband Rudolf's lectures on eurhythmics of 1927, insisted that the anthroposophical concept of rhythm had nothing to do with the use of 'rhythm' to describe jazz dances: '"Wir lieben daran den Rhythmus", sagten junge Mädchen, bei denen ich mich erkundigte, was denn an diesen Tänzen so faszinierend sei – Aber dieser Rhythmus ist eigentlich kein Rhythmus. [...] Die Dämonen der Maschine greifen hier ein und packen den Menschen in seinen Bewegungen, in seiner Vitalität' (Steiner IX) [When I asked young girls what was so fascinating about these dances, they answered: 'We love their rhythm'. But this rhythm is not a rhythm at all [...] The demons of the machine intervene and take hold of humanity in its movement, in its vitality]. It was this perceived subordination of vitality to the dictates of the machine that bothered these theorists about Jaques-Dalcroze's efforts to train the body through metric rhythms. As Bode put it: 'Diese unselige Verwechslung von toter Metrik mit lebendiger Rhythmik macht das System Dalcroze wertlos für alle, die andere Ziele verfolgen, als sie dem Menschen des Maschinenzeitalters bislang vorschwebten' (Bode 39) [This disastrous mistaking of dead metre for living rhythm makes the Dalcroze system worthless for anyone following other goals than those prescribed by the machine age]. Though Bode never mentioned jazz by name, one can nonetheless infer that he would have placed jazz in the same category as Dalcrozian gymnastics: for reform movements premised on the rejection of technological modernity as such, jazz represented a threat less on account of its imagined primitivity than because of its perceived proximity to the rhythms of modern technology.[34]

play with material is manifested more troublingly in the jazzification of classical compositions].

34 The Hellerau school, on the other hand, had no trouble publishing in the same pages as articles on jazz and mechanical music. Ernst Ferand, an Institute member, for example, wrote the following in an article for *Die Musikblätter des Anbruch* in 1926: 'Das Suchen nach dem Rhythmus ist eine charakterisctische Erscheinung unserer Zeit. Das soziale Leben, die Kunst, selbst die Wissenschaft

But the same technological associations that made jazz unacceptable to theorists of natural eurhythmics made it particularly attractive to those wishing to come to terms with the perceived Americanization of culture during the Weimar Republic. Thus alongside the well-known pedagogical programmes of Bode and others, the post-war decade witnessed a veritable explosion of education in jazz dances such as the foxtrot and the Charleston. In addition to courses, much of this industry relied on self-help media. Illustrated books such as Franz Wolfgang Koebner's *Tanz-Brevier* (1913, 1920) [*Dance Breviary*], Eduard Huppert's *Der moderne Tanz: ein Ratgeber für Tänzende* (1926) [*Modern Dance: A Guide for Dancers*] or Paul Moran's *Moderne Tänze* (1926) [*Modern Dances*] promised to help their readers master the latest dance steps (figure 3).[35] Like the work scientists, these writers associated jazz rhythms explicitly with the rhythms of labour and technology. Huppert, for example, after describing rhythm as the basic component of light, sound and electricity, expounded on its particular importance for productive labour. 'Der Rhythmus', he wrote, 'regelt und ordnet die Arbeitsbewegungen. Indem er dies tut, lehrt er uns die Arbeit unbewußt aufzuführen und nimmt ihr dadurch das Unlustmoment. [...] In jeder Tanzmusik spielt der Rhythmus die Hauptrolle' (Huppert 11) [Rhythm regulates and orders the movements of work. In so doing, it teaches us to execute movements automatically and thus strips labour of its unpleasurable element. [...] Rhythm plays the central role in all dance music]. Such passages suggest that part of the attraction of jazz dance lay precisely in the promise of rendering the body more efficient and thus more 'modern.' As the advertisement pages of these books make clear, moreover, the market for home gramophone sales in the 1920s came in no small part from the desire for self-training in the latest jazz

von heute widerhallt von diesem Ruf. Man sucht den Rhythmus in neuen Formen des sprachlichen Ausdrucks (Sprechchor), der Bühnenkunst (Raum, Bewegung), des Gesellschaftstanzes (Herrschaft der Synkope), des Straßenbildes (Verkehrsprobleme der Großstadt), der industriellen Produktion (Rhythmisierung der Arbeitsvorgänge)' [The search for rhythm is a characteristic phenomenon of our time. Social life, art and even contemporary science resound with this call. People seek out rhythm in new forms of verbal expression (the spoken chorus), of drama (space, movement), of social dance (the dominance of syncopation), of city streets (problems of city traffic) and of industrial production (the rhythmization of labour processes)], Ernst Ferand, 'Rhythmus und Tanz' [Rhythm and Dance], *Musikblätter des Anbruch* 8 (1926), 130.

35 See Franz Wolfgang Koebner, *Das neue Tanz-Brevier* [*The New Dance Breviary*] (Berlin: Eysler, 1920); Eduard Huppert, *Der moderne Tanz. Ein Ratgeber für Tanzende* [*Modern Dance. A Guide for Dancers*] (Graz, 1926); Paul Moran, *Moderne Tänze* [*Modern Dances*] (Wien: Tagblatt-Bibliothek, 1926).

Fig 3. Paul Moran, Moderne Tänze (1926)

dances. As one writer described it in an article for one of Koebner's many dance breviaries: 'Der Tänzer [...] kann trainieren und üben im eigenen Heim, soviel er Lust hat, er braucht nichts weiter, als ein Grammophon und gute Tanzplatten' [Dancers can train and practise in their own homes whenever they wish. All they need is a gramophone and good dance records].[36] Where scientists had once used phonograph recordings to collect audible evidence of primitive cultures, by the 1920s, the gramophone served as a training apparatus for modern life; with that, the record-player joined a host of other rhythmical media as an apparatus for mediating between the rhythms of the body and those of new technologies (figure 4). According to one image in Koebner's book, companies even sold black figurines that, attached to gramophone needles, performed mechanical dances to the rhythm of the record's rotation, which consumers could presumably imitate (figure 5). Finally, the practitioners of dance instruction were thoroughly aware of the potential of the time-based

---

36 W. Neumann, 'Konservenmusik' [Canned Music], in Franz Wolfgang Koebner (ed.), *Jazz und Shimmy. Brevier der neuesten Tänze* [*Jazz and Shimmy. A Breviary of New Dances*] (Berlin: Eysler, 1921), 89.

Fig 4. Heinz Loew, untitled photo (1927/28), courtesy of the Bauhausarchiv

Fig 5. Shimmy Liddy, illustration from Franz Wolfgang Koebner, Jazz und Shimmy (1922)

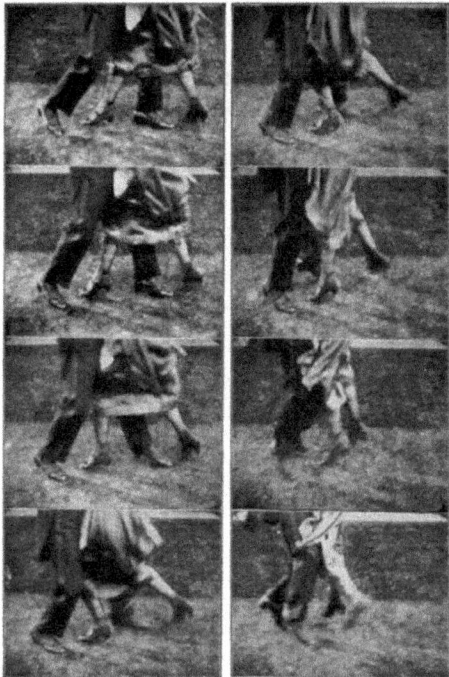

Fig 6. Filmed dance steps, from Franz Wolfgang Koebner, Das neue Tanz-Brevier *(1920)*

medium of film for training the body in the latest dance rhythms. Koebner who, alongside his career as an author of advice books and dance manuals, also worked as a film critic, illustrated his *Tanz-Brevier* with numerous sequential film-stills of dancing feet (figure 6). And he even created an instructional film, entitled *1000 Schritte Charleston* [*1000 Steps for the Charleston*], which ran in cinemas from Berlin to Munich (figure 7). According to one laudatory review article from the *Süddeutsche Filmzeitung*, Koebner's Charleston film consisted mostly of shots of legs dangling from a bench and performing various moves in slow motion, so that spectators in the cinema could imitate the filmic images from their seats. 'Der Charleston-Schritt ist mit einer derartigen Gründlichkeit [...] zerlegt', the reviewer concluded, 'daß man sich eine Tanzstunde kaum bequemer und billiger vorstellen kann' [The Charleston steps are so thoroughly analysed that one could hardly think of a more convenient or cheaper dance lesson].[37] Like the phonograph, then, film here assumed an eminently bodily

---

37 *1000 Schritte Charleston*, film review, *Süddeutsche Filmzeitung*, 14 January 1927 (n.p.).

Fig 7. Advertisement for 1000 Schritte Charleston *(1926), from* Der Film

function, being transformed from a medium of passive contemplation to one of active participation.

If one wishes to understand why such mediated lessons were so popular in the inter-war years, one might take a cue from Joel Dinerstein's work on American swing culture in the 1930s. Dinerstein understands the widespread adoption of African-American dance by Euro-Americans in 1930s as an effort to assimilate the experience of technology, which had taken on a decidedly less optimistic countenance in the wake of the Great Depression.[38] A similar dynamic, albeit beginning a decade earlier in the aftermath of the Great War, can be seen in Weimar jazz reception, where German observers conditioned to experiencing modernization as the imposition of Americanist technological rhythms found in jazz an imaginary training-ground for coming to terms with the new industrial technoscape characterized by the rhythms of Fordist production and consumption. In short, where eurhythmical gymnastics attempted to

---

38 Joel Dinerstein, *Swinging the Machine* (Amherst: University of Massachussetts Press, 2003), 17.

counter modernity's inhuman rhythms with a flight to nature, jazz dance held out the promise of adaptation.

One can see this fantasy of adaptation particularly clearly in the writing of Fritz Giese. In his popular 1925 study *Girlkultur. Verlgeiche zwischen amerikanischem und europäischem Rhythmus und Lebensgefühl* [*Girl Culture. Comparisons Between American and European Rhythm and Outlook on Life*], Giese argued – some two years before Kracauer's similar meditations on the parallels between the choreography of the Tiller Girls and the structure of the factory assembly line – that the rhythms of jazz dance and chorus lines offered an aesthetic objectification of the new rhythms of industrial production, urban traffic and mechanical media. Jazz, Giese wrote in a passage reminiscent of Engelke, gives musical expression to such signature urban rhythms as:

> das Rollen der Hochbahn, das Funktionieren des Warenautomaten, das Flügeln der Kaffeedrehtür, das Treppauf-treppab-Stürzen in der Untergrundbahn, das Rufen der Zeitungsverkäufer, das Pochen der Niethämmer im Hochhausbau, das Knirschen von Kränen, Heulen der Fabriksirenen oder was es sonst aus diesem Leben der Stadt gäbe. (Giese, *Girlkultur*, 33)
>
> [the rolling of the elevated railway, the noise of automatic product dispensers, the batting of revolving café doors, the throng of feet running up and down the steps of metro stations, the cry of the newspaper salesman, the pounding of pneumatic hammers in a skyscraper, the screeching of cranes, the wailing of sirens and all the other phenomena that make up the life of the city.]

Like Ludwig Klages before him, Giese drew a strict distinction between such industrial and urban rhythms – the 'technical-artificial' rhythms, as he put it, of Americanist work and leisure – and the 'biological-natural' rhythms cultivated by rhythmical gymnastics (25). Like Bücher and Simmel, moreover, he described this rhythm as a human creation that had emancipated itself from human control, an autonomous technological rhythm 'wie losgelöst vom menschlichen Schöpfer' (27) [as if detached from its human creator].[39] The sense of being overrun by an autonomous technological rhythm was doubly acute, Giese maintained, for European – and particularly German – observers faced with a new influx of Americanist forms of labour and leisure in the wake of Germany's defeat in the Great

---

39 See chapter 1, p. 30.

Fig 8. Tiller Girls, illustration from Fritz Giese, Girlkultur. Vergleiche zwischen amerikanischem und europäischem Rhythmus und Lebensgefühl *(1925)*

War.[40] But where practitioners of eurhythmics sought to counter such artificial rhythms with a flight to nature, Giese insisted that Europe – and Germany in particular – need to 'learn' from America's embrace of such rhythms in music and dance rather than rejecting it.[41] And this is precisely the role he assigned to chorus-line dance, which he described – along with filmic montage – as an 'education' for life amidst modernity's accelerated rhythms: 'Konzentration, Rhythmik, schnelle Auffassungen: das sind Erziehungswirkungen der Filmkultur und alles finden wir in der Girlidee wieder vereinigt' (54) [Concentration, rhythm and rapid comprehension: these are the educational effects of film culture, which we also find brought together in the figure of the chorus girl].[42] The chorus girl, Giese

40 See Giese, *Girlkultur*, 13.

41 Giese, *Girlkultur*, 13, 137–42.

42 The importance Giese ascribed to film as a representational form with a rhythmical structure analogous to dance is indicated by the fact that he included an entire chapter on film in *Girlkultur* – chapter 3, 'Filmkultur' (51–61). Giese later summarized his arguments on the proximity of chorus dance and film in an article entitled 'Revue und Film' for a special issue of *Der Auftakt* on variety shows. 'Revue und Film', he explained there, 'gehören kunstwissenschaftlich zusammen, da sie uns als Ausdruck einer im technischen Zeitalter geborenen Darstellungsgattung wesentlich werden' [From an art-historical perspective, chorus lines and film belong together since they are important to us as expressions of a genre of representation born in the technological age], Giese, 'Revue und Film', *Der Auftakt* 8 (1928), 172. Giese clearly understood both media in terms of rhythmical sensory training; a few pages later, he describes their analogous status as follows: 'Was ist das Entscheidende hier und dort? *Schneller Wechsel! Keine langatmige Exposition, keine epische Breite! Kein Überanstrengen der Gedanken! Dazu Spannung, Kurzweil, wohlweise, industriell erwogene Hin- und Herleitung über alle*

argued in his closing chapter 'Das Girl als Vorbild' [The Chorus Girl as Role Model], could thus serve as a model for living in the new technological landscape of post-war Europe (figure 8).

It is precisely here, moreover, that the racial constructions in Weimar jazz reception begin to take on contours more complex than the standard understanding of musical primitivism would allow. Behind its ostensible focus on girl groups, Giese's study is no less preoccupied with the history of African-American jazz which, in his account, emerges as the very model of an adaptation to life in a hostile technological world. In accordance with the ambivalent reception of jazz as both primitive and ultra-modern, Giese constructs a foundational myth of American jazz centred on the imitation of technological rhythms by African-Americans, whom he sees as most capable of reproducing modernity's rhythms aesthetically precisely on account of their 'primitive' sensibility:

> [Der Neger] war der erste Mensch, der diesen Rhythmus der Großstadt, der Technik, des Wirtschaftlichen und des Verkehrs ganz und gar intuitiv empfand. Er kam in diesem Sinne naiv wie ein Kind in die Welt der Großen. [...] Diese erwachsene Kulturkind reagierte ebenso unmittelbar motorisch wie rhythmisch und so entstand das, was heute von Amerika ausgehend Gemeingut ward: Jazzband und Negertanz. [...] Nicht die Erfindung des typisch amerikanischen Saxophons macht sie allein aus, sondern eben dieses negerhaft-naive Empfinden der unmittelbaren Umwelt, der Großstadt. (31–32)[43]

> [[The Negro] was the first person to experience this rhythm of the city, technology, economic life and traffic in a purely intuitive way. He

---

mengenmenschliche Instinkte' (174) [What is the decisive factor in chorus lines and film? *Rapid alternation! No long-winded exposition, no epic breadth! No overtaxation of thought! In their place excitement, amusement and the industrial channelling of all mass instincts*].

43 Certainly, it would be a mistake to see Giese's account of the origins of jazz in the imitation of machine rhythms by 'primitively' disposed African-American musicians and dancers as the only one available. But this explanation does seem to have enjoyed some popularity, particularly in the analysis of chorus lines and mass ornaments. In a 1928 article entitled 'Revue!', for example, the Czech writer E. F. Burian describes the origins of jazz as follows: 'Diese Neger, die ihrer Farbigkeit wegen mehr als im Mittelalter zu leiden haben, spielen am Broadway zum Tanze. Jasbo Brown, der schwarze Begründer des Jasz (*sic*), hat mit seinem eigentümlichen Rhythmus dem maschinellen Amerika die Maschinenmusik gebracht' [These Negroes, who suffer more than people did in the Middle Ages on account of their colour, play dance music on Broadway. With his unique rhythm, Jasbo Brown, the black founder of jazz, introduced the machinic America to machine music], E. F. Burian, 'Revue!', *Der Auftakt* 8 (1928), 182.

Fig 9. Illustration from Fritz Giese, Girlkultur. Vergleiche zwischen amerikanischem und europäischem Rhythmus und Lebensgefühl *(1925)*

arrived like a naïve child into this world of adults. [...] This grown-up cultural child reacted to the new environment in an immediate motor and rhythmical fashion, and the result was a phenomenon that has spread from America to become a common possession: jazz band and Negro dance. [...] They did not result from the invention of the typically American saxophone, but rather from this Negro-like naïve experience of our immediate environment: the city.]

In its comparison of African-Americans with children and its evolutionary assumptions about the history of culture as an acquisition of self-control, Giese's historical account trades in the kinds of racial stereotypes operative throughout early twentieth-century musicology (in both its mechanistic and nostalgic variants).[44] But this construction of 'primitivist' difference is matched, in Giese's account, by a marked fascination with the ability of the jazz dancer or musician to adapt to the new technological landscape; indeed, Giese's narrative of the origins of jazz abounds with the vocabulary

---

44 Such assumptions were underpinned by the writings of evolutionary psychiatrists such as Théodule Ribot, who had presented human evolution as the gradual progression from immediate instinctual bodily reactions through the mediated agency of affect and finally to the controlled actions of the will. See Ribot, *Les Maladies de la volonté* [*Pathologies of the Will*], 14th edn (Paris: Felix Alcan, 1900), 121.

of adaptation –'Der Neger passt sich dieser Welt an' (30) [The Negro adjusts to this world], etc. – to describe the historical experience of African-Americans within the hostile technological and legal conditions of white-dominated society. As such, Giese's imaginary narrative of the African American, thrown 'like a naive child' into the world of traffic, technology and mechanical media, can also be understood as a set of displaced fears and fantasies about *Germany's* own process of adaptation to the new Americanist cultural landscape of the mid-1920s (figure 9).[45]

Such an imaginary adaptation through jazz, moreover, goes well beyond any merely passive replication to involve a more active appropriation of the dominant culture through parody and caricature. As Giese describes it: 'Satire, Rache und Ironie entwickelt der Neger: an dieser Welt der Weißen, die ihn [...] ächtet, absondert, nicht für voll nimmt und doch benötigt. Er imitiert die Akustik der Großstadt und ahmt so die Menschen und ihren Rhythmus nach' (33) [The Negro develops satire, revenge and irony: he satirizes this world of whites which has ostracized, segregated and devalued him, even as it needs him. He imitates the sound of the city, its people and its rhythms]. Thus Giese understood the 'imitation' of urban rhythms in jazz not simply as an aesthetic reproduction or objectification but also as a form of *manipulation*, a symbolic form of mastery over the rhythms of an oppressive culture. Later – echoing several European writers on jazz including Claire Goll – Giese compared the African-American to the European Jew and describe jazz dance, with its satirical appropriation of industrial rhythm, as a symbolic 'revenge of the second-class citizen on the white man' (66) [Rache des Zivilisationsmenschen zweiter Klasse am Weißen].[46] Here, too,

---

45 'Die neue Zeit', Giese writes at one point, 'baute sich eine Welt in der natürlichen auf, und zwar in einem Ausmaß wie es keine Epoche vor uns, auch die der klassichen Zeit, kannte. Es entstand der Rhythmus der Großstadt aus den erwähnten Bedingungen. Was heißt das? Wer es noch nicht weiß, stelle sich an den Verkehrsturm auf dem Potsdamerplatz in Berlin' (26) [To a greater extent than any other epoch before us, including the classical, the modern era has constructed a world for itself within the natural world. The rhythm of the city arose from the conditions already mentioned. What is this rhythm? Whoever does not yet know the answer to this only needs to stand next to the traffic light on Potsdamerplatz in Berlin].

46 The entire passage reads: 'Er wird eine dem Kulturjuden nicht unähnliche Rolle spielen, je weiter die Zivilisationsbemühungen an ihm Früchte tragen; er wird dauernd an Minderwertigkeitsgefühl leiden müssen, und je mehr, je gebildeter er ist. Nicht unabsichtlich sprachen wir von der Rache des Zivilisationsmenschen zweiter Klasse am Weißen, als der Tanz nach dem Jazz und die Darstellungen des weißen Zeittempos durch das motorische Temperament

he was hardly alone. The cultural critic and cabaret artist Ernst von Wolzogen, for example, described jazz music as 'eine gerechte Rache des mißhandelten Negertums am Übermut der Weißen, [...] eine Rache durch Rhythmus' [a justified revenge of the abused Negro race on the arrogance of whites, [...] a revenge through rhythm].[47]

Jazz and Carnivalesque Agency

Integral to the German imagination of the black jazz musician in Weimar, this reading of jazz music as a symbolic revenge on the dominant culture formed part of a broader reception of jazz music as a forum for carnivalesque fantasies, a terrain for satire, caricature and the undermining of authoritative representations, particularly through the appropriation and transformation of classical motifs. Certainly, there was no shortage of conservative critics to decry the 'Verjazzung' (Bukofzer 388) [jazzification] of classical music as an alleged profanation of the European tradition, relating the practice specifically to the imagined national humiliation at the hands of black Senegalese troops in the Rhineland (the so-called 'schwarze Schmach' [black disgrace]).[48] More surprising, however, is the number of observers who celebrated the practice as the invention of a new genre of musical parody. Writing for *Der Auftakt* in 1926, Alfred Baresel explains it thus: '[D]ie vo[m Jazz] gern geübte Glossierung

der Afrikaner erwähnt ward' (66) [As the efforts of civilization begin to bear fruits, he will play a role not unlike that of the cultivated Jew; he will suffer constantly from feelings of inferiority, all the more so the more educated he is. Not by chance did we speak of the revenge of the second-class citizen on whites in our discussion of jazz dance and the representation of white tempo through the motor temperament of Africans]. In Goll's novel *Der Neger Jupiter raubt Europa* [*The Negro Jupiter Ravishes Europe*], the narrator makes repeated comparisons between the protagonist Jupiter Djilbuti and assimilated Jews: 'Neurasthenie der Erniedrigung', we read at one point: 'Er war empfindlich wie ein neugetaufter Jude, der sich einer Horde von Antisemiten assimilieren will. Als ob es für ihn, den Neger, jemals Assimilation gäbe!' [The neurasthenia of humiliation. He was as sensitive as a newly baptized Jew attempting to assimilate to a hoard of anti-Semites. As if there were any possibility of assimilation for him, the Negro!], Claire Goll, *Der Neger Jupiter raubt Europa* (Munich: Deutscher Taschenbuch Verlag, 1992), 11–12. Later Jupiter will claim: 'Vielleicht sind wir die schwarzen Juden des zwanzigsten Jahrhunderts' (76) [Perhaps we are the black Jews of the twentieth century].

47   Cited in Partsch 151.

48   On the role of the discourse around the 'schwarze Schmach' in jazz reception, see Lareau 43–44; Partsch 75–92.

bekannten oder verkannten und überschätzten Melodiematerials [...] gibt der Musik zum ersten Mal [...] die Möglichkeit zu einer *Kritik im eigenen Hause*, wie sie die Malerei in der Karikatur und die Dichtkunst in der Parodie längst besitzt' [The common jazz practice of glossing well known melodies [...] gives music for the first time the possibility [...] of a self-critique of the kind that painting has long possessed in caricature and poetry in parody].[49] In another article for the same journal appropriately entitled 'Jazz als Karikatur' [Jazz as Caricature], the Cologne music professor and editor of the journal *Musik im Leben*, Edmund Josef Müller, was even more enthusiastic about the rhythmical manipulation of traditional melodies in jazz:

> Hier nimmt er ein Kinderlied, dort eine Melodie von Schubert, dort einen bekannten Marsch – und diese bearbeitet er in der unbekümmersten Weise. [...] Um Würde ist es der Jazzmusik absolut nichts zu tun, und das ist gegenüber mancher gespreizten, hohlen Musik unserer Zeit ein Verdienst. Und was alles macht die Jazzmusik mit den gefundenen Melodien? Sie löst die langen Noten in kleine auf, bindet sie so, daß sie Synkopen bilden, [...] läßt die Melodiennoten vorschlagen oder nachkommen, ändert die Rhythmen auf mannigfache Weise. [...] Das ist alles Spott, Frechheit, Humor.[50]

> [Borrowing a children's song, a Schubert melody or an anonymous marching tune, he adapts them in the most carefree fashion. [...] Jazz music has no use for reverence or dignity, and this is a merit when compared with much of the overblown, hollow music of our time. The jazz musician transforms long notes into short ones, combines them into syncopated rhythms, plays notes in a melody before or after their normal position, and changes the rhythms in all sorts of ways. All this produces derision, irreverence and humour.]

As this passage suggests, syncopation, understood broadly as the creative manipulation of the basic rhythm, was *itself* understood as a mode of caricature, the central expression of jazz's irreverence for authoritative aesthetic traditions. It is hardly surprising that a musical form so associated with the undermining of authority would come to function as a forum for carnivalesque fantasies. To take one example from the category of ethnic representations, in Jean Renoir's surrealist jazz film *Sur un air de Charleston* [*Charleston Parade*] of 1926, a black protagonist (played by Johnny Huggins of the *Revue nègre*) travels by airship from a highly technological African city to the 'terres inconnues' [unknown territories] of France in order

---

49   Alfred Baresel, 'Jazz als Rettung', *Der Auftakt* 4 (1926), 215.
50   E. J. Müller, 'Jazz als Karikatur', *Der Auftakt* 4 (1926), 217.

to study the 'primitive' dances of an indigenous white woman. The film thus effects, as Henry Louis Gates has argued, a parodic reversal of 'the fundamental conventions' of colonialist narratives from the nineteenth and early twentieth centuries.[51] Renoir's film found an echo in Germany in Krenek's *Jonny spielt auf*, where the overturning of traditional hierarchies finds its central expression in Jonny's theft of Danielo's classical violin – a theft that allegorizes America's 'inheritance' of Europe's dominant cultural position thematized in the opera's famous refrain:

> Da kommt die neue Welt übers Meer
> gefahren mit Glanz
> und erbt das alte Europa durch den Tanz.[52]
> [The New World comes over the sea
> with an illustrious glance
> and inherits old Europe through dance.]

But alongside such racial fantasies, one would be remiss not to mention the frequent association of jazz with the overturning of gender hierarchies. An example can be seen in a satirical article entitled 'Saxophon und Jazzband' [Saxophone and Jazz Band] by Erwin Schulhof published in *Der Auftakt* in 1925. Purporting to explain the saxophone's increasing popularity with young women, Schulhof directly opposes its phallic, pipe-like appearance to the 'feminine' shape of the violin. '[K]ein geringerer als Prof. Dr. Sigmund Freud', he claimed, 'befaßt sich mt diesem Problem in einer ausführlichen Untersuchung, einer Parerga zu dessen *Totem und Tabu*, die sich *Fetisch Saxophon* betitelt' [No less an authority than Dr. Sigmund Freud is currently tackling the problem in an appendix to his *Totem and Taboo* entitled 'The Saxophone Fetish'].[53] In the figure of the female saxophone player – or 'Saxophonbläserin' [saxophone blower] as he called her – Schulhof saw the embodiment of changing gender hierarchies: 'Die Saxophonbläserin ist das Symbol der Aufforderung' [The female saxophone blower is the symbol of this challenge]. Schulhof's depiction of the saxophone-blowing woman forms a part of the broader discourse on the 'New Woman' in Weimar, and it is

---

51 Henry Louis Gates, Jr., *The Signifying Monkey. Theory of African-American Literary Criticism* (Oxford University Press, 1988), 108–11.

52 Ernst Krenek, *Jonny spielt auf*, CD booklet (Berlin: DECCA, 1993), 194.

53 Erwin Schulhof, 'Saxophon und Jazzband. Eine Entgegnung auf das Sonderheft *"Jazz"* der *"Musikblätter des Anbruch"'* [Saxophone and Jazz Band. A Response to the Special Issue of the *Musikblätter des Anbruch* on 'Jazz'], *Der Auftakt* 5 (1925), 181.

surely no coincidence that the phallic saxophone would often appear as the insignia of the new woman in jazz hits such as *Die Susi bläst das Saxophon* [*Susi blows the Saxophone*], which represented the female saxophonist as the pinnacle of a new autonomous and career-oriented womanhood. Thus, in the most popular rendition of the song from 1928, Irene Ambrus sang:

> Jedes Mädel unserer Zeit
> hat 'ne eigene Tätigkeit.
> Lili, die schreibt Bücher.
> Die Tilli, die malt Tücher.
> Greta Müller ist Dentist.
> Paula Hilla ist Jurist.
> Anna Stille predigt, erledigt, jedoch...
> Die Susi bläst das Saxophon.
> Die Susi hat den richtigen Ton.
> Sie macht 'ne feine Musi, die Susi, die Susi.
> Die Susi spielt so wundervoll.
> Mal süß in dur, mal weich in moll.
> Die Susi hat die Sache raus.
> Sie kennt sich aus.
>
> [Every girl today
> Has her own occupation.
> Lili writes books.
> Tilli paints pictures.
> Greta Müller is a dentist.
> Paula Hilla is a lawyer.
> Anne Stille preaches, teaches, but...
> Susi blows the saxophone.
> Susi hits just the right tone
> She makes fine music, Susi, Susi.
> Susi plays so wonderfully,
> Now hard in major, now soft in minor.
> Susi's a girl-about-town
> She knows her way around.]

The Susi figure also shows up in the hit film *Saxophon Susi* of 1928, starring one of the most successful Weimar actresses, Anny Ondra (figure 10). But echoes of the figure can also be seen in other domains such as Bauhaus photography and, not surprisingly, the 'Zeitoper'.[54] In Emerich Kálmán's popular opera *Die Herzogin von Chicago* (1928) [*The Duchess of Chicago*], the saxophone is associated with the

---

54 Among T. Lux Feininger's Bauhaus photographs, one photo from 1929 shows Lotte Gerson playing the saxophone for the Bauhaus jazzband.

Fig 10. Advertisement for Saxophone Susi
(1928), from Lichtbild-Bühne

American millionairess and jazz dancer Mary Lloyd, who crosses the ocean to conquer the Hungarian Prince Sándor Boris, buy his royal lineage and convert him from the Viennese Waltz to the American Charleston.[55]

Thus jazz, as the musical idiom for carnivalesque fantasies, could serve in the 1920s to work through any number of social upheavals characterizing the post-war years. However, inasmuch as it revolved specifically around questions of rhythm, the penchant for manipulating authoritative representations in jazz held a particular attraction for German observers wishing to come to terms with a sense of imposed 'Americanization' of work and leisure. Implicit, in Giese's celebration of the African-American's revenge on white culture, was thus a fantasy of agency in the face of a modern tragedy

---

55 On the reversal of gender roles in Kálmán's operetta, see Kai Sicks, 'Charleston, Girls und Jazztanzbar. Amerikanismus und die Identitätskrise der Operette in den zwanziger Jahren' [Charleson, Chorus girls and Jazz Dance Bar. Americanism and the Identity Crisis of Opera in the 1920s], in Oliver Kohns and Martin Roussell (eds.), *Einschnitte. Identität in der Moderne* [*Incisions. Modernity and Identity*] (Würzburg: Königshauen & Neumann, 2007), 153–68.

of culture that had come to be associated with the 'technologically superior opponent' across the Atlantic (*Girlkultur*, 213). In an article with the telling title 'Jazz als Rettung' [Jazz as Salvation], Alfred Baresel describes jazz syncopation precisely as a liberation from the new rhythms of work: '[Der] vielgepriesener Rhythmus [des Jazz] knüpft direkt an den Rhythmus unseres maschinellen, bürokratischen Alltags an; und gibt uns zugleich durch das Narkotikum der Synkope das Mittel zu unserer Selbstbefreiung' (Baresel, 'Jazz als Rettung', 216) [The much lauded rhythm of jazz music bears a direct relation to the machinic and bureaucratic rhythms of our everyday lives. But jazz also offers us a means of liberating ourselves from that monotony through its intoxicating syncopation]. Similarly, Manfred Bukofzer argued – in images reminiscent of Jaques-Dalcroze – that jazz could inculcate a polyrhythmical sensibility in listeners which would help them overcome the monotony of factory work:

> Heute will der Mensch den Alltag durch den Alltag vergessen, in der Kunst findet er den Alltag wieder. Er spürt in der Musik den Rhythmus der Maschinen, dem er dienen muß. Doch die improvisierte Polyrhythmik, die planvolle Destruktion des motorischen Prinzips, fängt das eintönige Stampfen mit entgegengeschalteter Bewegung auf. Sie zeigt den Triumph des Geistes über die Maschine, der der Mensch zwar körperlich unterworfen ist. – Jazz als Erlösungsform von der Maschine hat so seine ursprüngliche Funktion verloren – sie hat sich zu einer uns gemäßen gewandelt. (Bukofzer 391)

> [Today, people wish to forget the daily grind of work and find an image of that work life in art. In music, they feel the rhythm of the machines they serve in the factory. But the improvised polyrhythmics, the strategic destruction of motorized rhythm, counters the monotonous pounding with an opposing movement. It displays the triumph of the spirit over the machine, to which the body is still nonetheless subjected. As a form of salvation from the machine, jazz has lost its original function and taken on a significance corresponding to our own needs.]

One could, I think, hardly articulate the stakes behind a certain German infatuation with jazz rhythm better than Bukofzer does here in his reading of jazz as a 'salvation from the machine'. Among other motivations, the construction of such an extraordinary jazz imaginary in Weimar was driven precisely by a desire for a sense of agency amidst a new world of inhuman rhythms in work, technology and urban experience; whether imagined in terms of polyrhythmics or syncopation, the manipulation of rhythm in jazz promised to help people master, if only in the imagination, the rhythms to which they felt subjected.

Writing eight years after Bukofzer in 1936, Theodor Adorno famously criticized the fantasy of liberation through jazz syncopation as a deception fostered from above – a 'Trug' [deception] 'Schein' [appearance] or 'Pseudofreie[s]' [pseudo-freedom], which only serves to mask all the more forcefully the pervasive hold of the culture industry audible in the basic rhythm.[56] By now, Adorno's condemnation of jazz has spawned numerous debates, and it is not my intention to resolve them here. But I would point out the extent to which Adorno's reading of jazz takes up questions central not only to the Frankfurt school's cultural critique but also to Weimar jazz reception generally, which consistently sought in jazz rhythm answers to specific problems of technological and capitalist modernity. Not unlike the 'White Negro' phenomenon identified by Norman Mailer in the 1950s, Weimar jazz reception saw in the rhythmical African-American – beyond any fantasies of lost authenticity – a model for surviving in an inhospitable world of anxiety-provoking technologies.[57] Looking back today, we might say that what is problematic about such visions of blackness is less any failure of jazz to live up to this alleged emancipatory function of aesthetics than the instrumentalization of black suffering itself, the implied equivalence of victimhood across lines of oppression that were qualitatively and quantitatively incommensurable.[58] And not

---

56 Theodor Adorno, 'Über Jazz' (1936), in *Gesammelte Schriften 17. Musikalische Schriften 4: Moments musicaux, Impromptus* (Frankfurt am Main: Suhrkamp, 1982), 78, 80, 99.

57 Mailer famously argued that the 'Negro', and particularly the jazz musician, became a model for white Americans growing up in the 'age of anxiety' after WWII, faced with a world of concentration camps and nuclear technologies. See Norman Mailer, 'The White Negro: Superficial Reflections on the Hipster', *Dissent* IV (1957), www.learntoquestion.com/resources/database/archives/003327.html [accessed 20 July 2011].

58 As with later movements (e.g. Situationism), moreover, the discourse on blackness in the 1920s included attempts to draw equivalences between the racial violence of colonialism and class exploitation. A song by the Berlin group Rote Raketen [Red Rockets], for example, made the oppressed colonial subject into the embodiment of proletarian suffering: 'In Vergnügungsstätten der Bourgeois | tanzt ein Nigger – ha, ha, ha. | Begeistert schreibt der Zeitungsmob! | – Halt, stop! – | Versklavtes, schwarzes Arbeiterheer, | steht auf, steht auf! | Will nicht mehr! | [...] Ob schwarz, ob weiß | wir ziehn am selben Strick. | Ob Kanton, Budweis | Berlin, Kamerun – | nur eins ist zu tun: | Dem Unterdrücker ans Genick!' (cited in Lareau 54–55) [In the nightclubs of the bourgeoisie | A poor Negro dances – ha, ha, ha. | The press throng writes enthusiastically! | Cease and

even Adorno himself could entirely escape this dynamic. For although he explicitly denounced what he termed 'die Negerfabel' (88) [the myth of the Negro] in works such as Krenek's, underneath that exoticist mystification of blackness as spontaneity, Adorno posited a more fundamental – if less manifest – identification of the victims of the culture industry with the victims of slavery itself. 'Die Society', he insisted, 'hat ihre Vitalmusik [...] nicht von Wilden, sondern von domestizierten Leibeigenen bezogen. [...] Nicht alte und verdrängte Triebe werden in den genormten Rhythmen und genormten Ausbrüchen frei: neue, verdrängte, verstümmelte erstarren zu Masken der längst gewesenen' (84) [Society has harnessed its vital music [...] not from savages, but from domesticated slaves. [...] It is not ancient and repressed instincts that are set free in standardized rhythms and standardized eruptions; rather new, repressed and mutilated instincts harden into the masks of ancient instincts]. Equating the body of the jazz dancer with that of the slave, Adorno articulates a counter-image of blackness as a model for the 'mutilated' subjectivity under capitalism's culture industry – a metaphor surely no less problematic in its appropriation of historical suffering than the fantasy of the jazz man as a model for mastering technology.

Masters of Rhythm

The latter fantasy came in many forms, but perhaps the most obsessive version was that of the jazz drummer. Not surprisingly, Weimar musicologists consistently described jazz musical arrangements as a revalorization of those much neglected percussion instruments. As Alexander Jemnitz puts it in an already-cited article: 'Werden nicht heutzutage von Madrid bis Moskau Werke geschaffen, in denen das bis jetzt als Instrumentengruppe einer minderwertigen, barbarischen "zweiten Klasse" begutachtete Schlagzeug fast Vorzugsbehandlung, zumindest jedoch Gleichberechtigung genießt?' (Jemnitz 195) [Today, we see works being composed from Moscow to Madrid in which the drums – which were previously seen as instruments of an inferior and barbaric second class – now enjoy preferential treatment or at least

---

desist! | Enslaved black army of workers, | Arise, arise! | Refuses to continue! | [...] Whether black or white | We're all harnessed to the same rope | Whether in Canton, Budweis | Berlin or Cameroon – | There is but one thing to do: | Break the opressor's neck!].

Der „Schlagzeug-Mann"
Die wichtigste Person der Jazz Band

Fig 11. Illustration from Franz Wolfgang Koebner,
Jazz und Shimmy *(1922)*

equal rights?].⁵⁹ Jemnitz could have been referring to any number of compositions, including the much-discussed *Concert Piece for 28 Drums* of 1926 by the composer Jaap Kool, who incidentally also penned treatises on percussion instruments and the saxophone (in addition to primitive dances).⁶⁰ This musicological discourse helps to explain the frequent foregrounding of drummers in the jazz iconography of

---

59   Compare Iger 223: 'Daher kommt es auch, daß beim Jazz-Orchester die *Schlagzeuge* eine "ausschlag"-gebende Rolle spielen' [This is also the reason that the drums play a 'striking' role in jazz orchestras].

60   See Jaap Kool, *Tänze der Naturvölker. Ein Deutungsversuch primitiver Tanzkulte und Kultgebräuche* [*Dances of Natural Peoples. An Attempt to Interpret Primitive Dance Cults and Cult Rituals*] (Berlin: Fürstner, 1921); 'Geräuschinstrumente' [Noise Instruments], *Musikblätter des Anbruch* 8 (1926), 167–69; *Das Saxophon* (Leipzig: Weber, 1931). For mentions of Kool's *Konzertstück für 28 Trommeln*, see 'Geräuschinstrumente', 169; Rudolf Lämmel, *Der moderne Tanz. Eine allgemeinverständliche Einführung in das Gebiet der Rhythmischen Gymnastik und des Neuen Tanzes* [*Modern Dance. A Generally Comprehensible Introduction to Rhythmical Gymnastics and New Dance*] (Berlin: Peter J. Oestergaard, 1928), 212.

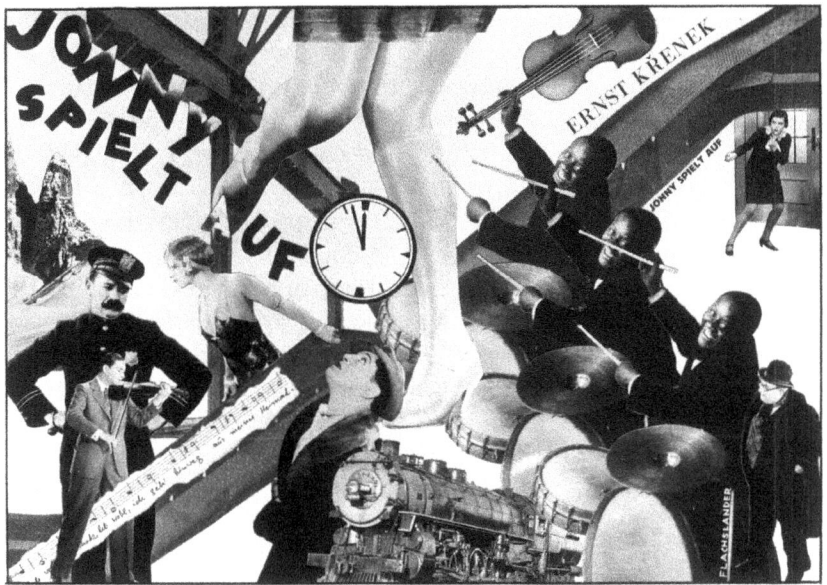

Fig 12. Ernst Krenek, Jonny spielt auf, *collage of elements from the opera (1927) © by kind permission of Universal Edition A.G., Wien*

the period; in books such as Franz Koebner's *Jazz und Shimmy*, the drummer appears as the central icon of a new rhythm-centred music for a technological age (figure 11). In the caption to this photo, Koebner describes the drummer as 'die wichtigste Person der Jazzband' [the most important person in the jazz band], and it was not unusual for jazz combos such as the legendary Weintraub Syncopators to be named after the drummer (Koebner, *Jazz und Shimmy*, 109).[61] Indeed, even Krenek's Jonny appears, on one promotional poster from the time, as a drummer, multiplied rhythmically by means of photomontage into several serial figures extending diagonally up the frame (in visual parallel to a locomotive) (figure 12). Whereas the first two figures can be seen holding drumsticks, the last figure clutches the prized European violin, now being used, however, as a rhythm instrument rather than one of melody: the violin has literally come to occupy the place of Jonny's drumstick. Such iconography went hand-in-hand with a genuine mythologization of the drummer in jazz writing. In an article printed in *Der Anbruch* in 1925, one writer described New York jazz bands as follows: 'Das Schlagzeug (die "Traps") war die Hauptsache und der Neger, der all die Trommeln, Becken, Glocken,

---

61 Stefan Weintraub began as a composer and pianist but switched to the drums on forming the Weintraub Syncopators, with Friedrich Hollaender on piano in 1927.

Holzschachteln, Sandpapiere etc. bearbeitete, war ein Dämon mit über- und unterirdischen Fähigkeiten. Es war unerhört, was er an grotesken rhythmischen Verzwicktheiten hineinphantasierte und wie er doch immer das Rückgrat des Ganzen blieb' [The drums or the 'traps' were the main attraction, and the Negro who worked all of the drums, cymbals, bells, woodblocks, sandpaper, etc., was a demon with the powers of heaven and hell. It was unbelievable to hear how many grotesque rhythmical tricks he could project into the music while nonetheless remaining the backbone of the whole ensemble].[62] For European observers, such 'demonic' powers over rhythm served as the object of a particular infatuation. In an article already cited towards the beginning of this chapter, Max Brod described his amazement upon witnessing the masterful ability of a jazz drummer to manipulate the basic rhythm through syncopation:

> Ich hörte einmal einen Jazzband-Trommler, der mit geradezu genialer Invention neue kühne Rhythmen erfand, von der die heutige Kunstmusik der ernsthaften Herren Komponisten noch nichts ahnt. Während sein Orchester einen strengen Vierviertaktake einhielt, ging [er] in einer ganz vertrackten Dreivierteltonung mit, so etwa, dass er den ersten und vierten Taktteil des ersten Taktes, den dritten des zweiten Taktes und den zweiten des dritten Taktes traf, im vierten Takt endlich mit seinem leise eigenwilligen, geradezu wahnsinnig ausgerenkten Rhythmus mit dem ersten Taktteil der neuen Periode sich zusammenfand. Dies aber war nur eines seiner vielen Kunststücke. Und wahrscheinlich das einfachste, denn nur dieses konnte ich theoretisch packen. (Brod 257)

> [I once heard a jazz drummer who could invent new and bold rhythms with a truly ingenious creativity, rhythms that our serious composers with their elite music can't even begin to fathom. While the rest of the band maintained a strict 4/4 measure, he accompanied them with a tricky 3/4 accent, in which he managed to hit the first and fourth beats of the first bar, the third beat of the second bar and the second beat of the third bar, only to meet up with the first beat of the new sequence in this idiosyncratic, insanely distended rhythm. But this was just one of his many tricks. And probably the simplest one – for it was the only one I could get my head around.]

If European observers were so fascinated by the figure of the polyrhythmical jazz drummer, this was not simply because of any interest in primitivism for its own sake. Rather, the virtuoso percussionist embodied a European – and particularly German

---

62 Cesar Saerchinger, 'Jazz', *Musikblätter des Anbruch* 7 (1925), 207.

Fig 13. Promotional photograph for Fritz Lang, Metropolis *(1927). Courtesy of the Deutsche Kinemathek*

– desire to master the new rhythms of Americanist labour and technology.

Metropolis Revisited

Before concluding, I want to consider one final image of the iconic jazz drummer within this context. Among the historical materials on file at the Deutsche Kinemathek for the film *Metropolis*, one can find a promotional photo showing Fritz Lang, Thea von Harbou and Brigitte Helm posing as a jazz band, in which Lang is positioned in the foreground commanding a large drum set (figure 13). Although the pose of the filmmakers has no direct counterpart in the film itself, the instruments do appear to have played a role, as we can see from a vision of the character Gyorgi in the newly-found footage from the original film print. Sent by Freder to Josaphat's apartment, Gyorgi is distracted en route by a mass of floating leaflets thrown down from a bridge, advertising the Yoshiwara pleasure palace, which morph into a collage of spinning jazz instruments before Gyorgi's enthralled gaze. Although cut after the original screening of the film, Gyorgi's jazz-inflected vision of Yoshiwara was hardly an anomaly; the robot Maria's costumes and gestures during her erotic dance in the club are not a little reminiscent of Josephine Baker's shows in Paris and Berlin, which had begun during the shooting of the film in 1925. And in Harbou's print version of *Metropolis*, Yoshiwara is described as a space saturated with jazz-like music: 'Frech war die Musik, von heißestem Rhythmus, von schreiender und peitschender Fröhlichkeit' (Harbou 41) [The music was uppity, set to a red-hot rhythm and roaring with frenzied jubilation].

If Harbou's description found its visual counterpart in the lost sequence of Gyorgi's vision, it found an acoustic echo in the *Metropolis* film score by Gottfried Huppertz, which specifically employed foxtrot rhythms to accompany the images of Yoshiwara. Like the composers of the 'Zeitoper' genre, Huppertz associated different characters and spaces with different musical idioms, opposing the Yoshiwara jazz rhythms in particular to the flowing Straussian waltzes that accompany images of the 'Eternal Gardens' where Freder passes his time at the beginning of the film in blissful ignorance of the deathly technology powering his father's city underground. What Freder discovers, immediately after leaving this Straussian paradise, is precisely an autonomous rhythmical machine, one which exists, to borrow Giese's description, 'as if detached from its human creator'. As we saw above, the city's factory whistle, the ten-hour work clock and its ever-increasing tempo all embody the kinds of inhuman technological rhythms discussed by Bücher, Simmel and Giese.[63] It is thus hardly by chance that Huppertz employed heavily rhythmical arrangements to convey such visions of technology, overlaying Freder's initial foray underground with a kettle-drum pounding in 4/4 time. Later, this foregrounding of rhythm finds an echo of sorts in the music accompanying Yoshiwara, and in particular in the prevalent solo woodblock rhythm which first introduces the erotic dance of the robot Maria – itself not a little reminiscent of the solo woodblock in Krenek's *Jonny spielt auf* that sounds from 'behind the stage' (as Krenek's score makes explicit) to introduce the figure of Jonny.[64]

Given the intersections between jazz and technological rhythms in *Metropolis*, I find the mysterious promotional photograph more than a little intriguing. While the instruments it shows may or may not have been intended to play a greater role in the film, their presence in a carefully staged promotional photo speaks to the self-fashioning of the filmmakers. Whereas Harbou, as the person responsible for the

---

63 See chapter 3 above.

64 As J. Bradford Robinson has pointed out, this rhythmical 'Jonny figure' is present in numerous 'Zeitoper' of the Weimar Republic and was taught in Baresel's *Jazzbuch* (Robinson).

film's narrative content, plays the piano, Brigitte Helm, in conformity with her role as the technological *femme fatale*, appears as a saxophone-blower in the tradition of Saxophon Susi. Finally, never one to miss a chance at self-promotion, Lang casts himself, the director of the film, in the role of drummer – a casting only comprehensible, I think, when one considers the myth of the virtuoso jazz drummer as a master of modernity's rhythms. Dominating the composition at the front of the frame, Lang appears as director of both the rhythmical jazz band and the rhythmical film. With his unfathomable ability to manipulate rhythm, the jazz drummer, one might speculate, offered a perfect analogy for Lang's own fantasy of the film director in a technological age: the technological artist as master of technological rhythms.

6. Epilogue – Rhythm and Moving Image Media: Some Afterthoughts

The preceding chapters have no pretension to thematic totality; indeed, it would be impossible to exhaust a topic as wide as 'modernity and rhythm' or even 'rhythm in modernist art', not only because of the sheer mass of material (the reader will, no doubt, think of many aspects and examples I have neglected here), but also because, as I discussed in chapter 1, the term 'rhythm' was itself open to so many competing interpretations. By no means does this book aspire to provide a definitive inventory of such efforts to define rhythm in one sense or another. However, through the selected examples I have analysed in depth here, I have attempted to outline the major contours of a shared historical investment in thinking about rhythm in the 1910s and particularly the 1920s as a phenomenon at the intersection of the body, technology and media in the modern world. As these analyses have shown, rhythm was itself seen as a kind of 'medium', or a key element of any number of artistic and mass media, providing an interface between the body and technology, the organic and the machinic, tradition and modernity. To varying degrees, this conception of rhythm as an interface – allowing a movement through technology back to nature or, conversely, an adaptation to the technological world – informed modern conceptions of dance and gymnastics, writing, painting, sound-recording and moving images; while obviously not the only parameter for defining media in the early twentieth century, this was nonetheless a powerful – and uniquely modern – one.

And it is one that has continued to resonate in recent decades, along with all the attempts to work through new forms of human-machine interface. One need only think, for example, of Paul Virilio's assertion that the invention of the pacemaker in the 1950s inaugurated a new type of biotechnological innovation in which the human body would be colonized by technological rhythms: 'l'hétérogénéité organique n'[est] plus celle d'un *corps étranger* adjoint au corps propre d'un patient, mais celle d'un *rythme étranger* susceptible de le faire vibrer à l'unisson de la machine' [organic heterogeneity is no longer that of a *foreign body* joined to the patient's own body, but rather that of a *foreign rhythm* capable of making the patient vibrate in unison with the machine].[1] Similar claims could have been made by any number of observers in the 1920s where, as we have seen, the mechanical heart returns again and again as a metaphor for modernity's subordination of the body to technological rhythms. Indeed, in biotechnological devices such as the pacemaker, as well as in various media technologies of the post-war years, Virilio himself saw the dystopic realization of Futurism's human-machine fantasies – an effort to overcome the sluggishness of bio- and neurorhythms in order to attain the 'vitesse absolue' (136) [absolute speed] of electromagnetic waves.

It would take several studies to examine the afterlives of thinking about rhythm, technology and the body since the 1920s, and the following pages can only suggest a few fragmentary starting-points, most of them located within the medium most central to the present investigation, that of moving images. Writing in 1928 for the journal *Süddeutsche Filmzeitung*, the critic Jean Lenauer argued: 'Seit kurzem vollzieht sich im Rhythmus des Films eine so entscheidende Änderung, daß es sich lohnt, davon zu sprechen' [Today, the rhythm of film has begun to change so dramatically that it is worth discussing it].[2] Citing films such as Viktor Sjöström's *The Scarlet Letter* (1926) and Alberto Cavalcanti's *En Rade* (1927), Lenauer argued that the modernist infatuation with 'Bewegung, Schnelligkeit, Rasen, Hasten' [movement, speed, rush and haste], which had now been accepted by mainstream films such as *Metropolis*, was giving way to an entirely new, more subdued rhythmical construction: '[Die jungen Filmleute] fanden ihr Ziel in einem sehr stillen, gemäßigten Rhythmus' (np) [Younger filmmakers sought to create a very quiet, moderated rhythm]. On one level, one could read Lenauer's article as a premonition of the later, better-known analyses of André Bazin who, writing from the vantage-point of the 1950s, would famously characterize the development of film language in the 1930s and 40s as a move away from montage towards a 'more realistic' staging through depth of field.[3] Lenauer's 1928 article posits a fundamental

---

1 Paul Virilio, *L'art du moteur* [*The Art of the Motor*] (Paris: Galilée, 1993), 135–36.
2 Jean Lenauer, 'Innerer Rhythmus', *Süddeutsche Filmzeitung* 7:23 (1928), n.p.
3 André Bazin, 'The Evolution of the Language of Cinema', in *What is Cinema?*, trans. by Hugh Gray (Berkeley: University of California Press, 1967), 35.

opposition between the external rhythm of montage and the 'inner rhythm' (the article is entitled 'Innerer Rhythmus') of movement within a sustained shot. Although not discussing depth of field *per se*, Lenauer nonetheless seems to foreshadow Bazin's conceptual framework when he argues that the new 'inner rhythm' of filmic narration was made possible by the increased use of panchromatic film stock which, reacting to a greater range of colours and transforming them into shades of grey, created more three-dimensional – Lenauer's term is 'reliefhafter' [higher relief] – images. At the same time, Lenauer hardly shares Bazin's post-war faith in the cinema's 'realist' calling. On the contrary, precisely through examples such as that of Cavalcanti, Lenauer argues that, whereas the older avant-garde rhythm sought to reflect the tempo of technological life, the new rhythm offers a poetic alternative to the world of industrial modernity: 'diese Langsamkeit, die uns aus dem Hasten unseres Lebens in ein Bilderzauberreich versetzt, uns mit Stille und Sanftheit umgibt' (np) [this slowness, which transports us from the hurried tempo of our lives into a magical realm of images, surrounds us with a gentle silence].

It would be a mistake to overestimate the relevance, let alone the prophetic power, of an article such as this one. Nonetheless, Lenauer does seem to have sensed certain transformations in filmic rhythm already taking place in the late 1920s and a certain diminishing of the modernist fascination with accelerated montage à la Ruttmann or rapid visual counterpoints à la Seeber. This is not to repeat once again the thesis of the end of the avant-garde (whether attributed to the coming of sound film or of fascism). Malte Hagener has argued convincingly that the trajectory of avant-garde culture in the 1930s is not a story of failure, but rather of functional differentiation in which once allied affiliations split up into movements leading to the development of documentary, advertising, state-sponsored industry and propaganda films, film archives, art-house cinemas and cineclubs.[4] But while some of these filmic practices – such as the ever developing field of advertising – did continue to allow for more accelerated rhythms, the dominant trend of documentary and narrative film in the 1930s could be captured by what Sabine Hake has, in another context, labelled 'the domestication of modernism'.[5]

4　See Malte Hagener, *Moving Forward, Looking Back. The European Avant-Garde and the Invention of Film Culture 1919–1939* (Amsterdam: Amsterdam University Press, 2007), 105–20.

5　See Sabine Hake, *Popular Cinema of the Third Reich* (Austin: University of Texas Press, 2002), 46–67.

In the cinema of the Third Reich, in particular, urban or modern rhythms – and specifically 20s-style montage – tend, when present at all, to be coded negatively. Hake offers the example of the urban montage of New York from Luis Trenker's 1934 film *Der verlorene Sohn* [*The Prodigal Son*], where the anomie of the protagonist's New York experience is juxtaposed with the ritual and seasonal rhythms of his Tirolean homeland.[6] Another striking example can be found in a film from the same year co-directed by Ruttmann himself: namely the Nazi-propaganda film *Blut und Boden: Grundlagen zum neuen Reich* [*Blood and Soil: The Foundations of the New Reich*]. In many ways, this *Kulturfilm* – commissioned by the Stabsamt des Reichsbauernführers [Office of the Reich Peasant Leader] to argue for the necessity of populating the Eastern farmlands – offers a representative, if particularly egregious example of one line within the functional differentiation of the 1920s avant-garde: namely the area of state-sponsored documentary. In several scenes, *Blut und Boden* recalls 1920s avant-garde work in its use of techniques such as animation, superimposition, found footage and a mixture of narrative and documentary forms (reminiscent of films such as *Menschen am Sonntag* [*People on Sunday*] of 1929). But here these techniques undergo a thorough re-evaluation. Most strikingly, Ruttmann recycles the very train sequence from *Berlin: die Sinfonie der Großstadt*, which had formed the pinnacle of a machinic, urban avant-garde in the 1920s, to argue for the dangers of urbanization now coded unequivocally as an uprooting of rural peasants thrown into the malaise of urban traffic, dark tenement buildings, joblessness and crime. Inserted just at the point where the main family in the film is forced to migrate to the city because they can no longer pay for their farm equipment, the sequence is meant to illustrate – here retaining its 'cross-section' function – how common their plight is. Flanked by titles reading 'Von den Schollen vertrieben zieht es den Bauer in die Stadt' [Driven from the land, the peasant is drawn to the city] and 'Der Zug der Landflüchtigen füllt die Großstädte' [The cities are filled with streams of peasants fleeing the countryside], the sequence cuts from the opening train montage to a newly edited sequence of several shots from *Berlin* most easily coded as negative: the spinning newspapers with their messages of 'murder', 'stock market' and 'money'; montages of empty, impersonal building façades; shots of frenzied production lines with their serial repetition; images of pedestrians frantically trying to work their way through the throng of street traffic; and endless images of cars, buses, carriages and trams moving in clashing directions.

---

6 See Hake 57.

Given the resources available for propaganda film under Nazism and the obvious care that went into the other scenes of *Blut und Boden*, it seems unlikely that the use of recycled footage from Ruttmann's *Berlin* film was the result of merely financial considerations. Rather, critics and audience-members would have clearly recognized these scenes as quintessential embodiments of *Weimar*, the era blamed throughout the film – as it was in Nazi culture generally and specifically in documentary and propaganda films such as Leni Riefenstahl's *Triumph des Willens* (1935) [*Triumph of the Will*] or Albert Speer's *Die Bauten Adolf Hitlers* (1938) [*Adolf Hitler's Constructions*] – for Germany's current woes. Notably absent from the *Berlin* footage are any of the more pleasurable sequences from Ruttmann's original film: the leisurely lunch scenes, for example, or the entertainment sequences from the final act.

This is not to say that Nazi film or Nazi culture rejected the discourse on rhythm *per se*. On the contrary, as much recent research has shown, vitalist concepts of rhythm à la Klages and Bode, as well as the pairing of rhythm and race, became a staple component of official Nazi body culture and ethnography.[7] In *Blut und Boden*, more positively coded images of natural rhythm can be seen in the film's opening, where a slow montage of shots of swaying wheat, threshing farmers, the baking and cutting of bread and the feeding of children depicts the former life of German peasants in harmony with the seasonal rhythms of agriculture. It is this traditional, peasant rhythm that the frantic, urban rhythms associated in the film with the Weimar Republic will destroy. But through a tripartite narrative structure, the film also shows the restoration of those opening rhythms on a higher plane, as it were, during the closing credits; in the final shots of the film, we see a group of frolicking peasant children, their faces shown in a steady rhythmical montage of close-ups, who gradually morph into an older group of Hitler Youth, marching in disciplinary formation and singing Willy Geisler and Heinrich Bolten-Baecker's *Die Jugend marschiert* [*Youth is on the March*]. Through this ending, *Blut und Boden* reveals itself not as a simple call for a return to natural rhythms in the tradition of the *Lebensreform* movement, but rather as a reflection of Nazism's reactionary modernism: that particular combination of 'blood and soil' nature cult and a militant discipline

---

7 See especially Golston, *Rhythm and Race*; MacKenzie, 'From Athens to Berlin'; Guilbert, *Danser avec le troisième Reich*. See also Andrew Hewitt, *Social Choreography. Ideology as Performance in Dance and Everyday Movement* (Durham: Duke University Press, 2005), 30.

that Goebbels described as a 'stählerne Romantik' [romanticism of steel].⁸

While the propagandistic content of *Blut und Boden* might locate it specifically within the culture of Nazi Germany, the new infatuation with the rhythms of rural life formed part of a broad international tendency in the art of the 1930s.⁹ In the context of European film history, *Blut und Boden* also exemplifies a growing trend towards state and political sponsorship of film and a corresponding tendency to tame the avant-garde aesthetics of 1920s experimental montage. If such tendencies are visible in the rise of socialist realism in the Soviet Union, they can also be seen in the development of the documentary by John Grierson in the UK under the aegis of government agencies such as the Empire Film Board and the General Post Office, as well as the work of Jean Renoir for the Popular Front in France.¹⁰

Where post-war neorealism – and Bazinian film aesthetics – largely continued the tradition of restraining rhythmical montage, rhythmical filmmaking would return in force in the late 1950s and early 1960s with the advent of formalist and structural filmmaking. Particularly relevant, for my purpose here, is the pioneering work of Viennese filmmaker Peter Kubelka, whose meticulously constructed 'metric films' inaugurated a decade or more of formalist filmmaking in Austria. In some respects, Kubelka's filmmaking looks back to the work of Richter, Eggeling or Seeber; in works such as *Adebar* (1957), *Schwechater* (1958) and the 'flicker' film *Arnulf Rainer* (1960) Kubelka, whose background lay in music, meticulously and rigorously constructed his rhythmical patterns or 'Partituren' [scores] frame by frame.¹¹ Like the constructivist filmmakers of the 1920s, he had little use for Bergsonian or Klagesian notions of continuous flow. Indeed, although he saw rhythm as a basic component of nature and life, Kubelka repeatedly insisted that it functioned to lend structure to what he otherwise referred to disparagingly as the 'amorphous' experience of real time. As he described it in a lecture of 1974 at New York University, the aim of films such as *Adelbar* was precisely to

---

8   Jeffrey Herf, *Reactionary Modernism: Technology, Culture and Politics in Weimar and the Third Reich* (Cambridge: Cambridge University Press, 1986), 3.

9   On the international revalorization of rural life in the 1930s, see the chapter 'Mother Earth' in *The 1930s: The Making of 'The New Man'*, ed. Jean Clair (Ottawa: National Gallery of Canada, 2008), 209–19.

10 On this point, see also Hagener 109.

11 For analyses of the rhythmical patterns in these films, see Stefano Masi, 'Der gemeißelte Zeit' [Sculpted Time], in Gabriele Jutz und Peter Tscherkassky (eds.), *Peter Kubelka* (Vienna: PVS, 1995), 73–123.

suspend this formless flow of reality: 'I wanted to make myself an ecstatic time, to take me out of the amorphousness of daily life'.[12] Throughout Kubelka's lecture, terms such as 'regulatory rules' (148), 'law and order' (148), structure (152), 'exactly ruled' (153) and 'systems' (157) recur to reveal his understanding of filmic rhythm as an *ordering* principle, which serves to subject nature to precise laws rather than reproduce its formless flow.

Indeed, Kubelka insists that what film can and should show is precisely *not* movement, but rather a series of still moments or cuts. In an eminently Bergsonian formulation, he argues that no matter how close such cuts occur together, they will always miss the movement occurring between them: 'but there is always an in between which I can never get out' (158). For Bergson, as we have seen, it is precisely this in-between moment that constituted the authenticity of movement, an experience available only to the intuition and not to the intellect. Similarly, Klages located genuine rhythm between the two beats of the train tracks, in the non-quantifiable forward thrust of the train's movement. Norman McLaren may have had something similar in mind when he famously proclaimed that in animation 'what happens between each frame [sic] is more important than what happens on each frame.'[13] For Kubelka, however, the movement 'between' two points is precisely *not* the goal of rhythmical filmmaking. On the contrary: 'In cinema, [the dancer] can be here, and in the next 24th of a second he can be there. I am not dependent on the natural flow of events in cinema' (158).

While such an anti-natural conception of filmic rhythm displays certain affinities with constructivist filmmaking, however, it may have had other reference points than that of industry or conveyor belt. In her study *Chronophobia*, Pamela M. Lee has argued that the obsession with time in the art of the 1960s should be read against the background of the simultaneous waning of the 'Machine Age' and the highly publicized race to develop digital information technologies in the late 1950s and early 1960s: '[T]he rise of the Information Age and its emphasis on speed and accelerated models of communication serve as the cultural index against which many

---

12 Peter Kubelka, 'The Theory of the Metrical Film', in P. Adams Sitney (ed.), *The Avant-garde Film. A Reader of Theory and Criticism* (New York: Anthology Film Archives, 1987), 148.

13 Cited in Bill Schaffer, 'The Riddle of the Chicken: The Work of Norman Mclaren', *Senses of Cinema*, March 2005, www.sensesofcinema.com/2005/cteq/norman_mclaren [accessed 20 July 2011].

artists and critics gestured'.[14] Seen in relation to the new sense of acceleration associated with digital communications media, Kubelka's films would seem to react in a way opposed to the *longue-durée* art of Warhol and On Kawara, which attempted to recapture the experience of time. Whereas Warhol's real-time films sought to provoke, in Lee's description, 'an experience of duration so unwieldy that it implicitly screamed out for something to happen' (Lee 278), Kubelka's rhythmical films themselves compress time by means of both accelerated montage and an explicit rejections of the desire to capture temporal *durée*.[15]

Indeed, it is not a little paradoxical that Kubelka, who would famously reject all requests to archive his films using the media of video and DVD, often characterized the filmic medium in terms that resonate with the understandings of new informational technologies in the 1960s. Describing the rapid montage of still images in *Schwechater* – which would also become a defining aesthetic in films by Kurt Kren and other actionist filmmakers – he stated: 'The strength of film is that I can give you visual information each 24th of a second' (150). Such 'information' could readily be compared to the concept of information in the digital age. By contrast to Bazin and Kracauer, Kubelka explicitly sought to detach the filmic medium from any relation to photography with its iconic and indexical sign system: 'This whole argument is directed against the belief in photography and the value of reporting the real world' (143). By contrast to 1920s abstraction, however, Kubelka's abstract films aimed not to set constructivist blocks or machine parts into choreographed movement but rather to reduce the visual field to a system of opposites. Already in *Adebar*, he not only increased the contrast in order to reduce the figures to black shadows on a white background, but also, by doubling these positive images with an equal quantity of negative film, to create an equilibrium of white and black ('When a positive appears I want it to be succeeded by a negative' 148). This principle would find its ultimate development in the 'flicker film' *Arnulf Reiner*, where the screen is reduced to alternations of light and dark calculated according to a complex mathematical formula. The film is accompanied by a soundtrack juxtaposing silence to white noise, which contains every tone frequency, just as the colour white

---

14   Pamela M. Lee, *Chronophobia. On Time in the Art of the 1960s* (Cambridge: MIT Press, 2006), xiii.

15   'When you just film what is happening in time, and then project it, you have only a loss. Filmed reality is inferior to real reality' (150). For Lee's analysis of Warhol and On Kawara, see pp. 218–58.

contains every visual wavelength. Thus, as Stefano Masi has written, the entire film is based on a fundamental opposition of positive and negative, presence and absence: 'Die Stille [...] ist die Negation aller Geräusche, so wie das Schwarze die Negation aller Farben ist. Ton, Licht, Stille, Dunkel: in *Arnulf Rainer* gibt es nichts anderes' (Masi 100) [Silence is the negation of all sound, just as blackness is the negation of all colour. Sound, light, silence darkness: in *Arnulf Rainer* there is nothing else]. In its absolute reduction of 'information' to presence and absence, *Arnulf Rainer* is not a little reminiscent of computer technology with its reduction of information to ones and zeros. The film, which Kubelka himself often insisted on displaying spatially spread out on the wall, physically resembles the kind of punchcard and 'paper tape' systems that were still in use in computers in the 1960s. It is thus perhaps not by chance that Kubelka employs the term 'programming' – a term traceable to his own early field of music, but increasingly used in reference to computers in the 1960s – to describe his activity as a filmmaker.[16] Like musical compositions and much of the concrete poetry of the 1960s, his metric films were 'programmed' to produce specific patterns of combinations: the combinations between freezeframes and movements in *Adebar* or between positive images, negative images, black and red frames in *Schwechater*, etc.

These observations are not intended to reduce Kubelka's mathematical films to reflections of discourses around digital technologies, and critics have rightly pointed to his repeated invocations of his own first field of music, as well as his preoccupation with Greek classicism and his comparison of his complex patterns to the harmony of Greek temples.[17] Yet it is hard to avoid the impression that a certain conception of filmic 'programming' involving the creation of complex combinations of opposites resonates with the new forms of data-processing made possible by digital technologies.

More generally, Kubelka's constructions of filmic rhythm around complex patterns of opposites might find a counterpart in the structuralist anthropology of the 1950s and 1960s. More than

---

16 Describing the mistaken attempts to represent real movement on film, Kubelka stated: 'Only if you program the projector so that the form of these images which are projected are very similar, will movement appear' (149). Kubelka's point here is that making a film *is* fundamentally an act of 'programming', and he criticizes those who would hide artificial, programmed quality of filmic spectacle behind a claim to reproduce nature. (Kubelka argues on the same page that all such attempts, even in their most 'realistic' manifestations, ultimately lead back to the 'magic' of Méliès.)

17 See Kubelka, 144, 146; Masi, 83; Dominique Norguez, 'Der Weltmensch' [The Worldly Human], in *Peter Kubelka*, 131.

anything else, Kubelka saw rhythmical filmmaking as a fundamental act of overcoming nature, an act of processing or – a term he often employs to describe filmic language – 'articulation': 'What I say that you must do in cinema is not try to report or bring the real world – to use the qualities of the cinematographic camera to mirror the real world, but that you have to articulate as you do when you talk or draw' (143). Again and again, he represents rhythmical filmmaking as a fundamental act of creating 'culture' out of 'nature', and it is hardly a coincidence that he relates this act, once again, to 'primitive' Africa. Already for *Adebar*, Kubelka chose music coded as 'primitive': 'I took a very old, very primitive and ecstatic piece of music for the film [*Adebar*]. It was pygmy music with one motif, exactly 26 frames long' (145). The keyword of this passage is *ecstatic*. Kubelka returns to the concept throughout his lecture on the 'metrical film' to define it as a form of liberation from nature: 'Now to come to ecstasy, which comes from the Greek, and it means being situated out of it, and it's a means to beat the laws of nature, not to be slaves of nature. It means to get out of the prison of nature' (158). Through this concept of 'ecstasy', Kubelka develops a vision of primitive cultures – and primitive rhythm – far removed from Rousseauean fantasies of a return to nature. On the contrary, primitive rites – for Kubelka as for contemporary anthropology – form the most basic technique of culture, the moment when one can observe the articulation of nature in its most elementary form. Kubelka describes witnessing such a primal act of cultural articulation during a trip to Africa in which he supposedly attended the preparations by members of a 'stone age village' for an 'ecstasy which would last all night' (158). The moment that moved him to tears, he recounts, came as the villagers waited, drums in hand, for the setting sun to cross over the horizon, at which moment the chief struck the drum. Although Kubelka does not state the point of his story explicitly, it seems to have everything to do with achieving a kind of elementary ordering of the world. By pounding the drum, he suggests, the chief created a 'sync event' (158) of the same kind he himself sought to create with *Arnulf Rainer*. 'What I wanted to do with sound and light, they did too. This was a fantastic, beautiful sound sync event. [...] They had one day. I had every 24th of a second. That doesn't make mine better, but it's faster' (158).

In a sense, then, despite Kubelka's rejection of nature, his film theory did incorporate a certain kind of 'primitivism', and he explicitly described his *Arnulf Rainer* film as an effort to create 'filmische Ekstase' (66) [filmic ecstasy] similar to the one he believed he experienced in an African village. However, like the structural anthropologists of the post-war period, he understood the primitive as an elementary system of culture rather than a pre-historical state of nature, as the originary ordering and 'articulation' of the universe. And this view of primitivity profoundly informed his understanding of filmic rhythm; far from a return to nature, rhythm was, for Kubelka, the first ordering principle, the basic act and origin of human culture. If film and new technologies had accelerated the rhythms of primitive cultures, this hardly made them superior. But Kubelka did hope that such technologies could be used to lend current audiences a sense of the ecstatic moment of cultural creation – a moment he also located, like Lévi-Strauss in *Le Cru et le cuit* (1964) [*The Raw and the Cooked*], in the act of cooking. More than a metaphor for cultural production in general, cooking figures in Kubelka's genealogy of cultural creation as the most ancient of arts and the primal act by which humanity takes leaves of nature to create something anew.[18]

Given Kubelka's invocation of Africa in his description of the 'metric film', one is tempted to test his understanding of rhythm against the images of *Unsere Afrikareise* (1966) [*Our Trip to Africa*]. This is hardly the place for a detailed reading of Kubelka's most complex film; I will simply suggest a possible deviation from a received interpretation. Shot when Kubelka accompanied a group of Austrian tourists on an African hunting safari, *Unsere Afrikareise* has long been interpreted as a critique of neo-colonial relations, in which the repeated killing of animals stands as both metaphor and synecdoche for the exploitative relations between Europe and Africa, its resources and people.[19] Certainly, the Austrian tourists in *Unsere Afrikareise* hardly come across as benign. But there may be reason to

---

18 'Das Kochen ist die älteste Ausdruckskunst, die älteste Formulierung einer Weltsicht, aus der sich die anderen Künste erst entwickelt haben. [...] [Der Koch] stellt Wesen her, die es im Universum vor ihm nicht gab' [Cooking is the oldest expressive artform, the most ancient act of formulating a world view, from which all other artforms first arose. [...] The cook creates entities that did not exist in the universe before him], Peter Kubelka, 'Was bedeutet Essen und Kochen für die Menschen?' (1987) [What is the Significance of Eating and Cooking for Humanity?], in *Peter Kubelka,* 176.

19 In her article 'Der Welt-Mensch', for example, Dominique Noguez argues: 'In Kubelkas Film [*Unsere Afrikareise*] ist das Signifikat, das sich in letzter Instanz aus einem komplexen Bedeutungsspiel [...] erbigt, begrifflich und "pathetisch" zugleich. Es ist das "Thema" (oder die Form) des *Raubzugs* – Mord oder Vergewaltigung –, auf das die Beziehung der weißen Besucher, Touristen und Jäger zu Afrika, seinen Menschen und Tieren letzendlich hinauslaufen' (Norguez 147) [In Kubelka's film [*Unsere Afrikareise*], the complex play of meaning produces in the final instance a signified that is both conceptual and affective. It is the 'subject' (or the form) of the *raid* – murder or rape – to which

question a reading of the film that would align indigenous peoples and animals as victims on the one side and white Europeans as perpetrators on the other. Such a reading runs into difficulties not only because it contradicts Kubelka's own celebration of animal meat in his cooking presentations, but also because, within the film itself, the African characters participate in the hunting nearly as much as the Europeans.[20]

More significantly, perhaps, in addition to the three groups of protagonists already mentioned – Europeans, Africans and animals – there is a fourth protagonist unmistakably present in *Unsere Afrikareise*: namely the filmmaker himself. It is the filmmaker who, like the African drummer or the primal cook, takes nature apart to establish artificial synchronic events, thus creating something new. In *Unsere Afrikareise*, such constructed synchronous events tend to revolve around the ever-present motif of the gunshot: whether blending the sound of a gunshot with the image of a hat flying from a tourist's head; the sound of a tourist letting out an 'aua!' [ouch!] in German with the image of a zebra being shot in the head; the sound of rapid gunfire with the image of a tourist shaking the hands of locals; or – probably the most famous example – the sound of a tourist's voice mentioning the 'Schuss [Schluss] von Goethes *Faust*' [ending of Goethe's *Faust*] with the image of a shot ('Schuss') killing a crocodile. In their flaunted artificiality, such image-tone constructions clearly reveal the hand of a filmmaker who refuses to copy nature and its synchronicities but instead constructs something new in an act of artistic articulation. The omnipresence of gunshots, then, does not in itself justify a reading of *Unsere Afrikareise* as an anti-colonialist film. It seems no less plausible to argue that they were mean to flaunt the way in which *Unsere Afrkareise* – as a film commissioned to document a safari – took the conditions imposed upon it and transformed them into something new. Indeed, in the repeated soundtrack leitmotif 'Was hab'n wir da g'schoss'n?' [What've we shot?], one can hear something of this appropriation: for the point of *Unsere Afrikareise* is not to answer the question of what game the *tourists* have shot, but rather what images the *filmmaker* has shot and above all how he has processed and recombined them into a structural novelty. Kubelka often emphasized his ability to transform conditions of reproduction imposed by the commissions he received – whether Schwechater beer

---

the relation of the white visitors (tourists and hunters) to Africa, its people and animals ultimately leads].
20 See Kubelka, 'Über das Wiener Schnitzel' [On Wiener Schnitzel], in *Peter Kubelka*, 168.

or the Adebar café – and transform them into something new, and it is this ability to create something new out of imposed conditions that he understood as analogous to primitive culture and its relation to nature.[21] 'Rhythm', as Kubelka understood it, was a central mode of such primary acts of data-processing, a fact that may also explain the many images of rhythmical work – pounding or rowing – and the sounds of rhythmical dance scattered throughout *Unsere Afrikareise*.

In its various guises, Kubelka's work exemplifies an ambiguous relation to rhythm during the 1960s, one that was caught between structuralist notions of human culture, new digital technologies and nostalgic narratives of a lost primitivism. It is perhaps telling that, within his metrical films, images of industry are neither celebrated (as in constructivist film) nor demonized (as in the 'blood and soil' ideology of the Third Reich), but hardly present at all, the repetitive rotations or back-and-forth movements of industrial technology having been replaced by complex rhythmical combinations.

This would change once again with the more definitive and widespread transition to a post-industrial – and increasingly post-celluloid – culture of the late twentieth century, where one can detect an intense renewal of interest in the industrial rhythms of 1920s film. The most salient illustration here might be offered by the fate of Fritz Lang's *Metropolis*. Whereas the film had largely been understood in political terms since the publication of Siegfried Kracauer's influential *From Caligari to Hitler* (1947), the release by Giorgio Moroder of a newly colourized version with a rock and electronic soundtrack in 1984 helped to bring questions of rhythm and music back into focus. Moroder's release came only shortly after the *Metropolis*-inspired *Blade Runner* (1982) – the most influential meditation on human-machine interfaces of the 1980s – and was most certainly motivated in part by its success. In particular, much of the electronic music Moroder composed for the colourized *Metropolis* is reminiscent of Vangelis's synthetic music for *Blade Runner*. When one watches the film today, this droning soundtrack seems strangely out of place over the Fordist images of pumping machine halls. But perhaps that very discordance points towards the real stakes of the renewed interest in *Metropolis* in the 1980s: as the most important modernist film to grapple with the (then) new technologies and Fordist rhythms of industrial labour, Lang's 1927 film stood as an obvious model for any attempt to grasp the new synthetic media- and techno-scapes replacing industrial technologies in the 1980s.

21 See, for example, Kubelka's description of the making of Schwechater (Kubelka, 'Theory of the Metrical Film', 149–55).

This, at least, is one way to understand the importance of *Metropolis* for 80s music videos such as David Fincher's extremely successful video for Madonna's *Express Yourself* (1989). Fincher's video, which divides its world into a vertical hierarchy similar to that of *Metropolis* and ends with the famous allegory about the need for a heart to mediate between the mind and the body, is an obvious homage to Lang's film. But in Fincher's version, rather than appearing as the agent of modernity's suppression of vitality, industrial technology becomes *identified* with that lost vitality. *Express Yourself* has rightly been understood in terms of changing gender relations, where a destabilization of gender codes can be observed in the way in which Madonna appears by turns in the roles of an elegant Garbo-like figure, a chained woman, the factory boss (i.e. Fredersen) in his office tower high above the city, and even Fritz Lang himself – wearing the director's signature monocle and a striped suit – emerging from the mouth of the Moloch machine.[22] In the last guise, which would be repeated countless times on stage for the opening number of the 'Express Yourself' concert tour, one might see a reference to the pairing of femininity and technology that had already informed *Metropolis* and stood at the centre of most critical readings of the film throughout the 1980s.[23] But the video is just as much – if not more – concerned with questions of *masculinity* in a postmodern age, and specifically a sense of 'lost' masculine vitality now identified with industrial technology.

One can see this identification of industrial technology and masculine vitality right from the opening sequence, where the establishing shot of the city is rhythmically intercut with an image of a spinning crankshaft graphically melded with what looks conspicuously like a male biceps. This pairing of industry and the

22 For feminist readings of the song and video, see for example Melanie Morton, 'Don't Go for Second Sex Baby!', in Cathy Schwichtenberg (ed.), *The Madonna Connection: Representational Politics, Subcultural Identities, and Cultural Theory* (Boulder: Westview, 1993), 213–38; Douglas Kellner, *Media Culture. Cultural Studies, identity and politics between the modern and the postmodern* (London: Routledge, 1995), 278–79.

23 The reading of *Metropolis* as a film about modernity's projections of a dichotomous concept of femininity – the virgin and the vamp – onto technology was first proposed by Andreas Huyssen in an article of 1982, a version of which was reprinted in 1986 in his book, *After the Great Divide*. See Huyssen, 'The Vamp and the Machine: Technology and Sexuality in Fritz Lang's *Metropolis*', *New German Critique* 24/25 (Autumn 1981–Winter 1982), 221–37. See also Ludmilla Jordanova, 'Fritz Lang's *Metropolis*: Science, Machines and Gender', *Radical Science* 17 (1985), 4–21, reprinted in *Fritz Lang's Metropolis: Cinematic Visions of Technology and Fear*, 173–95.

muscular male body will only become more pronounced when we see the underground workers – now appearing as a group of shirtless muscle-men whose glistening biceps are set into relief by the rainwater and chiaroscuro lighting – engaged in rhythmical pumping movements on the machines. Again and again, the video operates with such graphic matches, likening the rhythmical motions of industrial technology to the pumping, dancing or fighting of shirtless male bodies.

That the *Express Yourself* video reads technology more in terms of masculinity than femininity can also be seen in the fact that the video's central *Doppelgänger* is no longer the female robot but the masculine worker himself. Specifically, the most prominent male worker – who will join Madonna for a bout of love-making at the end of the video – has an obvious double in the prominent figure of a factory manager (another variant on the Fredersen figure) played by the same actor. Wearing a tight suit and a bald wig, the manager is as desexualized as the worker is hypersexualized. The first time we see him, the manager appears troubled on hearing the music blaring from a loudspeaker and looks down to catch the gaze of his hypermasculine double below. A few shots later, the manager figure reappears, this time seated on a leather chair and holding a remote control with which he illuminates a giant glass cylinder containing a rotating jazz band. The sequence is particularly revealing for the media relations at stake in Madonna's appropriation of *Metropolis* for the music video. While the viewing situation visualized here – the remote contol and virtual (untouchable) quality of the spectacle – clearly evoke the television medium for which Madonna's video was made, the jazz spectacle within the glass case, which is displayed spinning like a phonograph, recalls the modernist dream of investing industrial technology with vitality. But the glass tube also suggests – not unlike the manager's constrictive costumes – a phenomenon of containment, where new technologies have repressed the vitality now identified with old technologies. Thus where *Metropolis* constructed a dichotomous vision of femininity projected onto opposing visions of obedient and rebellious technology, *Express Yourself* constructs a dichotomous vision of masculinity, which is projected in turns onto the vital pumping of industrial technologies and the sterile virtuality of televisual media serving to contain that former virility. The promise of *Express Yourself* is thus not only – in accordance with the song's lyrics – to help men liberate their suppressed masculinity, but also to use the virtual medium of television (the medium of music videos and thus of Madonna's clip itself) to liberate that lost virility retrospectively projected onto industrial technology and film.[24]

A similar nostalgia for industrial rhythms characterized many of the attempts to refashion the image of Berlin into a thriving capital of German and European cultural life during the 1990s. Particularly relevant here is the revival of the city-symphony genre in films such as Hubertus Siegert's *Berlin Babylon* (2001), which documented post-wall construction projects in the city to the industrial music of Einstürzende Neubauten, and Thomas Schadt's *Berlin: Sinfonie einer Großstadt* (2002) [*Berlin: Symphony of a City*], which sought to remake Ruttmann's *Berlin* film nearly sequence-for-sequence in luscious black and white, to picture the Berlin of the new millennium. This return to the rhythmical aesthetics of the city symphony could be analysed in the context of a broad renewed interest in the rhythms of urban life. Henri Lefebvre's *Éléments de rythmanalyse* (1992) [*Elements of Rhythmanalysis*], for example, proposed the reintroduction of time, and specifically rhythm, into Lefebvre's better-known sociology of spatial practices. This academic interest in urban rhythms found an echo, moreover, in the rise of symbolic rituals such as the Love Parade techno festival, which took place annually in Berlin throughout the 1990s before moving to the industrial Ruhr area from 2006 to 2010. But the revival of the city symphony in Berlin films after 2000 also played into a broader marketing strategy, as it were, which sought to refashion the image of the 'New' Berlin into that of a vibrant centre of cultural and economic production after German reunification.

Such depictions of the neoliberal city as a conglomerate of vital rhythms were not without their critics. Harun Farocki, in particular, saw this anachronistic gesture as the sign of a failure to engage with the actual developments of labour and urban life in recent decades. In a text accompanying his own video installation *Contre-chant* [*Counter Music*], in which he juxtaposed found footage from the city symphonies of Ruttmann and Dziga Vertov with images taken from surveillance cameras in Lille in 2003, Farocki explained:

> On peut encore montrer, de nos jours, des marées humaines sortant des transports en commun pour se rendre à leur travail, mais il est trop évident que les grandes industries ont quasiment disparu de nos villes. De plus, le rythme des machines ne produit plus la moindre

---

[24] This treatment of masculinity with reference to older media seems to form something of a pattern in Fincher's work, which reappears in *Fight Club* (1999), where the relationship between the repressed protagonist (Edward Norton) and his libidinous *Doppelgänger* played by Brad Pitt recalls any number of German *Doppelgänger* films such as Paul Wegener's *Der Student von Prag* (1913).

mélodie. La société de masse n'étonne plus. La distorsion des horaires de travail, le caractère visuellement abstrait de la plupart des métiers, la moindre densité de l'habitat, voilà qui ôte leur force aux imitations de Ruttmann.[25]

[In our time, one can still show human crowds pouring out of public transport systems and heading for their workplaces, but everyone knows that the major industries have all but disappeared from our cities. Moreover, the rhythm of machines no longer produces the slightest melody. Mass society is no longer novel. The spreading-out of working hours, the visually abstract character of most work, the reduced density of habitation – these factors rob Ruttmann imitations of their force.]

If the classical city symphony is no longer appropriate for representing post-industrial cities, this is, for Farocki, not least because the city itself is no longer the locus of audible or visual rhythms. Work is no longer coordinated – as it was in Ruttmann's *Berlin* as well as in *Metropolis* – by the hours and minutes of a common clock, but rather 'spread out' over various work schedules. Such a lack of coordination also makes for a 'reduced density' of bodies in any given space of the city. Moreover, post-industrial technologies themselves no longer operate according to the visible or audible rhythms of cranks, gears or levers, to which the hand might adapt. Repeating a theme that runs throughout his recent work, Farocki argues that labour itself has become 'abstract' in the digital age, automatized and increasingly inaccessible to the human hand or eye.[26]

All these factors form central themes in Farocki's *Contre-chant*, which depicts a city *not* functioning to coordinate the productive movement of working bodies according to common rhythms. Rather, Farocki's city is depicted as much more centrally concerned with occupying bodies – youths, immigrants and the unemployed – that have become superfluous amidst a world of automatized technologies increasingly able to do without them.[27] Whereas industrial society exploited human labour by making it, in the words of one intertitle in Farocki's installation, an 'appendage to the

---

25 Harun Farocki, 'Contre-chant', in Alain Guiheux (ed.), *La ville qui fait signe* (Paris: Le Fresnoy, 2004), 106–07, translation mine.

26 For more on this theme, see the essays on Farocki collected in Philippe Despoix and Johanne Lamoureux (eds.), *Travailler: Farocki*, special issue of *Intermédialités* 11 (Spring 2008).

27 On this point, see my article in the above-mentioned special issue: Michael Cowan, 'Rethinking the City Symphony after the Age of Industry: Harun Farocki and the "City Film"', *Intermédialités* 11 (2008), 69–89.

machine', it was still marked by an unmistakeable human-machine interface, one that is increasingly disappearing from post-industrial society, as digital technology surpasses the capacities of human work or perception. Again and again, *Contre-chant* juxtaposes images of industrial society (from Vertov's cameraman to the workers of the erstwhile textile industry of Lille), in which bodies conform to the rhythms of machines, with images of post-industrial society, where bodies are shown rather as the objects of technological surveillance, imaging technologies designed to count metro passengers, identify loiterers, monitor sleep patterns, etc. Put differently, *Contre-chant* juxtaposes the *disciplinary* nature of modern industrial cities, where technology trained bodies to move to common (machinic) rhythms in well defined circuits and spaces, with the *control* structure of post-industrial cities, where technology now serves to monitor bodies set adrift in an increasingly diffuse urban environment.[28] If, for Farocki, the city is no longer 'rhythmical', this is because rhythm was the hallmark of such disciplinary formations.

Perhaps nowhere is this discrepancy more striking than in Farocki's reference to the paradigmatic train-sequence from Ruttmann's *Berlin* film. In Ruttmann, the train transported its spectators into the enclosed, disciplinary space of the city, while the jarring montage demanded an adaptation to the technological rhythm that would characterize the activities depicted in that urban space. At one point, Farocki cites this opening sequence from Ruttmann, overlaying the image with a pulsating rhythmical percussion. But the footage of Ruttmann's train montage soon gives way to a series of images of the technology regulating the contemporary TGV network around Lille, which no longer transports spectators into a bustling urban centre, but links the city to a diffuse network of destinations throughout Europe. In place of Ruttmann's filmic montage, we now see digital maps and train simulators designed to regulate every aspect of train travel with minimal input from human workers, now reduced to the role of merely monitoring computer programmes. At this point, Farocki replays Ruttmann's montage while intersplicing various shots from the TGV simulator, as if to question the validity of trying to recreate Ruttmann's rhythms with digital technologies at a time when urban life and labour no longer assume rhythmical form. Unlike the initial

---

28 On the concept of control society, see Gilles Deleuze, 'Postscript on the Societies of Control', *October* 59 (1992), 3–7. Farocki was clearly influenced by Deleuze's concept. See, for example, his essay 'Controlling Observation', in Thomas Elsaesser (ed.), *Harun Farocki: Working on the Sight-Lines* (Amsterdam: University of Amsterdam Press, 2004), 293.

citation of Ruttmann's train, however, Farocki's combined montage remains curiously unmoving, accompanied not by rhythmical percussion but rather by a mundane droning background noise.

Once again, then, Ruttmann's train sequence has emerged as a privileged vector of modernist ideas about rhythm in the 1920s and the fate of those ideas in subsequent decades: whereas Nazi propaganda could use Ruttmann's train to discredit the cultivation of urban and 'Americanist' rhythms in Weimar culture (while nonetheless proposing its own disciplinary rhythms in the form of communal marching), the same footage in Farocki's installation serves to suggest the sheer impossibility – or at least the disingenuousness – of such a rhythmical imaginary in a post-industrial and post-disciplinary society of control. No doubt, the recurrence of the train sequence, as well as its prominent place in Ruttmann's original film, is no accident. From Engelke to Klages, the train returns again and again as a charged symbol of industrial modernity and its rhythmical movement.[29] As Lynn Kirby has shown, moreover, the train was closely associated in the modern imagination with moving images themselves, both embodying in a privileged way the perceptual shocks constitutive of modern experience.[30] The paradigmatic representations of trains in these films can thus be read as indirect commentaries on moving images: whereas Nazism wanted to discredit the rhythm of modernist montage, Farocki questions the very validity of rhythmical filmmaking à la Ruttmann in a post-industrial era.

But this is not to argue that modernist rhythmical utopias have no relevance for contemporary society. On the contrary, as I pointed out in chapter 1 in the case of *Rhythm is it!*, the infatuation with polyrhythms in Stravinsky and Jaques-Dalcroze appear once again to have caught the desires and imagination of contemporary educators. And yet, having examined the stakes of rhythm and industrialization in German modernism over the preceding chapters, we can now sense a shift in emphasis in such projects compared to their modernist predecessors. In another interview from *Rhythm is it!*, Simon Rattle suggests such a shift when he argues that Stravinsky has become more relevant than ever for a post-industrial generation precisely because we no longer adhere to disciplinary forms of collective labour:

---

29   See in particular Engelke's poem 'Lokomotive'. Klages's discussion of the train has already been treated in chapter 1.

30   See Lynn Kirby, *Parallel Tracks. The Railroad and Silent Cinema* (Durham: Duke University Press, 1997).

> We have been educated for many years to be a certain type of person. We've been educated for a society that maybe is gone. We need more and more creative people in society. We need more and more people who will make things connect together, who will go in strange directions. We don't only need good workers. These days are over.

While Rattle's critique of obedient workers could find many precedents in modernist discourses on rhythm (including the examples of *Metropolis* and jazz music examined in the chapters of this book), his assertion that this disciplinary society has now disappeared points toward a new situation; for the creativity associated with polyrhythm and syncopation is no longer seen as a form of liberation from the dominant rhythms of work and daily life but rather as a form of adaptation to life in a post-industrial world. Although Rattle does not state it specifically, his contention that 'we need' people who think creatively evokes all the values of flexibility, adaptability, multi-tasking and (in the academic field) interdisciplinarity that have come to structure normative labour in our own societies of control.[31] And this might just be what really differentiates the project documented in *Rhythm is it!* from Stravinsky's ballet in 1913. If the idea of a rhythmical education has gained a new urgency today, this is not because it promises to help people adapt to factory rhythms or, as the case may be, to escape such rhythms through syncopation and polyrhythms. But neither can one say that the 'liberation' of the body through polyrhythms has succeeded. Rather, perhaps what we are experiencing today is a paradoxical new kind of polyrhythmical discipline, one more appropriate to the post-industrial imperatives of flexibility and constant change than to the rigid schedules and repetitive gestures of Fordism, one better suited to societies of control than the disciplinary space of the factory.

---

31 On the key place of 'flexibility' in post-industrial labour, see David Harvey, *The Condition of Postmodernity* (Cambridge: Blackwell, 1990), 141–72; Zygmunt Bauman, *Liquid Modernity* (Cambridge: Polity, 2000), 130–68.

Bibliography

'1000 Schritte Charleston', film review, *Süddeutsche Filmzeitung,* 14 January 1927, n.p.

Abel, Richard, *French Cinema. The First Wave 1915–1929* (Princeton: Princeton University Press, 1984)

Adorno, Theodor, 'Abschied vom Jazz', in *Gesammelte Schriften,* vol. 18, *Musikalische Schriften V* (Frankfurt am Main: Suhrkamp, 1984), 795–99

— 'Über Jazz', in *Gesammelte Schriften,* vol. 17, *Musikalische Schriften 4: Moments musicaux, Impromptus* (Frankfurt am Main: Suhrkamp, 1982), 74–109

Agawu, Kofi, 'The Invention of "African Rhythm"', in *Journal of the American Musicological Society* 48:3 (1995), 380–95

Ägde, Günter, *Flimmernde Versprechen. Geschichte des deutschen Werbefilms im Kino seit 1897* (Berlin: Verlag Das Neue Berlin, 1998)

Agnew, Vanessa, 'The Colonialist Beginnings of Comparative Musicology', in Eric Ames, Marcia Klotz and Lora Wildentahl (eds.), *Germany's Colonial Pasts* (Lincoln: University of Nebraska Press, 2005), 41–61

Altenberg, Pete, *Aschantee. Afrika und Wien um 1900,* ed. Kristin Kopp and Werner Michael Schwarz (Vienna: Löcker, 2008)

Ames, Eric, 'The Sound of Evolution', in *Modernism/modernity* 10:2 (2003), 297–325

Amsler, André, *'Wer dem Werbefilm verfällt, ist verloren für die Welt.' Das Werk von Julius Pinschewer 1883–1961* (Zürich: Chronos Verlag, 1997)

Andriopoulos, Stefan. *Possessed: Hypnotic Crimes, Corporate Fiction and the Invention of the Cinema,* trans. Peter Jensen and Stefan Andriopoulos (Chicago: University of Chicago Press, 2008)

Anz, Thomas and Michael Stark (eds.), *Expressionismus: Manifeste und Dokumente zur deutschen Literatur 1910–1920* (Stuttgart: Metzler, 1982)

Aros, 'Die Woche der Kipho', in *Kinematograph* Nr. 971 (1925), 1–2

Asendorf, Christoph, *Ströme und Strahlen. Das langsame Verschwinden der Materie um 1900*, Werkbund-Archiv 18 (Gießen: Anabas-Verlag, 1989)

'Aus dem Programm der Kipho', in *Lichtbildbühne* Nr. 159 (1925), 13

Autsch, Sabine, 'Von Lichtbildern und Lichtfreunden. Zur Beziehung von Fotografie und Lebensreform um 1900,' in Kai Buchholz, Rita Latocha, Hilke Peckmann and Klaus Wolbert (eds.), *Die Lebensreform. Entwürfe zur Neugestaltung von Leben und Kunst um 1900*, vol. 1 (Darmstadt: Häusser, 2001), 303–06

Awramoff, Dobri, *Arbeit und Rhythmus. Der Einfluss des Rhythmus auf die Quantität und Qualität geistiger und körperlicher Arbeit, mit besonderer Berücksichtigung des rhythmischen Schreibens* (Leipzig: Wilhelm Engelmann, 1902)

Bachmann, Holger, 'The Production and Contemporary Reception of Metropolis', in Michael Minden and Holger Bachmann (eds.), *Fritz Lang's Metropolis. Cinematic Visions of Technology and Fear* (Rochester: Camden House, 2000), 3–46

Bahr, Hermann, *Expressionismus* (Munich: Delphin-Verlag, 1916)

Balász, Bela, *Der sichtbare Mensch oder die Kultur des Films* (Frankfurt am Main: Suhrkamp, 2001)

Baresel, Alfred, 'Jazz als Rettung', in *Der Auftakt* 4 (1926), 213–16

— *Das Jazz-Buch*, 4th edn (Berlin: Julius Heinrich Zimmermann, 1926)

— *Das neue Jazz-Buch* (Leipzig: Wilhelm Zimmermann, 1929)

Baudelaire, Charles, *Curiosités esthétiques, L'Art romantique et autres Oeuvres critiques* (Paris: Garnier, 1962)

Baumann, Zygmunt, *Liquid Moderity* (Cambridge: Polity, 2000)

— *Society under Siege* (Cambridge: Polity Press, 2002)

Baxmann, Inge, *Mythos: Gemeinschaft. Körper- und Tanzkulturen in der Moderne* (Munich: Fink, 2000)

Bazin, André, *What is Cinema?* trans. Hugh Gray. Berkeley (University of California Press, 1967)

Behn, Siegfried, *Der deutsche Rhythmus und sein eigenes Gesetz. Eine experimentelle Untersuchung* (Strassburg, Verlag von Karl J. Trübner, 1912)

Benjamin, Walter, 'Das Kunstwerk im Zeitalter seiner technischen Reproduzierbarkeit', in *Illuminationen*, ed. Hannah Arendt (Frankfurt a.M.: Suhrkamp, 1961), 136–70

— *Einbahnstrasse* (Frankfurt am Main: Suhrkamp, 1955)

— 'Über einige Motive bei Baudelaire', in *Illuminationen*, 201–45

Bergson, Henri, *L'évolution créatrice* (Paris: Presses universitaires de France, 2003)

— *Matière et mémoire. Essai sur la relation du corps à l'esprit* (Paris: Presses Universitaires de France, 2008)

— 'Bericht von der "Kipho"', in *Lichtbildbühne* 189 (1925), 12–13
Bernhard, Paul, *Jazz: eine musikalische Zeitfrage* (Munich: Delphin-Verlag, 1927)
Die Bildungs-Anstalt für Musik und Rhythmus E. Jaques-Dalcroze in Dresden-Hellerau. Ein Bericht mit 8 Abbildungen (Jena: Eugen Diederichs, 1910)
Bode, Rudolf, *Rhythmus und Körpererziehung*, 2nd edn (Jena: Eugen Dietrichs, 1925)
Bolton, Thaddeus, 'Rhythm', in *The American Journal of Psychology* 6:2 (1894), 145–238
Borck, Cornelius, 'Communicating the Modern Body: Fritz Kahn's Popular Images of Human Physiology as an Industrialized World', in *Canadian Journal of Communication* 32:3 (2007), www.cjc-online.ca/index.php/journal/article/view/1876 [accessed 20 July 2011]
Brain, Robert, 'The Pulse of Modernism: and Aesthetic Avant-Gardes circa 1900', *Studies in the History and Philosophy of Science* 39 (2008), 393–417
Braun, Andreas. *Tempo, Tempo! Eine Kunst- und Kulturgeschichte der Geschwindigkeit im 19. Jahrhundert* (Frankfurt am Main: Anabas, 2001)
Brod, Max, 'Shimmy und Foxtrott', in *Der Auftakt* 2 (1922), 256–59
Brüstle, Christa, Nadia Ghattas, Clemens Risi and Sabine Schouten (ed.) *Aus dem Takt. Rhythmus in Kunst, Kultur und Natur* (Bielefeld: transcript-Verlag, 2005)
Bücher, Karl, *Arbeit und Rhythmus* (Leipzig: S. Hirzel, 1897)
— *Arbeit und Rhythmus*, 6th edn (Leipzig: Emmanuel Reinicke, 1924)
Bukofzer, Manfred, 'Soziologie des Jazz', in *Melos* 8 (1929), 387–91
Buñuel, Luis, 'Metropolis', film review, in *Fritz Lang's Metropolis: Cinematic Visions of Technology and Fear*, 106
Burian, E. F., 'Revue!', in *Der Auftakt* 8 (1928): 181–83
Clair, Jean (ed.), *The 1930s: The Making of 'The New Man'* (Ottawa: National Gallery of Canada, 2008)
Cook, Susan, 'Jazz as Deliverance: the Reception and Institution of American Jazz during the Weimar Republic', in *American Music* 7:1 (1989), 30–47
— *Opera for a New Republic: The Zeitopern of Krenek, Weill, and Hindemith* (Ann Arbor: U.M.I. Research Press, 1988)
Cowan, Michael, 'Americanism, Popular Culture and the Primitive around 1900: Johannes V. Jensen's *Madame d'Ora* (1904)', in *Orbis Litterarum* 60:2 (2005), 109–32
— *Cult of the Will: Nervousness and German Modernity* (University Park: Pennsylvania State University Press, 2008)

- 'The Heart Machine: Rhythm and Body in Weimar Film and Fritz Lang's Metropolis', in *Modernism/modernity* 14.2 (April 2007), 225–48
- 'Imagining the Nation through the Energetic Body: the Royal Jump', in Michael Cowan and Kai Sicks (eds.), *Leibhaftige Moderne. Körper in Kunst und Massenmedien 1918–1933* (Bielefeld: transcript-Verlag, 2005), 55–74
- 'Rethinking the City Symphony after the Age of Industry: Harun Farocki and the "City Film"', in *Intermédialités* 11 (2008), 69–89
- 'Theater and Cinema in the Age of Nervousness: *Der Andere* by Paul Lindau (1893) and Max Mack' (1913), in *Cinema & Cie* 5 (2004), 65–91

Crary, Jonathan, *Techniques of the Observer. On Vision and Modernity in the Nineteenth Century* (Cambridge: MIT Press, 1992)

Darwin, Charles, *The Descent of Man and Selection in Relation to Sex*. 2nd edn (London: John Murray, 1874)

'Das neueste der Woche: das Programm der Kipho', in *Der Film* 10:38 (20 September 1925), 27

Deleuze, Gilles. *Cinéma I. L'image-mouvement* (Paris: Éditions de Minuit, 1983)

- 'Postscript on the Societies of Control', in *October* 59 (1992), 3–7

Demetz, Peter, 'The Futurist Johannes R. Becher', in *Modernism/modernity* 1:3 (1994), 179–94

Derrida, Jacques. *De la grammatologie* (Paris: Les Éditions de Minuit, 1967)

Didi-Huberman, Georges and Laurent Mannoni, *Mouvements de l'air. Étienne-Jules Marey, photographe des fluides* (Paris: Gallimard, 2004)

Dinerstein, Joel, *Swinging the Machine* (Amherst: University of Massachussetts Press, 2003)

Doane, Mary Ann, *The Emergence of Cinematic Time. Modernity, Contingency and the Archive* (Cambridge: Harvard University Press, 2002)

Dohrn, Wolf, 'Aufgaben der Bildungsanstalt Jaques-Dalcroze', in *Der Rhythmus. Ein Jahrbuch* (Jena: Eugen Diederichs, 1911), 2–19

Donald, James. 'Jazz Modernism and Film Art: Dudly Murphy and *Ballet mécanique*', in *Modernism/modernity* 16:1 (2009), 25–49

Dulac, Germaine, 'Les esthétiques, les entraves, la cinégraphie intégrale', in *Écrits sur le cinéma (1919–1937)*, ed. Prosper Hillairet (Paris: Paris Expérimental, 1994), 98–104

Dulac, Nicolas and André Gaudreault, 'Circularity and Repetition at the Heart of the Attraction: Optical Toys and the Emergence of a New Cultural Series', in Wanda Strauven (ed.), *The Cinema of Attractions Reloaded* (Amsterdam: Amsterdam University Press, 2006), 227–44

Duncan, Isadora, *The Art of the Dance* (New York: Theater Arts Inc., 1970)

Eckstein, Modris, *The Rites of Spring* (Boston: Houghton Mifflin, 1989)

Eisenstein, Sergei, 'The Dialectical Approach to Film Form', in *Film Form. Essays in Film Theory*, ed. and trans. Jay Leda (San Diego: Harcourt, 1977)

Elsaesser, Thomas, *Weimar Cinema and After: Germany's Historical Imaginary* (London: Routledge, 2000)

Engelke, Gerrit, *Rhythmus des neuen Europa. Das Gesamtwerk* (Hannover: Postskriptum, 1979)

Epstein, Jean, 'Le cinéma et les lettres modernes', in *Écrits sur le cinéma*, vol. 1 (Paris: Seghers, 1974) 65–69

'Die Eröffnung der "Kipho"', in *Der Film* 10:39 (1925), 33

Farocki, Harun, 'Contre-chant', in Alain Guiheux (ed.), *La ville qui fait signes* (Paris: Le Fresnoy, 2004), 106–18

— 'Controlling Observation', in Thomas Elsaesser (ed.), *Harun Farocki. Working on the Sight-Lines* (Amsterdam: Amsterdam University Press, 2004), 289–97

Felber, Erwin, 'Primitive und moderne Musik', in *Der Auftakt* 5 (1925), 307–12

Ferand, Ernst, 'Rhythmus und Tanz', in *Musikblätter des Anbruch* 8 (1926), 130

Fichna, Wolfgang, '"Die Überfahrt beginnt": schwarze Körper und Amerikanismus in Ernst Kreneks Zeitoper *Jonny spielt auf*', in Michael Cowan and Kai Sicks (eds.), *Leibhaftige Moderne: Körper in Kunst und Massenmedien 1918–1933* (Bielefeld: transcript, 2005), 292–304

Fischer, Hans, *Rhythmus des kosmischen Lebens. Das Buch vom Pulsschlag der Welt* (Leipzig: Voigtländer, 1925)

Fließ, Wilhelm, *Der Ablauf des Lebens. Grundlegungen zur exakten Biologie* (Leipzig: Franz Dueticke, 1906)

Ford, Henry, *My Life and Work* (London: William Heinemann, 1923)

Fritzsche, Peter, *Reading Berlin 1900* (Cambridge: Harvard University Press, 1998)

Fülöp-Miller, René, *Die Phantasiemaschine. Eine Saga der Gewinnsucht* (Berlin: Paul Zsolnay Verlag, 1931)

G., F., 'Rhythmus und Resonanz als ökonomisches Prinzip in der Reklame', review article, in *Die Reklame* 19 (1926), 513

Gates, Henry Louis Jr., *The Signifying Monkey. Theory of African-American Literary Criticism* (Oxford University Press, 1988)

Gebhardt, Wilhelm Walther, *Wie werde ich energisch*, 9th edn (Leipzig: Verlag von F. W. Gloeckner & Co, 1912)
Giese, Fritz, *Girlkultur. Vergleiche zwischen amerikanischem und europäischem Rhythmus und Lebensgefühl* (Munich: Delphin-Verlag, 1925)
— *Methoden der Wirtschaftspsychologie* (Berlin: Urban und Schwarzenberg, 1927)
— 'Revue und Film', in *Der Auftakt* 8 (1928), 172–76
Göktürk, Deniz, *Künstler, Cowboys und Ingenieure... Kultur- und mediengeschichtliche Studien zu deutschen Amerika-Texten, 1912–1920* (Munchen: Fink, 1998)
Goergen, Jeanpaul, 'Julius Pinschewer: A Trade-Mark Cinema', in Thomas Elseasser (ed.), *A Second Life. German Cinema's First Decades* (Amsterdam: Amsterdam University Press, 1996), 168–74
Goll, Claire, *Lyrische Films* (Basel, Leipzig: Rhein Verlag, 1922)
— *Der Neger Jupiter raubt Europa* (Munich: Deutscher Taschenbuch Verlag, 1992)
Goll, Yvan, 'Die Neger erobern Europa' (1926), in Anton Kaes (ed.), *Weimar Republik. Manifeste und Dokumente zur deutschen Literatur 1918–1933* (Stuttgart: Metlzler, 1983), 256–59
Golston, Michael, '"Im Anfang war der Rhythmus" — rhythmic incubations in discourses of mind, body and race from 1850–1944', in *Stanford Electronic Humanities Review. Supplement 5: Cultural and Technological Incubations of Fascism* (1996), www.stanford.edu/group/SHR/5-supp/text/golston.html [accessed 20 July 2011]
— *Rhythm and Race in Modernist Poetry and Science* (New York: Columbia University Press, 2008)
Grevelli, Maria, 'Tänzertum und Menschlichkeit', in *Die Tanz-Gemeinschaft* 3 (1929), 4–5
Grosse, Ernst, *Die Anfänge der Kunst* (Freiburg: Akademische Verlagsbuchhandlung von J. C. B. Mohr, 1894)
Guido, Laurent, *L'Âge du rythme. Cinéma, musicalité et culture du corps dans les théories françaises des années 1910–1930* (Lausanne: Payot, 2007)
Guilbert, Laure, *Danser avec le IIIe Reich. Les danseurs modernes sous le nazisme* (Paris: Édtion Complexe, 2000)
Gunning, Tom, 'The Cinema of Attractions: Early Film, its Spectator and the Avant-garde', in Thomas Elsaesser (ed.), *Early Cinema: Space, Frame, Narrative* (London: BFI, 1989) 56–62
— *The Films of Fritz Lang. Allegories of Vision and Modernity* (London: British Film Institute, 2000)
— 'Loïe Fuller and the Art of Motion. Body, Light, Electricity and the Origins of Cinema', in Richard Allen and Malcolm Turvey

(eds.), *Camera Obscura. Camera Lucida. Essays in Honor of Annette Michelson* (Amsterdam: Amsterdam University Press, 2003), 75–90

Hagener, Malte, *Moving Forward, Looking Back. The European Avant-Garde and the Invention of Film Cuture 1919–1939* (Amsterdam: Amsterdam University Press, 2007)

Hake, Sabine, *Popular Cinema of the Third Reich* (Austin: University of Texas Press, 2002)

Hansen, Miriam, *Babel and Babylon: Spectatorship in American Silent Film* (Cambridge: Harvard University Press, 2005)

Harbou, Thea von, *Metropolis* (Frankfurt am Main: Ozeanische Bibliothek, 1984)

Hartungen, Christoph von, *Psychologie der Reklame* (Stuttgart: C.E. Poeschel, 1921)

Harvey, David, *The Condition of Postmodernity* (Cambridge: Blackwell, 1990)

Heidegger, Martin, 'Wozu Dichter', in *Holzwege* (Frankfurt am Main: Vittorio Klostermann, 2003), 269–320

Hein, Birgit, *Film im Untergrund* (Frankfurt am Main: Ullstein, 1971)

Hellpach, Willy, *Nervosität und Kultur* (Berlin: Verlag von Johannes Räde, 1902)

Herf, Jeffrey, *Reactionary Modernism: Technology, Culture and Politics in Weimar and the Third Reich* (Cambridge: Cambridge University Press, 1986)

Hewitt, Andrew, *Social Choreography. Ideology as Performance in Dance and Everyday Movement* (Durham: Duke University Press, 2005)

Holmes, C. G., 'Stray Thoughts on Rhythm in Painting', *Rhythm* 1:3 (1911), 1–3

Huppert, Eduard, *Der moderne Tanz. Ein Ratbeger für Tänzende* (Graz, 1926)

Huyssen, Andreas, 'The Vamp and the Machine: Technology and Sexuality in Fritz Lang's *Metropolis*', in *New German Critique* 24–25 (Autumn 1981–Winter 1982), 221–37

Iger, Artur, 'Jazz Industrie', *Der Auftakt* VI (1926), 222–25

Jaques-Dalcroze, Emil, *Rhythmus, Musik und Erziehung*, trans. Julius Schwabe (Basel: Verlag Beno Schwabe & Co., 1922)

Jemnitz, Alexander, 'Der Jazz als Form und Inhalt', *Musikblätter des Anbruch* 7 (1925), 188–96

'Jonny spielt auf', review, *Der Auftakt* 7 (1927), 43–44

Jordanova, Ludmilla, 'Fritz Lang's *Metropolis*: Science, Machines and Gender', in *Radical Science* 17 (1985), 4–21

Kaes, Anton, 'Leaving Home: Film, Migration and the Urban Experience', in *New German Critique* 74 (1998), 179–92

Keightley, Archibald, *Das Gesundheitsproblem: Der Rhythmus des Lebens*, trans. Therese Panizza (Berlin: Paul Raatz Verlag, 1912)
— *The Rhythm of Life: Character Building as an Aid to Health* (London: Henry J. Glaisher, 1907)
Kellner, Douglas, *Media Culture. Cultural Studies, Identity and Politics between the Modern and the Postmodern* (London: Routledge, 1995)
Kirby, Lynn, *Parallel Tracks. The Railroad and Silent Cinema* (Durham: Duke Universtiy Press, 1997)
Kittler, Friedrich, *Aufschreibesysteme 1800/1900* (Munich: Fink, 1985)
— *Discourse Networks 1800/1900*, trans. Michael Metteer (Stanford University Press, 1992)
Klages, Ludwig, *Ausdrucksbewegung und Gestaltungskraft*, 3rd edn (Leipzig: Johann Ambrosius Barth, 1923)
— *Vom Wesen des Rhythmus* (Kampfen auf Sylt: Niels Kampmann Verlag, 1934)
Klar, Gustav, *Der Rhythmus und seine Bedeutung für den Unterricht* (Langensalza: Verlag von Julius Beltz, 1919)
Klein, Alfred, *Im Auftrag ihrer Klasse. Weg und Leistung der deutschen Arbeiterschriftsteller 1918–1933* (Berlin und Weimar: Aufbau, 1972)
Koch, Bernhard, *Der Rhythmus. Untersuchungen über sein Wesen und Wirken in Kunst und Natur und seine Bedeutung für die Schule* (Langenzala: Hermann Beyer & Söhne, 1922)
Koebner, Franz Wolfgang (ed.), *Jazz und Shimmy. Brevier der neuesten Tänze* (Berlin: Eysler, 1921)
Koebner, Franz Wolfgang, *Das neue Tranz-Brevier* (Berlin: Eysler, 1920)
Koffka, Kurt, *Experimenal-Untersuchungen zur Lehre vom Rhythmus* (Leipzig: Barth, 1908)
König, Theodor, *Reklamepsychologie*, 2nd edn (Munich: R. Oldenbourg, 1924)
Kool, Jaap, 'Geräuschinstrumente', in *Musikblätter des Anbruch* 8 (1926), 167–69
— *Das Saxophon* (Leipzig: Weber, 1931)
— *Tänze der Naturvölker. Ein Deutungsversuch primitiver Tanzkulte und Kultgebräuche* (Berlin: Fürstner, 1921)
Kracauer, Siegfried, *From Caligari to Hitler. A Psychological History of the German Film* (Princeton: Princeton University Press, 1947)
— *Das Ornament der Masse. Essays* (Frankfurt am Main: Suhrkamp, 1977)
Krenek, Ernst, *Jonny spielt auf*, CD booklet (Berlin: DECCA, 1993)
Kristeva, Julia, *La Révolution du langage poétique* (Paris: Seuil, 1986)
Kubelka, Peter, 'The Theory of the Metrical Film', in P. Adams Sitney (ed.), *The Avant-garde Film. A Reader of Theory and Criticism* (New York: Anthology Film Archives, 1987), 139–59

— 'Über das Wiener Schnitzel', in Gabriele Jutz und Peter Tscherkassky (eds.), *Peter Kubelka* (Vienna: PVS, 1995), 168
— 'Was bedeutet Essen und Kochen für die Menschen?' in *Peter Kubelka*, 170–86
Kühn, Gustav, 'Wir begrüßen die Kipho', in *Der Film* 10:39 (27. September 1925), 1
'Die Kundgebung des deutschen Films', in *Der Film* 10:38 (1925), 28
Kurtzig, Käthe, 'Die Arten des Werbefilms', in *Industrielle Psychotechnik* 3:10 (1926), 311–14
Kurz, Rudolf. *Expressionismus und Film* (Berlin: Verlag der Lichtbild-Bühne, 1926)
Lämmel, Rudolf, *Der moderne Tanz. Eine allgemeinverständliche Einführung in das Gebiet der Rhythmischen Gymnastik und des Neuen Tanzes* (Berlin: Peter J. Oestergaard, 1928)
Lang, Fritz. 'Ausblick auf Morgen. Zum Pariser Kongress', in *Lichtbild-Bühne* 19:229 (September 25, 1926), 9–10
Lareau, Alan. 'Jonny's Jazz: From *Kabarett* to Krenek', in Michael Budds (ed.), *Jazz and the Germans: Essays on the Influence of 'Hot' American Idioms on 20th-century Germanic Music* (Hilsdale, NY: Pendragon, 2002), 19–61
Lawder, Standish, *The Cubist Cinema* (New York: New York University Press, 1975)
Lee, Pamela M, *Chronophobia. On Time in the Art of the 1960s* (Cambridge: MIT Press, 2006)
Lenauer, Jean, 'Innerer Rhythmus', *Süddeutsche Filmzeitung* 7:23 (1. Juni 1928), n.p.
Lessing, Gotthold Ephraim, *Laokoon*, in *Gesammelte Werke*, vol. 5, ed. Paul Rilla (Berlin: Aufbau, 1955)
Lethen, Helmuth, *Verhaltenslehren der Kälte. Lebensversuche zwischen den Kriegen* (Frankfurt am Main: Surhkamp, 1994)
Levinson, André, 'Pour une poétique du film', *L'art cinématographique* 4 (1927), 51–88
Lubkoll, Christine, 'Rhythmus. Zum Komplex von Lebensphilosophie und ästhetischer Moderne', in Christine Lubkoll (ed.), *Das Imaginäre des Fin de siècle. Ein Symposion für Gerhard Neumann* (Freiburg: Rombach, 2002), 83–110
Lucretius, *On the Nature of Things*, trans. W. H. D. Rouse, Loeb Classical Library (Cambridge: Harvard University Press, 1975)
Lukács, Georg, *Werke. Ästhetik I*, vol. 11 (Berlin: Luchterhand, 1972)
— *Werke. Probleme des Realismus*, vol. 4 (Berlin: Luchterhand, 1971)
McCaren, Felicia, *Dancing Machines: Choreographies of the Age of Mechanical Reproduction* (Stanford: Stanford University Press, 2003)

Mackenzie, Michael, 'From Athens to Berlin: The 1936 Olympics and Leni Riefenstahl's Olympia', in *Critical Inquiry* 29 (2003), 302–36

Macrae, David, 'Ruttmann, Rhythm, and "Reality": A Response to Siegfried Kracauer's Interpretation of *Berlin. The Symphony of a Great City*', in Dietrich Scheunemann (ed.), *Expressionist Film. New Perspectives* (Rochester: Camden House, 2003)

Mailer, Norman, 'The White Negro: Superficial Reflections on the Hipster', in *Dissent* 4 (1957), www.learntoquestion.com/resources/database/archives/003327.html [accessed 20 July 2011]

Marcinowski, Johannes, *Im Kampf um gesunde Nerven: Ein Wegweiser zum Verständnis und zur Heilung nervöser Zustände für Ärzte und Laien*, 4th edn (Berlin: Verlag von Otto Salle, 1911)

Marinetti, Filippo Tommaso, *Teoria e invenzione futurista*, ed. Luciano De Maria (Milan: Arnoldo Mondadori, 1968)

Masi, Stefano, 'Der gemeißelte Zeit', in *Peter Kubelka*, 73–123

Mauss, Marcel, *Manuel d'ethnographie* (Paris: Payot, 1947)

Merz, Max, *Körperbildung und Rhythmus* (Vienna: Duncan, 1926)

Meumann, Ernst, *Psychologie und Ästhetik des Rhythmus* (Leipzig, Wilhelm Engelmann, 1894)

Mierendorff, Carlo, *Hätte ich das Kino!* (Berlin: Erich Reiß Verlag, 1920)

Mitry, Jean, *Esthétique et psychologie du cinéma* (Paris: Cerf, 2001)

'Das moderne Filmatelier', *Der Film* 10:39 (1925), 52, 57–58

Moholy-Nagy, László, *Malerei, Fotografie, Film*, Neue Bauhausbücher (Berlin: Gebr. Mann Verlag, 1986)

Moran, Paul. *Moderne Tänze*. Wien: Tagblatt-Bibliothek, 1926

Morawietz, Kurt, *'Mich aber schone, Tod': Gerrit Engelke 1890–1918* (Hannover: Postskriptum, 1979)

Morawietz, Kurt, Karl Riha and Florian Vaßen (eds.), *Zwischen Wolken und Großstadtrausch. Warum Engelke lesen? Dokumentation zum 100. Geburtstag des hannoverschen Dichters Gerrit Engelke* (Hannover: Postskriptum-Verlag, 1992)

Morton, Melanie, 'Don't Go for Second Sex Baby!' in Cathy Schwichtenberg (ed.), *The Madonna Connection: Representational Politics, Subcultural Identities, and Cultural Theory* (Boulder: Westview, 1993), 213–38

Müller, E. J., 'Jazz als Karikatur', in *Der Auftakt* 4 (1926), 216–18

Müller, Robert, *Tropen* (Munich: H. Schmidt, 1917)

Musner, Lutz, 'Stadt. Masse. Weib: Metropolenwandel, Massenphobie und Misogynie im Fin-de-Siècle', in Günther Hödl, Fritz Mayrhofer and Ferdinand Opll (eds.), *Frauen in der Stadt* (Linz: Österreichische Arbeitskreis für Stadtgeschichtsforschung, 2003), 63–83

Muthesius, Hermann, *Die Einheit der Architektur. Betrachtungen über Baukunst, Ingenieurbau und Kunstgewerbe* (Berlin: Curtius, 1908)
Naumann, Barbara (ed.), *Rhythmus. Spuren eines Wechselspiels in Künsten und Wissenschaften* (Königshausen und Neumann, 2005)
Nettl, Paul, 'Die Lustquellen des Rhythmus', *Der Auftakt* 3 (1923), 244–48
Neumann, W., 'Konservenmusik', in Franz Wolfgang Koebner (ed.), *Jazz und Shimmy. Brevier der neuesten Tänze* (Berlin: Eysler, 1921), 87–89
Nichols, Bill, *Representing Reality: Issues and Concepts in Documentary* (Bloomington: Indiana University Press, 1991)
Norguez, Dominique, 'Der Weltmensch', in *Peter Kubelka*, 129–49
Oksiloff, Assenka, *Picturing the Primitive. Visual Culture, Ethnography, and Early German Cinema* (New York: Palgrave, 2001)
Partsch, Cornelius, *Schräge Töne. Jazz und Unterhaltungsmusik in der Kultur der Weimarer Republik* (Stuttgart: Metzler, 2000)
Pauli, Fritz, 'Das Problem des Werbefilms', in *Die Reklame* 19 (1926), 616–17
— 'Der rhythmische Film', in *Die Reklame* 20 (1927), 441
— *Rhythmus und Resonanz als ökonomisches Prinzip in der Reklame* (Berlin: Verlag des Verbandes deutscher Reklamefachleute, 1926)
— 'Tönende Lichtreklame', in *Die Reklame* 20 (1927), 302
Pfeiffer, Theodor, *Studien bei Hans von Bülow* (Berlin, 1894)
Pierre Boulez Conducts Stravinsky. Le Sacre du printemps, DVD (Image Entertainment, 1993)
Platzer, Monika and Ursula Storch (eds.), *Kinetismus. Wien entdeckt die Avantgarde* (Ostfildern: Hatje Cantz Verlag, 2006)
Plessner, Helmuth, *Die Stufen des Organischen. Gesammelte Schriften*, vol. 4, ed. Günter Dux, Odo Marquard und Elisabeth Ströker (Frankfurt am Main: Surkamp, 1981)
'Primitivismus', *Der Auftakt* 5 (1925), 50
'Quer durch die Kipho', *Der Film* 10:40 (1925), 23–24
Rabinbach, Anson, *The Human Motor* (Berkeley: University of California Press, 1992)
Radkau, Joachim, *Das Zeitalter der Nervostät: Deutschland zwischen Bismarck und Hitler* (Munich: Carl Hanser Verlag, 1998)
Rancière, Jacques. *La fable cinématographique* (Paris: Seuil, 2001)
Christian Rapp, *Höhenrausch. Der deutsche Bergfilm* (Wien: Sonderzahl, 1997)
Rhythm is it!, dir. Thomas Grube and Enrique Sánchez Lansch, DVD (Boomtown Media, 2005)

Ribot, Théodule, *Les maladies de la volonté*, 14th edn (Paris: Felix Alcan, 1900)

Richter, Hans, *Filmgegner von heute, Filmfreunde von morgen* (Berlin: Hermann Reckendorf, 1929)

— 'Rhythm', in Jeanpaul Georgen (ed.), *Hans Richter: Film ist Rhythmus* (Berlin: Freunde der Deutschen Kinemathek, 2003), 38

— 'Der Gegenstand in Bewegung', *Hans Richter: Film ist Rhythmus*, 42

— 'Die schlecht trainierte Seele'. *Hans Richter: Film ist Rhythmus*, 28–30

Rippey. Theodore F, 'Rationalization, Race, and the Weimar Response to Jazz', *German Life and Letters* 60:1 (2007), 75–97

Robinson, J. Bradford, 'Jazz Reception in Weimar Germany: In Search of a Shimmy Figure', in Gillam Bryan (ed.), *Music and Performance during the Weimar Republic* (Cambridge University Press, 1994), 107–34

Roth, Joseph, *Bekenntnis zum Gleisdreieck* [1924], www.berlin-gleisdreieck.de/Seiten/projekte/projekte_Frameset.htm [accessed 20 July 2011]

Rückler, Christoph, *Ideologie der Arbeiterdichtung 1914–1933. Eine wissenssoziologische Untersuchung* (Metzler, Stuttgart, 1970)

Ruprecht, Lucia, 'Ambivalent Agency. Gestural Performances of Hands in Weimar Dance and Film', in Michael Cowan and Barbara Hales (eds.), *Moving Bodies, Moving Pictures: Dance in Early German Cinema*, special issue of *Seminar* 46:4 (2010), 257–78

Saerchinger, Cesar, 'Jazz', in *Musikblätter des Anbruch* 7 (1925), 205–10

Sauvanet, Pierre, *Le rythme et la raison*, 2 vols. (Paris: Kimé, 2000)

— *Le Rythme grec d'Héraclite à Aristote* (Paris: Presses Universitaires de France, 1999)

Sauvanet, Pierre and Jean Jacques Wunenburger (eds.), *Rythmes et philosophie* (Paris: Kimé, 1996)

Schaffer, Bill, 'The Riddle of the Chicken: The Work of Norman Macleran', in *Senses of Cinema* (March 2005), www.archive.sensesofcinema.com/contents/cteq/05/35/norman_mclaren.html [accessed 20 July 2011]

Schieferstein, Heinrich von. 'Die Ausnützung mechanischer Schwingungen im Maschinenbau', *Bayerisches Industrie- und Gewerbeblatt* 111:19 (1 October 1925), 117–23, 125–29

Schiller, Friedrich, 'Über naive und sentimentalische Dichtung', in *Werke und Briefe in zwölf Bänden*, vol. 8: *Theoretische Schriften*, ed. Rolf-Peter Janz (Frankfurt am Main: Bibliothek deutscher Klassiker, 1992), 707–810

Schneider, Albert, 'Der deutsche Film und die Öffentlichkeit', in *Der Film* 10:39 (1925), 41–42

Schoennemann, Annika, *Der deutsche Animationsfilm von den Anfängen bis zur Gegenwart 1909–2001* (Sankt Augustin: Gardez! Verlag, 2003)

Schulhof, Erwin, 'Saxophon und Jazzband. Eine Entgegnung auf das Sonderheft "*Jazz*" der "Musikblätter des Anbruch"', in *Der Auftakt* 5 (1925), 179–83

Schulz, Gerhard, 'Nachwort', in Arno Holz, *Phantasus,* ed. Gerhard Schulz (Stuttgart: Reclam, 1968)

Schulz, Hans Hermann, *Das Volkstumserlebnis des Arbeiters in der Dichtung von Gerrit Engelke, Heinrich Lersch und Karl Bröger. Ein Beitrag zur Morphologie des Problems. Stadion — Arbeiten aus dem Germanistischen Seminar der Universität Berlin*, vol. 5, ed. Franz Koch (Würzburg: Triltsch, 1940)

Schwarz, Frederic J. 'The Eye of the Expert: Walter Benjamin and the Avant Garde', in *Art History* 24:3 (2001), 401–44

Schwarz, Werner, *Anthropologischer Spektakel. Zur Schaustellung 'exotischer' Menschen in Wien 1870–1910* (Vienna: Turia und Kant, 2001)

Seeber, Guido, *Der Trickfilm in seinen grundsätzlichen Möglichkeiten* (Frankfurt am Main: Deutsches Filmmuseum, 1979)

Senti-Schmidlin, Verena, *Rhythmus und Tanz in der Malerei. Zur Bewegungsästhetik im Werk von Ferdinand Hodler und Ludwig Hoffmann* (Hildesheim: Georg Olms Verlag, 2007)

Serner, Walter, 'Kino und Schaulust', in *Die Schaubühne* 9:34/35 (1913), 807–11

Sicks, Kai, 'Charleston, Girls und Jazztanzbar. Amerikanismus und die Identitätskrise der Operette in den zwanziger Jahren', in Oliver Kohns and Martin Roussel (eds.), *Einschnitte. Identität in der Moderne* (Würzburg: Königshausen & Neumann, 2007), 153–68

Simmel, Georg, 'Die Großstädte und das Geistesleben', in *Aufsätze und Abhandlungen I: 1901–1908* (Frankfurt am Main: Suhrkamp, 1995), 16–131

— *Philosophie des Geldes,* 4th edn (Munich: Duncker & Humboldt, 1922)

Simon, A. 'Jazz', in *Der Auftakt* 6 (1926), 211–13

Smith, Margaret Keiver, *Rhythmus und Arbeit* (Leipzig: Wilhelm Engelmann, 1900)

Sontag, Helmut, *Sidi: eine Hommage an den Kameramann und Filmpionier Guido Seeber* (Hannover: Kronsberg-Verlag, 1986)

Spencer, Herbert, *First Principles,* 4th edn (New York: Appleton, 1883)

Stam, Robert, *Film Theory. An Introduction* (Oxford: Blackwell, 2000)
Steiner, Rudolf, *Eurhythmie als sichtbare Sprache. Ein Vortragszyklus vom 24. Juni bis 12. Juli 1924 im Goetheanum* (Dornach: Philosophisch-Anthroposophischer Verlag am Goetheanum, 1927)
Stercken, Angela, 'Die Gesolei als Schaubild des Körpers. Sektionen, Überblick', in Hans Körner and Angela Stercken (eds.), *Kunst, Sport und Körper / GeSoLei 1926–2002* (Düsseldorf: Hatje Cantz Verlag, 2002), 99–123
Stuckenscmidt, H. H., 'Aeroplansonate', in *Der Auftakt* 6 (1926), 178–81
Toepfer, Karl, *Empire of Ecstasy. Nudity and Movement in German Body Culture, 1910–1935* (Berkeley: University of California Press, 1997)
Turvey, Malcolm, 'Dada Between Heaven and Hell: Abstraction and Universal Language in the *Rhythm* films of Hans Richter', in *October* 105 (2003), 13–36
U., E., 'Kunst und Geschäftsregisseure', in *Der Kinematograph* 971 (1925), 23–24
'Unsere Kipho-Enquete', *Der Film* 10:39 (1925), 38–40
Valéry, Paul, *Degas Danse Dessein*, in *Œuvres*, vol. 2 (Paris: Gallimard, 1960), 1163–240
Vasold, Georg, 'Optique ou haptique : le rythme dans les études sur l'art au début du 20e siècle', in *Intermédialités* 16 (automne 2010), 35-55
Virilio, Paul, *L'art du moteur* (Paris: Galilée, 1993)
Das wandernde Bild. Der Filmpionier Guido Seeber, ed. Stiftung Deutsche Kinemathek (Berlin: Elefanten-Press, 1979)
Ward, Janet, 'Metropolis and the Technosexual Woman of German Modernity', in Katharina von Ankum (ed.), *Women in the Metropolis: Gender and Modernity in Weimar Culture* (Berkeley: University of California Press, 1997), 128–44
— *Weimar Surfaces. Urban Visual Culture in 1920s Germany* (Berkeley: UC Press, 2001)
'Was wird aus der Kipho?' in *Der Kinematograph* 952 (1925), 16
Wees, William C, *Recycled Images. The Art and Politics of Found Footage Films* (New York: Anthology Film Archives, 1993)
Weiner, Marc, 'Urwaldmusik and the Border's of German Identity: Jazz in Literature of the Weimar Republic', in *German Quarterly* 64:4 (1991), 475–87
Westbrock, Ingrid, *Der Werbefilm. Ein Beitrag zur Entwicklungsgeschichte des Genres vom Stummfilm zum frühen Tonfilm* (Hildesheim: Georg Olms Verlag, 1983)

Wipplinger, Jonathan, 'The Aural Shock of Modernity: Weimar's Experience of Jazz', in *The Germanic Review* 82:4 (2007), 299–320

Wolbert, Klaus. 'Das Erscheinen des reformerischen Körpertypus in der Malerei und Bildhauerei um 1900', in *Die Lebensreform. Entwürfe zur Neugestaltung von Leben und Kunst um 1900*, vol. 1, 215–22

Wundt, Wilhelm, *Grundzüge der physiologischen Psychologie*, 6th edn (Leipzig: Kröner, 1911)

— *Völkerpsychologie. Eine Untersuchung der Entwicklungsgesetze*, vol. 3, 4th edn (Leipzig: Alfred Kröner Verlag, 1923)

Index

absolute film. *See* abstract film
abstract film, 93-4, 97, 109, 128-31, 139, 146, 163, 216
acceleration, 56-8, 60, 63-4, 95-104, 210, 215-17
Adorno, Theodor, 177, 200-1
advertising, 46, 127-66
Altenberg, Peter, 169
Ambrus, Irene, 197
Americanism, 30, 43, 48, 176-8, 184, 188-200, 205, 227
Antheil, George, 180n.
Anthroposophy, 96, 183
Asendorf, Christoph, 34n., 53
Ashanti, 169
avant-garde, 68, 91-3, 106, 109, 128, 138-9, 146-7, 152, 163-6, 211-14

Bade zu Hause, 127
Bahr, Hermann, 70-1
Baker, Josephine, 123, 174n., 205. *See also* Revue nègre
Balázs, Béla, 118-119
Balla, Giacomo, 67
Baresel, Alfred, 174, 180-1, 194-195, 199
Baudelaire, Charles, 62-3
Bauhaus, 160-1, 163, 165, 197
Bauman, Zygmunt, 16, 19
Baxmann, Inge, 38n., 78
Bazin, André, 210-11, 216
Becher, Johannes, 51
Behn, Siegfried, 40n.
Benjamin, Walter, 63, 108, 127, 136, 157n., 160, 177
Bergson, Henri, 32, 34, 44-6, 105-8, 214-15
Bernhard, Paul, 171-2
Big Brother, 16
Blade Runner, 221
Boccioni, Umberto, 68
Bode, Rudolf, 21, 38-9, 41, 50, 87, 101-2, 104, 115-18, 178, 183, 213
Bolten-Baecker, Heinrich, 213
Bolton, Thaddeus, 40n.
Boulez, Pierre, 21-2
Brecht, Bertolt, 56
Brod, Max, 48, 173-4, 178-9, 204
Broughton, Susannah, 16, 20
Bücher, Karl, 22-7, 38-41, 43, 45-47, 54, 56, 62, 70, 77, 84, 86, 95, 100, 105, 128, 131-3, 149, 165-6, 167-9, 178, 180-1, 189, 206. *See also* rhythm and work

Bukofzer, Manfred, 179, 182, 199
Bülow, Hans von, 17-18, 167
Buñuel, Luis, 111

carnivalesque, 194-8
Cavalcanti, Alberto. *See En rade*
Cendrars, Blaise, 92
Chocolate Kiddies, The, 177
chronophotography, 31, 46, 65, 68, 88, 90, 105, 108. *See also* photography; rhythm and media
continuous rotation, 26-7, 47, 77, 86-7, 92n., 97, 135, 146-151, 153. *See also* restlessness
Clair, René, 93-4, 146
  Entr'acte, 93
colour organs, 92, 173
conflict of culture, 29-30, 69-71, 73-4, 80, 83, 169n., 189-90, 198-9. *See also* Simmel, Georg
Correll, E. H., 142
Crary, Jonathan, 44
Cubism, 68-69, 165

Dada, 66, 68, 94, 104
dance, 15-21, 24, 34-5, 40, 44, 48, 49, 61-2, 78-83, 87, 100-101, 105, 108, 113, 116, 121, 123-4, 136-7n., 151, 169-170, 173, 178, 181-94, 196, 201, 205-6. *See also* gymnastics
Darwin, Charles, 23
Dehmel, Richard
  'Predigt ans Großstadtvolk', 60
Deleuze, Gilles, 45, 87, 92, 105-8, 226n.
Deutscher Werkbund, 18
Diaghilev, Sergei, 21
Didi-Huberman, Georges 106n., 108

Dinerstein, Joel, 188
Dohrn, Wolf, 23
Doumet, Christian, 43n.
drums, 201-7
Dulac, Germaine, 92-5, 141
Dulac, Nicholas, 147
Duncan, Elisabeth, 21
Duncan, Isadora, 34-5, 40, 82, 87, 183

Eckstein, Modris, 21
efficiency. *See* energy
Eggeling, Viking, 93, 105, 109-10, 214
  Symphonie diagonale, 131-132n.
Eisenstein, Sergei, 99, 103-105, 109
  concept of rhythm, 103-4
  Strike, 99
Elsaesser, Thomas, 141n.
En rade, 210
energy, 24-7, 41, 53-4, 56, 61-3, 64n., 66n., 67, 73, 76-86, 88, 90, 137, 173, 180-3. *See also* continuous rotation; restlessness; rhythm and efficiency; rhythm and work
Engelke, Gerrit 45, 51-86, 189, 227
  'Auf der Straßenbahn', 57, 61-62
  'Blut-Strom', 74-78
  'Der ewige Herzklang', 74-75, 78
  'Die Fabrik', 55, 61
  'Gott braust', 74
  'Die große Uhr', 56, 59-60
  'Heimkehr', 84-6
  'Ich klopfe mit dem Schallwort-Hammer', 84
  'Ich weiß: ich bin ein Leben', 62-63

'Ich will heraus aus dieser Stadt', 60
'Der Mittler', 79-83
'Der rasende Psalm', 56-8, 84
'Rhythmus', 52-3, 78
'Seele', 60
'Sonne', 56
'Stadt', 54, 57, 61
'Die Stadt lebt', 56
'Von innen nach außen', 74
'Weltfrühling', 75
'Weltgeist', 63-4
Epstein, Jean, 92, 97, 101
ethnographic displays. *See* Völkerschauen
Expressionism, 45, 51-2, 69-71, 109-110, 157, 165

Fanck, Arnold, 46
Farocki, Harun, 224
 Contre-chant, 224-7
Felber, Erwin, 22n., 168, 171n., 172n.
film, 45-6, 87-166, 179, 187-8, 190, 205-7, 210-28. *See also* rhythm and media
Fincher, David, 222
Fischinger, Oskar, 139
 Kreise, 139
Fließ, Wilhelm, 31
Fülöp-Miller, René, 90-91
Fuller, Loïe, 82
fascism, 39-40, 48, 124, 137n. 212-214
Fordism, 29, 39, 42, 116, 134, 153, 156-7, 159, 165, 177-8, 188, 221, 228
Futurism, 57, 61, 63-69, 71-2, 90-1, 97, 164-5, 210

Gance, Abel, 92-3, 98, 101, 144
 La Roue, 92-3, 95, 98, 111n.

Gates, Henry Louis, 196
Gaudreault, André, 147
Gebrauchsmusik, 182
Geisler, Willy, 213
Gerling, Reinholt, 64n.
Gesolei (exhibition), 90, 129
Giese, Fritz, 29-30, 47-8, 62, 159, 181, 189-94, 198, 206
Gilman, Sander, 177
Goebbels, Joseph, 214
Goll, Claire, 49, 61, 193, 194n.
Goll, Yvan, 61, 174n.
Golston, Michael, 25n., 38n., 40n.
Gosse, Ernst, 23-24
gramophone. *See* phonograph
Grierson, John, 214
Guido, Laurent, 40n., 42n., 90-2
Guilbert, Laure, 40n.
Gunning, Tom, 108, 146n.
gymnastics, 19-20, 24-5, 27n., 38-9, 72, 87, 96, 100-2, 104, 115, 181, 188-9. *See also* dance

Hagener, Malte, 211
Hake, Sabine, 211
Harbou, Thea von
 Metropolis (novel), 112-16, 120, 205-7
Heidegger, Martin, 39, 84
Hellpach, Willy, 58-9
Helm, Brigitte, 205-7
Heym, Georg, 45
Hindemith, Paul, 18, 177
Hirschfeld-Mack, Ludwig, 93
Hodler, Ferdinand, 71-2
 Eurythmie, 72
 Tag, 72
Holz, Arno, 49, 50, 52-3
Huggins, Johnny, 195
Huppert, Eduard, 184
Huppertz, Gottfried, 206

hypnosis, 47, 131, 134-6, 153-157

Iger, Artur, 167, 202n.

Jaques-Dalcroze, Emil, 19-25, 27, 38, 41-2, 72, 87, 101, 105, 167-8, 181, 183, 199, 227
jazz, 47-8, 167-207, 223, 228.
Jemnitz, Alexander, 171, 172, 201

Kaes, Anton, 98n.
Kafka, Franz
'Das Urteil', 55
Kálmán, Emerich, 197
  Die Herzogin von Chicago, 197-198
Kantor, Franziska, 67
Kawara, On, 216
Keightley, Archibald, 40n., 96
Kinetismus, 66, 68, 90, 164-5
Kipho (exhibition), 141-3, 152, 156-7
Kipho (film), see 'Seeber, Guido'
Kittler, Friedrich, 44, 159-160, 182n.
Klages, Ludwig, 30-9, 41-2, 50, 97, 100-1, 103-5, 107n., 109, 111, 113-14, 118, 151, 157-9, 170, 178, 183, 189, 213, 214-15, 227
Klar, Gustav, 18n., 21, 131n.
Koch, Bernhard, 21, 31n., 41-42
Koebner, Franz Wolfgang, 184-8, 202-3
  1000 Schritte Charleston, 188
Koffka, Kurt 40n.
Kool, Jaap, 202
  Concert Piece for 28 Drums, 202
Kracauer, Siegfried, 29, 69, 98n., 99-100, 124, 189, 216, 221
Kren, Kurt, 216

Krenek, Ernst
  Jonny spielt auf, 175-6, 196, 203, 206
Kristeva, Julia, 49n.
Kubelka, Peter, 214-221
  Adebar, 214, 216-218
  Arnulf Rainer, 214, 216-18
  Schwechater, 214, 216-17
  Unsere Afrikareise, 219-21
Kühn, Gustav, 142
Kurtzig, Käthe, 129-32, 138
Kurz, Rudolf, 109-10

Laban, Rudolf von, 21, 88, 101, 105
Lang, Fritz, 46, 205-207
  Die Nibelungen, 141, 143
  Metropolis, 46, 56, 75, 110-25, 127, 135n., 205-7, 210, 221-3, 225, 228
Lawder, Standish, 47, 92, 120, 140-1
Le Bon, Gustave, 117
Lebensreform, 60, 66n., 213
Lee, Pamela, 215
Lefebvre, Henri, 224
Léger, Fernand, 92, 94, 120, 130, 141, 146
  Ballet mécanique, 92, 93, 97, 147
Lenauer, Jean, 210-211
Lessing, Gotthold Ephraim, 65, 87
Lethen, Helmut, 16n.
Levetzow, Karl Freiherr von, 49-50
Lévi-Strauss, Claude, 219
Levinson, André, 104
L'Herbier, Marcel, 92
  L'Inhumaine, 120-4
Lipps, Theodor, 36
Love Parade, 224

Lubkoll, Christine, 19, 38n., 49, 105, 108-9
Lukács, Georg, 41, 69
Lucretius, 80-1

Mach, Ernst, 90
Mackenzie, Michael, 40n., 103n.
Macrae, David, 99-100
Madonna, 222-4
    Express Yourself, 222-4
Mailer, Norman, 48, 200
Maldoom, Royston, 16-17
Mallarmé, Stéphane, 49
Mann, Thomas, 69n.
Marcinowski, Johannes, 58-9
Marey, Étienne-Jules, 30-2, 34n., 90, 106n., 108
Mauss, Marcel, 40n.
McLaren, Norman, 215
mechanical music, 179-80. See also rhythm and media
Meisel, Edmund, 97
Menschen am Sonntag, 212
Mensendieck, Bess, 104
Merz, Max, 39n.
Messter, Oskar, 127n., 128
metre, 49-51, 53-4, 103. See also poetry; *Takt*
Meumann, Ernst, 36, 40n.
Mierendorff, Carlo, 146n.
Milhaud, Darius, 18
Mitry, Jean, 107
Moholy-Nagy, László, 160-161
montage, 92, 95-100, 103, 106, 153, 190, 210-12, 214, 216, 226-7
    in-camera montage (Seeber), 144-6
    photomontage, 203
Moran, Paul, 184-5
Moroder, Giorgio, 221
Müller, Edmund Josef, 195

Müller, Robert, 26
Murnau, Friedrich Wilhelm
    Der letzte Mann, 144
Murphy, Dudley, 92
Muthesius, Hermann, 18-19
Muybridge, Eadweard, 88, 90

Nazism, see 'fascism'
nervousness, 58-60, 70, 77-8, 80, 83, 96, 99, 101
Nettl, Paul, 180
Neue Sachlichkeit, 77, 109, 163, 175n.
neurasthenia, see 'nervousness'
New Objectivity, see 'Neue Sachlichkeit'
Nijinsky, Vaslav, 21

Ondra, Anny, 197

painting, 65-8, 71-2. See also rhythm and media
Partsch, Cornelius, 178
Parufamet, 141-142n.
Pauli, Fritz, 46, 131-40, 153, 156-9, 163-6, 181-2
percussion, see 'drums'
phonograph, 170-171, 184-187. See rhythm and media
photography, 66n., 87-8, 90, 93, 108, 157-8, 197, 206, 216. See also chronophotography
Picabia, Francis
    Entr'acte, 93
Pinschewer, Julius, 47, 128, 138, 140, 143
pleasure of looking. See Schaulust
Plessner, Helmuth, 33n.
poetry, 45, 49-86. See also metre; rhythm and media

polyrhythms, 19-22, 168, 199-200, 204, 227-8. *See also* jazz; rhythm and primitivity; syncopation
Pommer, Erich, 141, 152
post-industrial society, 221-8
Prager, Wilhelm
  Wege zu Kraft und Schönheit, 100-3, 144, 151, 165
Pudovkin, Vsevolod, 103-104

Rabinbach, Anson, 19n., 24
Radkau, Joachim, 99
Rancière, Jacques, 53, 106n.
Rattle, Simon, 15-17, 22, 227-8
Ray, Man, 131n.
Reinhardt, Heinrich, 132
Reiniger, Lotte, 128-9, 163
  Das Geheimnis der Marquise, 128
  Die Barcarole, 129
Renoir, Jean, 214
  Sur un air de Charleston, 195-196
restlessness, 26-8, 45, 54-7, 63-5, 77-9, 86. *See also* continuous rotation; energy
Revue nègre 174n., 195. *See also* Baker, Josephine
rhythm
  and attention, 46, 129, 133-8, 153-6, 159-63
  and efficiency, 24-6, 41, 134-7, 153, 164-5, 181-4. *See also* continuous rotation; energy; rhythm and work
  and flow, 32-34, 39, 41n., 71, 75-8, 82-3, 97, 100-3, 106, 108, 114-17, 122, 124. *See also* wave movement
  and media, 44, 47, 51, 84, 102-10, 119-26, 138, 157-62, 184-8, 209-10;
  and nature, 19, 24, 30, 32-4, 49-50, 52-3, 78, 82, 94, 97, 101, 109, 117-18, 120, 183, 190, 213. *See also* dance; gymnastics; wave movement
  and pleasure, 23, 25, 95n., 129-33, 136, 180-1
  and primitivity, 18, 22-6, 38, 45, 52-4, 91, 109-10, 121-3, 168-75, 177-8, 191-192, 218-19. *See also* rhythm and race
  and race, 38-39, 191-196, 199-201, 213
  and technology, 26-29, 55-7, 61, 77-8, 113-15, 120-5, 149, 151. *See also* conflict of culture; rhythm vs. *Takt*
  and vitalism, 30-31, 33, 35, 39, 54, 71, 73-8, 85-6, 91, 95, 104-5, 108-9, 114-16, 122, 213, 222-3. *See also* rhythm and primitivity
  and work, 22-8, 56, 76-7, 95n., 113-14, 131-4, 149-51, 180-181, 184, 199, 227-8. *See also* energy
  as integrative force, 22-4, 105
  as irresistible force, 94-95, 131-6, 153. *See also* hypnosis
  as mediator between the organic and the technological, 42-3, 46, 51, 84, 102-10, 119-25, 178, 184-92, 209-10
  vs. *Takt*, 30-3, 37-8, 97-102, 111-14. *See also* modernity and subordination of natural rhythm to technological rhythm; rhythm and technology

Rhythm is it!, 15, 16, 17, 22, 100, 227-8
rhythmical gymnastics, see 'gymnastics'
Ribot, Théodule, 192n.
Richter, Hans, 46, 93-4, 97, 99, 104-5, 109-10, 127, 128, 130, 131, 134, 141, 149, 182, 214
 Inflation, 99
 Rhythmus 21, 46, 94, 131n.
 Rhythmus 23, 46, 94
 Zweigroschenzauber, 138
Riefenstahl, Leni, 46, 103
 Triumph des Willens, 213
Riegl, Alois, 40n.
Roth, Joseph
'Bekenntnis zum Gleisdreieck', 61
Russack, Hermann, 40n.
Russolo, Luigi, 66, 90
Ruttmann, Walter, 46, 93, 97-100, 109, 127, 128, 130, 139, 141, 146, 163, 211-14
 Der Aufstieg, 129, 138
 Berlin. Die Sinfonie der Großstadt, 46, 97, 97-100, 103, 157, 212-213, 224-227
 Blut und Boden: Grundlagen zum neuen Reich, 212-214
 Melodie der Welt, 131n.
 Opus films, 138
 Der Sieger, 128, 138
 Spiel der Wellen, 138
 Das wiedergefundene Paradies, 138
 Das Wunder, 138

Sauvanet, Pierre, 43n.
Saxophon Susi (film), 197-8
Schadt, Thomas
 Berlin: Sinfonie einer Großstadt, 224

Schaulust, 124
Schieferstein, Heinrich, 134
Schiller, Friedrich, 60
Schmarsow, August, 40n.
Schulhof, Erwin, 196
Schwarz, Frederic, 161
Seeber, Guido, 47, 128, 140n., 143-4, 162-3, 211, 214
 Kipho, 47, 129, 139-62
Siegert, Hubertus
 Berlin Babylon, 224
Simmel, Georg, 27-9, 41, 54, 56-7, 60n., 62, 69-71, 80, 84, 95-6, 99, 188, 206
Simon, A., 172n.
Sjöström, Viktor
 The Scarlet Letter, 210
Smith, Margaret Keiver, 25n.
Speer, Albert
 Die Bauten Adolf Hitlers, 213
Spencer, Herbert, 30, 180
Steiner, Marie, 96, 183
Steiner, Rudolf, 96, 178, 183
Stoicism, 80
Stravinsky, Igor
 Rite of Spring, 15-18, 21-2, 167, 168, 170, 227, 228
Struwe, Friedrich, 21
synaesthesia, 92, 173. See also colour organs
syncopation, 48, 169, 171-172, 195, 199-200, 204, 228. See also jazz
Taeuber, Sophie, 105
Takt, 30-2, 37-8, 46, 98, 101, 108, 111-14, 118, 159, 183. See also Klages, Ludwig
Taylorism, 22, 39, 42, 101, 112-13
technology, 26-28, 30, 39, 55-58, 62-4, 75-9, 84-6, 91, 95-100, 102-4, 110-14, 120-5, 134, 146, 149-53, 170-1, 173-4, 179, 183,

189-91, 209, 221-7. *See also* continuous rotation; rhythm vs. *Takt*
television, 223
Theosophy, 96
Tiller Girls, 29, 189-90
Toepfer, Karl, 38n.
tragedy of culture, see 'conflict of culture'
Trenker, Luis
   Der verlorene Sohn, 212
Turvey, Malcolm, 105

Valéry, Paul, 82-3
Vangelis, 221
Verband deutscher Reklamefachleute, 137
Vertov, Dziga
   The Man with a Movie Camera, 152, 157, 224, 226
Virilio, Paul, 209-210
Völkerschauen, 22, 169

Wagner, Richard, 17, 139
Wald-Lasowski, Aliocha, 43n.
Ward, Janet, 124n., 136
Warhol, Andy, 216
wave movement, 33-4, 81-3, 97, 101, 116. *See also* rhythm and flow; rhythm and nature
The Weakest Link (TV series), 16
Weill, Kurt, 177
Weintraub, Stephan, 203n.
Weintraub Syncopators, 203
Westbrock, Ingrid, 127n., 129n., 139
Whiteman, Paul, 178
Wiene, Robert
   Das Cabinet des Dr. Caligari, 47, 141, 144, 153, 156-8, 161, 164-5
Wigman, Mary, 21, 101, 151
Wipplinger, Jonathan, 177
Wolzogen, Ernst von, 194
Wooding, Sam, 177
Wundt, Wilhelm, 24n., 36, 40n.
Zeitoper, 174-5, 177, 197, 20. *See also* jazz